A History of Organized Labor
in Peru and Ecuador

A History of Organized Labor in Peru and Ecuador

ROBERT J. ALEXANDER

WITH THE COLLABORATION OF
ELDON M. PARKER

Westport, Connecticut
London

Library of Congress Cataloging-in-Publication Data

Alexander, Robert Jackson, 1918–
   A history of organized labor in Peru and Ecuador / Robert J. Alexander ;
with the collaboration of Eldon M. Parker.
      p. cm.
   Includes bibliographical references and index.
   ISBN 0–275–97741–2 (alk. paper)
   1. Labor unions—Peru—History.   2. Labor unions—Ecuador—History.
I. Parker, Eldon M.   II. Title.
   HD6642.A44   2006
   331.880985—dc22   2006026018

British Library Cataloguing in Publication Data is available.

Library of Congress Catalog Card Number: 2006026018
ISBN: 0–275–97741–2

First published in 2007

Praeger Publishers, 88 Post Road West, Westport, CT 06881
An imprint of Greenwood Publishing Group, Inc.
www.praeger.com

Printed in the United States of America

The paper used in this book complies with the
Permanent Paper Standard issued by the National
Information Standards Organization (Z39.48–1984).

10 9 8 7 6 5 4 3 2 1

To Ligia Herasme-Alexander

Contents

Preface

My interest in the history of organized labor in Latin America was first aroused when I took a course in Latin American history with Dr. Frank Tannenbaum at Columbia University in the late 1930s. In that course, I wrote an extensive term paper for Dr. Tannenbaum on the history of the Argentine labor movement. Subsequently, I wrote my MA thesis on the history of Chilean organized labor and my PhD dissertation on labor relations in Chile.

After World War II, I was fortunate to associate with two men who greatly facilitated my gaining a much more extensive acquaintance with the labor movements of Latin America: Serafino Romualdi, the self-styled "ambassador" of the American Federation of Labor (AFL), and subsequently of the AFL-CIO (Congress of Industrial Organizations), to Latin American organized labor; and Jay Lovestone, head of the Free Trade Union Committee of the AFL and then virtual "foreign minister" of the AFL-CIO. I helped Mr. Romualdi edit the English-language version of the periodical of the Inter-American Confederation of Workers (CIT), and I traveled numerous times to Latin America in the 1950s and early 1960s for Mr. Lovestone, to report to him on the labor movements, as well as on the general economic and political situations of the countries that I visited on his behalf.

In later decades, I continued to visit some part of Latin America in virtually every year until the mid-1990s. In all such visits, I always tried, among other things, to keep myself current with the state of organized labor in the various countries that I visited.

In the last few years, I have been working on a general history of organized labor in Latin America and the Caribbean. This opus became so extensive as to make it unlikely to see print as a single work, and so I have been breaking it down into a number of volumes, dealing with specific countries or neighboring nations. The present work is one of these volumes.

Generally, this volume carries the story of the labor movements of Peru and Ecuador up to the year 1990. Although the closing parts of the material on both countries presage what might have been written beyond that date, I have not in fact carried the study beyond 1990.

As is the case with all authors, I owe numerous intellectual and other debts to many people who in one way or another helped bring this work to fruition. Of course, I owe one of these debts to the many trade unionists and other people in the two countries who over the years have recounted to me details of the history of the labor movements in their respective countries and who frequently made available to me printed material of one kind or another, which otherwise would not have been readily available.

I also obviously owe much to the late Messrs. Romualdi and Lovestone for having facilitated my knowledge of the organized labor movements of Peru and Ecuador.

This volume would not have been brought to fruition without the aid of my former student and continuing friend Eldon Parker. Not only has he prepared the camera-ready manuscript, but he has also been an expert copyeditor, catching innumerable errors of one kind or another. Of course, the responsibility for any continuing errors is mine, not his. We both owe much to Lindsay Claire of the Greenwood Publishing Group for her careful work in preparing final copy for the volume.

Finally, as always, I am much obliged to my late wife, Joan, who over the years put up patiently with my researches and writing when, often I am sure, she might have felt that my time might better have been spent on more domestic matters.

Rutgers University
New Brunswick, NJ

Introduction

Both present-day Peru and Ecuador were part of the Inca Empire before the arrival of the Spaniards early in the sixteenth century. In fact, Atahualpa, the last of the Inca emperors, was born in Ecuador and from there moved south to win control of the whole of the Inca domain shortly before the arrival of the Spaniards.

In both Peru and Ecuador, the colonial regime established by the Spaniards was based on control of the land by the Conquistadors and their white and mestizo heirs. In both countries, too, the American Indians, who made up the great majority of the population, were fighting a losing battle to maintain their traditional rural communities in the face of constant encroachment by the white and nearly white landowning elite. It was not until the closing decades of the twentieth century that agrarian reforms—more widespread in Peru than in Ecuador—were undertaken to destroy the traditional landholding pattern that had existed for nearly half a millennium.

In both countries there was a sharp contrast, economically and socially, between the highland parts of the country and the lowland coastal areas. In the latter, there developed in the twentieth century an economy based largely on modern plantation agriculture, producing crops for export, principally sugar and cotton in Peru and bananas and sugar in Ecuador. Also, the population of the coastal areas differed markedly from that of the highlands in both countries. Along the coast in both countries were people of mixed racial background—indigenous, or Indian, and Caucasian, with some people of African descent, mingled with people of Asian origin (Chinese and Japanese in Peru, Arabs in Ecuador)—in contrast with the overwhelmingly American Indian population of the highlands.

Mining was an important economic activity in Peru from before the colonial period, with the search for precious metals being a major reason for the Spanish conquest. By the twentieth century, copper and iron ore had supplanted gold as the principal minerals being exploited in Peru. Petroleum had also become an important national product. In Ecuador, mineral mining was less significant, and it was the second half of the twentieth century before petroleum production became a significant part of the national economy.

During the twentieth century, both countries developed a significant manufacturing sector. In Ecuador this tended to be concentrated in the capital of Quito in the highlands and the port city of Guayaquil, whereas in Peru, although there was a heavy concentration of industry in the Lima region, there were also significant concentrations of industries in a number of provincial cities.

Organized labor understandably had in both countries one center of concentration in the industrial sector. However, transport workers—whether on railroads, in the ports, or in buses, trucks, and taxis—were another important sector insofar as the trade union movement was concerned, as were mining, petroleum, and construction workers. Only in the post–World War II period were the plantation workers (and to a lesser degree sharecroppers, tenants, and other peasant groups) recruited into the labor movement in both countries on a substantial scale.

The exact boundaries separating Peru and Ecuador long remained a matter of dispute. This conflict led to a short but violent war in the 1940s, as a result of which Peru acquired much of the eastern part of the territory claimed by Ecuador. Still uncertain boundaries continued to cause occasional military confrontations between the two countries as late as the 1990s. These conflicts sometimes impacted labor relations in both countries.

The organized labor movement in both Peru and Ecuador had its origins in mutual-benefit societies, which began to appear in the later decades of the nineteenth century. Although by the second decade of the twentieth century these organizations had been largely superseded by *sindicatos*, or trade unions, in Peru, they continued to be an appreciable part of organized labor in Ecuador until after World War II.

As elsewhere in Latin America, the labor movements of Peru and Ecuador have been highly politicized. During much of the history of organized labor in the two countries, one particular party tended to be dominant. In Peru this party was the Partido Aprista; in Ecuador, it was the Communist Party. However, by the 1970s, other political groups had challenged, with varying degree of success, the hold of the Apristas and Communists in the labor movements of the two countries.

At least in part because of its highly political nature, the workers' movement in Peru and Ecuador tended to run afoul of the governments of the two countries. This tendency was also attributable to the fact that the government of the day often was a military dictatorship that had seized power by force. Political events as well as changes in the economy helped explain the ebb and floe of militancy in the two countries' labor movements.

In both Peru and Ecuador, organized labor developed against a background of a particular kind of economic development. This was characterized by a process of import-substitution industrialization, with the state playing a major role not only through development of the economic infrastructure and social services such as education and health care, but also through itself owning important parts of the economy, as well as regulating foreign investment and protecting the growth of domestic manufacturing through tariffs, exchange controls, and other measures.

However, with the advent of the "lost decade" of the 1980s, which Peru and Ecuador shared with the rest of Latin America, the economic situation changed dramatically. In the previous decade both countries had assumed very large foreign debts (as had most other Latin American countries). They had done so with the strong encouragement not only of the lenders but also of the U.S. government.

This situation arose as a response to the so-called oil crisis of the 1970s, when the United States and other industrial countries had been recipients of drastically larger deposits from the oil-producing countries and were desperate to find borrowers who could, through their interest payments, help those U.S. banks pay the much larger interest payments to the depositors from the oil-producing nations.

This drastically changed the international economic relations of Peru, Ecuador, and other Latin American countries. They had borrowed abroad before, but in the post–World War II period, principally from the World Bank, the Inter-American Development Bank, and other sources, which offered long-term loans at below-commercial interest rates. But by 1980, these countries' foreign debts were in the form of short-term, high-interest loans from commercial banks, and inflation was increasingly rampant.

Consequently, by the 1980s, Peru, Ecuador, and many other Latin American nations had found themselves unable to deal with their foreign debt burden and rising inflation and had to turn to the International Monetary Fund (IMF) for help. But the IMF, with the enthusiastic support of the U.S. government, refused aid except under very exigent terms. On the one hand, the IMF insisted on adoption of drastic austerity measures, involving wage freezes, freeing of interest rates, and major reductions in government expenditures, to reduce the rate of inflation. But the IMF's requirements also included the adoption of much more long-range policies, those of "neoliberalism." These included the ending of government ownership of important sectors of the economy, establishment of "favorable conditions" for foreign investment, permanently balanced fiscal budgets, and end of all measures to protect segments of their national economies from foreign competition. In a word, the IMF insisted on the dismantling of the institutions and policies under which economic development had taken place and organized labor had been able to grow and defend its members' interests and livelihood through most of the twentieth century.

Virtually all of these changes militated against the organized labor movement. They resulted in massive increases in unemployment, drastic reductions in real wages, elimination of all attempts to guarantee workers security in their jobs (as an inducement for foreign and domestic investors alike), and reduction of government expenditures on education and social services.

By the end of the twentieth century, therefore, organized labor in Peru and Ecuador (and throughout Latin America and the Caribbean) was faced with the most serious challenge that it had encountered in all of its history: the overwhelming acceptance of the philosophy and policies of neoliberalism by governments and political leaders. The trade union movement was faced on the one hand with the need to incorporate into the movement the workers in the "informal" economy—victims of neoliberalism—and on the other hand the need to develop a philosophy and set of policies to successfully confront those policies of unmitigated neoliberalism. Failure to meet this challenge may well mean that the future of organized labor will be problematical at best and may be a tale of the disappearance of a movement that for most of the twentieth century was able to defend, and advance the interests of, an important segment of the less advantageously placed elements of the population of these countries.

CHAPTER 1

Organized Labor in Peru through 1948

Present-day Peru was the center of the Inca Empire, one of the major pre-Columbian civilizations in America. After the Spaniards overthrew and pulverized the Inca Empire early in the sixteenth century, Peru became the center of one of the principal divisions of the Spanish Empire in America. The capital of the viceroyalty of Peru was Lima, a city that was built by the Iberians on the Pacific coast and that became the capital of the Republic of Peru early in the nineteenth century.

When the Spaniards overran Peru, they divided much of the country's land among the conquerors and their heirs, although some of it continued to be in the hands of local native, or Indian, communities. Until well into the twentieth century, the majority of the Peruvians were Quechua-speaking descendants of the pre-Columbian "native Americans," living in the plateaus and valleys of the central highland third of the country or in the easternmost (and geographically largest) third, raising into the Amazon and Rio de la Plata river systems.

The most "modern" part of Peru developed along the Pacific coast, with oil fields and plantation agriculture in the north and the capital city of Lima and its port in Callao in the south. Lima-Callao became the principal location of manufacturing. By the latter part of the twentieth century, largely as a result of migration from the interior, Lima contained one-quarter of Peru's population. Lima-Callao, the soon-major interior cities Cuzco, Arequipa, Trujillo, and Iquitos, the coastal plantations, and the mining centers in the highlands also have been the most important centers of the trade union movement.

THE BEGINNINGS OF ORGANIZED LABOR IN PERU

Castilla Larrea has pointed out that during the colonial era there had existed in Peru *gremios,* or guilds, among the craftsmen and apprentices of the towns and cities. Although these were officially abolished by the Constitution of 1860,[1] they apparently continued to exist for some time.

James Payne noted with regard to the *gremios* that "the decline of the hand craftsman, the growth in importance of the labor unions, and the entrance of revolutionary doctrines into their own organizations finally drove them into near oblivion."[2]

A dozen years after the official banning of the colonial guilds an event occurred that may be said to have inaugurated the labor movement of Peru. The first strike in the country's history took place in September 1872 among the workers who were demolishing the colonial walls of Lima, in preparation for construction of boulevards around the city.[3] There is no record of any organization, permanent or otherwise, resulting from this walkout.

The year 1886 saw the formation of the first important labor organization, the Confederación de Artesanos "Unión Universal." This group was established under the leadership of a blacksmith, Manuel Gómez. It included organizations of shoemakers, tailors, painters, and plasterers, among others. It was very conservative politically and was reported to have begun receiving a subsidy from the government in 1905.[4]

There is a legend that the stimulus for the formation of the Confederación de Artesanos came from a representative of the First International who arrived in Peru, with the proposal of establishing an organization to bring together the various artisans of the capital.[5] Of course, the International had ceased to exist, even formally, several years previous to the date of the organization's formation, but it does seem conceivable that the arrival of some immigrant from Europe who had been active in the labor movement there gave an impetus to the establishment of this early member of the Peruvian organized labor movement. As Castilla Larrea argued, it also seems unlikely that the idea for formation of such a group, with sections consisting of workers of various crafts and skills, could have taken root spontaneously in Peru at such an early date.[6]

Poblete Troncoso seemed to be of the opinion that the formation of the Confederación de Artesanos followed the establishment of a number of mutual benefit societies that were then brought together into a united group.[7] Castilla Larrea, on the other hand, thought that the confederación was established first and that groups covering specific kinds of workers then were organized by the central society.[8] In any case, the confederación soon came to include blacksmiths, carpenters, cigar makers, shoemakers, painters and paperhangers, bricklayers, tailors, typographical workers, barbers, plumbers, and gasfitters. A number of other groups were added later, including florists, millers, newsboys, agricultural workers, and some provincial groups.[9]

The confederación had a wide range of activities, including establishment of a night school for children and adults, the provision of legal services for members, and establishment of consumers' cooperatives.[10] It also maintained a recreation center and a restaurant. On the occasion of anniversaries or other holidays, it organized festivities.[11] The confederación also had an employment agency that guaranteed the quality of the workers whom it sent out to take jobs.[12]

A similar organization, the Sociedad de Artesanos, was established in the provincial city of Cuzco, once the capital of the Inca Empire, in 1875. It was principally a mutual benefit society, although it engaged in some activities more appropriate to a trade union.[13]

The printing-trades workers were among the first to become organized, and the second strike in Peru of which we have found record seems to have been a walkout of typographical workers in 1895. The workers sought a wage increase and were successful after a few days.[14] The first organization of printers was the Sociedad Tipográfica del Perú de Auxilios Mutuos, founded in 1877. This was followed in 1882 by the Sociedad Gutenburg and in 1883 by the Unión Tipográfica del Perú. The printers formed the Sociedad Unión Tipográfica in 1889 and the Sociedad Tipográfica Confederada in 1896. Each organization arose and then disappeared and was succeeded by the next one. However, the rapid succession of organizations indicates the continuing desire of the printing-trades workers to band together for self-defense.[15]

In 1895 the workers of the gas company of Lima went out on the country's third strike, and the capital city remained in the dark until this walkout was settled.[16]

The first of a memorable series of walkouts among the textile workers of the Vitarte plant took place in 1896. In an attempt to break this strike, the government put a policeman alongside each machine to force the workers to remain on the job. The Confederación de Artesanos stepped in to help and asked Deputy Rosendo Vidaurre to aid the strikers. He put their case before the authorities, and the workers finally won some improvements in the food and housing provided them by the company.[17]

During the first decade of the twentieth century, a number of mutual benefit societies appeared that were not affiliated with the Confederación de Artesanos.[18] One mutualist group of much importance was the Sociedad de Empleados de Comercio, formed in 1903. It was destined to become one of the strongest working-class groups in the country, with its own headquarters and many activities. Sometime later, it changed its name to Asociación de Empleados del Perú.[19] A rival to the Confederación de Artesanos, the Asamblea de Sociedades Unidad, was also formed. It was more radical than the confederación.[20]

The Confederación de Artesanos went into politics, and a number of its important figures won posts in Parliament. These included Juan Goschet, a printing-trades worker who took the leadership in a number of strikes during the early years and who gave some eloquent defenses of the workers in Parliament; Pedro H. Osma, a carpenter who also apparently made an impression on the parliamentarians; and textile worker and deputy Luis B. Casteñeda, who was a foreman in the "El Inca" factory in Lima.[21]

ANARCHIST BEGINNINGS

Considerable anarchist influence began spreading among the Peruvian organized workers. This came principally through contacts with the labor movement of Argentina, much of which was at that time under the leadership of the anarchists. Another important element in the early organization of the Bakuninists in Peru was the influence of a number of Spanish anarchists who migrated there in the early years of the twentieth century.[22] The Peruvian anarchists also had contacts with their counterparts in Brazil.[23]

The cigar workers' union was one of the first anarchist unions to be organized, and it called its first strike in 1904 in protest against the introduction of cigar-making machines. The workers tried to break up the machinery during this walkout.[24] The Sindicato de Construcción Civil (construction workers' union) was also organized at this time, under the influence of the anarchists.[25]

There was also some Socialist organization and influence in the labor movement during this period. It was reported in 1907 that a group of Socialists had been arrested in connection with a strike.[26]

The Centro de Estudios Sociales was the rallying point for all of the left-wing elements of the labor movement. It included both anarchists and Marxists. Its periodical, *Centro Socialista,* directed by José Barrera, first appeared in 1907. However, conflict between anarchists and Socialists made it impossible for them to stay in the same organization for long, and in 1910 the anarchists broke away to form the group known as Luchadores por la Verdad (Fighters for the Truth). Among the group's founders were Delfín Levano, Manuel Caracciolo Levano, M. Elias Mendola, J. D. Tapia, F. Vallejos, and Emilio Castilla Larrea.

These Peruvian anarchists, having received copies of the *Almanque de la Protesta,* published by the Argentine anarchosyndicalists' daily paper, were fired with the idea of founding a Peruvian *La Protesta.* Delfín Levano made the arrangements for this, and on February 15, 1911, the first issue of the paper appeared. J. D. Tapia was its administrator, and the editor of the first issue was Elías Mendiola. After the second issue, Gliserio Tassar was the editor. The paper was at first a monthly, but in 1913 the anarchists of Callao, organized into the group Luz y Amor (Light and Love), took it over and turned it into a weekly. However, after months the Lima group once more took charge of the paper. Among its contributors were

Manuel González Prada, Gliserio Tassara, Juan Manuel Carreno, Erasso Roca, and university people. It republished works of important anarchist writers of other countries. In 1913 the paper acquired a small print shop, which it continued to use until it was seized by the government during disturbances in May 1919. *La Protesta* never recovered from this seizure, although a previous closing by the police in 1914 did not do very much damage to the paper. The group that finally gathered around La Protesta provided most of the leadership for the labor movement of Peru during the first two decades of the twentieth century.[27]

LABOR MILITANCY

During the first years of the twentieth century, the labor movement was quite militant. There were walkouts by many workers' groups. Most of the strikes ended relatively favorably for the workers, in spite of severe opposition from the government. Wage increases, regular payment of wages, and better sanitary conditions were among the demands of the workers in these early walkouts.[28]

The first celebration of May Day in Peru took place in 1905, when a musical-literary meeting was held under the sponsorship of the Federación de Panaderos "Estrella del Perú" (Star of Peru Bakers Federation). Among those who spoke were Manuel Caracciolo, Leopoldo Urmachea, Teodoro Rodríguez, and Juan Guerrero. Mauel González Prada delivered a lecture that became famous as "The Intellectual and the Worker."[29]

Early in 1907 there was a successful strike by the trolley-car motorists and conductors in Lima.[30] The first general stoppage by textile employees in the Lima area took place when workers in the Inca, Victoria, Progreso, and San Jacinto factories went out at the end of 1906. The strike was highlighted by a meeting of the strikers in front of the Victoria factory, which was addressed by the Levanos, Pedro Otzu, and a Spanish Socialist named Cirilo Martín. This walkout was victorious after one week.[31]

In March 1911, the Vitarte textile workers went on strike for a wage increase. This walkout was more violent than its predecessor, and there were several clashes with the police. However, the workers were partially successful, as a result of a general strike in Lima called in support of the textile stoppage. As a consequence of this strike, the Unificación Obrera Textil de Vitarte was formed as a permanent organization. A number of students took a prominent part in leading this movement.[32]

The anarchist leadership of the labor movement was probably best demonstrated by the frequency with which general strikes were called. We have noted such a walkout to celebrate the first of May in 1906 and another in 1911 to support the Vitarte textile workers, and in the years that followed, such walkouts were frequent. On May 1, 1912, the first really successful general strike in celebration of the international workers' holiday took place in Lima.[33]

Somewhat later in 1912, a general strike was organized in protest against President B. Leguía's attempts to have his brother Roberto succeed him and in favor of the presidential candidacy of Guillermo Billinghurst, the mayor of Lima. During the demonstration accompanying this walkout, one of the people held up a large loaf of bread, one meter long, with the slogan on it, "Este es el Pan Grande que nos Dara Billinghurst" ("This is the large loaf Billinghurst will give us"). From then on, Billinghurst, who became president soon afterward, was known as "Pan Grande."[34]

James Payne noted the frequently violent nature of labor relations in Peru during the first decades of the twentieth century, writing,

When strikes were called the employers simply continued production with those who stayed on the job and proceeded to fill the vacant positions from the surrounding abundance of labor. The strikers, deprived of their livelihood, resorted to violence: mass demonstrations and assaults on the factory or the owner's house, smashing of machinery, attacks on strikebreakers, and, in one instance, mass thefts of provisions to replenish the dwindling food supply. The government was naturally drawn in to protect life and property and maintain public order. Bitter clashes broke out between police forces and masses of agitated workers on strike. One of the first such clashes occurred in 1906; others followed in 1908, 1912, 1913, and 1914.[35]

THE FEDERACIÓN OBRERA REGIONAL PERUANA

The first national central labor organization was established in October 1912, when a number of workers' organization formed the Federación Obrera Regional Peruana (FORP). The groups joining this federation included the Unificación Textil de Vitarte and other textile workers' groups of Lima, as well as unions of white-collar workers, day laborers, and the Federación de Obreros Panaderos "Estrella de Peru." A declaration of principles and statutes was drawn up by Mauel Carraciolo Levano, Eulogio Otazu, and Adelberto Fonken.[36] Fonken was the son of a Chinese father and Peruvian mother. The anarchist orientation of the FORP was indicated by its name, copied from the Argentine anarchosyndicalist federation, the FORA. Both names reflected the anarchists' opposition to national patriotism and belief in the unity of the international working class. Workers were thought to reside in different "regions," not in "nations," to which they owed their loyalty.

THE 1912–1913 STRUGGLE FOR
THE EIGHT-HOUR DAY

The most spectacular victory of the labor movement in Peru prior to World War I came in 1912–1913 in a general movement in the Lima-Callao area for an eight-hour workday. The strike wave for this objective began in November 1912, when the dockworkers of Callao, led by the Unión

General de Jornaleros (General Union of Day Laborers) struck for the eight-hour day. It called a meeting of other unions in the port city for the purpose of turning their strike into a general movement. On December 22, 1912, a Comité de Agitación del Paro General (Committee for Agitation for a General Strike) was organized by the Federación Obrera Regional Peruana and other unions. Mauel and Delfín Levano, José Montesi, and Eulogio Otazu were among the leaders of the group, and Fernando E. Vera was elected its president, and Emilio Castilla Laarera its secretary-general.[37]

The government took strong measures against the strike movement. A decree of January 24, 1913, prohibited strikes, prescribing severe penalties for those engaging in them. The employers took the offensive, and lock-outs were declared in the brewery, metallurgical, and other industries.[38]

However, by February 1, a number of settlements, which granted all or some of the workers' demands, had been reached. Thus, the millers, gas workers, grain-elevator workers, and customs-house employees won the eight-hour day and a 10 percent wage increase. The canal workers got the eight-hour day, the municipal employees won a 20 percent wage rise, and woodworkers and the sailors of the C.P.V.D. Company got promises of wage increases and other concessions. The bakers received a 3 percent wage increase.[39]

The bakers' federation a boycott against the flour of one of the milling companies. There was some sabotage in the gas company and a number of metallurgical firms.[40]

The movement spread from Callao to Lima, and although it did not reach such proportions there as in the port, there were walkouts of cigar workers, woodworkers, coal-depot employees, and telephone workers. The metalworkers of four plants received a 5 percent wage increase; the bakers in Lima won a 10-hour day in place of the previous 12 hours. The Bakus and Johnston brewery was subjected to a boycott when it refused to give in to its workers' demands.[41]

Throughout the rest of 1913, there was much labor unrest. There was a general strike in Lima on May Day.[42] In the same month, the oil workers in the northern field of Talara called on the FORP for aid, and some of those who had been active in the Lima-Callao strikes were there. An agreement favorable to the workers was reached, but soon afterward, all leaders of the walkout were fired, giving rise to another strike that was quickly smashed, while the strike leaders were taken to Callao and jailed.[43] Later in the year, there were strikes among telegraph workers and employees of the El Inca textile factory in Lima.[44]

THE FEDERACIÓN OBRERA MARÍTIMA Y TERRESTRE

As a result of the eight-hour–day movement, workers organized the Federación Obrera Marítima y Terestre del Callao, which included stevedores, truck drivers, seamen, ship carpenters, launch workers, metallurgical workers, match-factory employees, gas workers, custom-house employees, and others.[45] In the middle of 1913, the federation opened a big headquarters.[46]

The leadership of the 1912–1913 walkouts was principally in the hands of Peruvians such as the Leavnos and Otazu, but there were also some foreigners, particularly Italians and Spaniards. For instance, a Spanish anarchist, Belén de Zárraga, was one of the intellectual leaders of the Peruvian anarchist labor movement at that time,[47] and José Spagnoli and Antonio Gastinelli, two Italian anarchists, were among the most prominent figures in the strike movements in Lima and Callao.[48]

Although anarchists were the principal leaders of organized labor in Lima and Callao, other political groups also were active. More moderate leaders were predominant in a move to bind more closely together the workers of Peru and Chile. Relations between those two countries had not been friendly since the 1879 War of the Pacific, and this national enmity had permeated the working class. In a move to counteract this, a group of moderate Chilean labor leaders, including Nolasco Cárdenas and Lindolfo Alarcón, arrived in Peru at the time of the Peruvian national holiday in July 1913, and a delegation of Peruvian workers went to Chile, chosen from among leaders of the Sociedades Unidad and Confederación de Artesanos.[49]

The anarchists, to counteract this exchange, sent the secretary-general of the FORP, Eulogio Otazu, to Chile, with credentials from several anarchist-controlled unions. There Otazu had some clashes in public meetings with the Peruvian "reformist" delegates.[50] As a result of the exchange between the more moderate labor leaders of Chile and Peru, the short-lived Confraternidad Obrera Peruana-Chilena was established.[51]

PERUVIAN LABOR DURING WORLD WAR I

For some time after 1913, there was a lull in labor activities in Peru. However, in January 1915 there was another strike of Vitarte textile workers, and this was backed by most other anarchist labor organizations of Lima and Callao, although there was no general strike at the time.[52] In May 1916 there was a labor campaign against the high cost of living, led by the shoemakers and bricklayers. The high point of this drive was a public meeting, during which Carlos Barba, one of the principal union leaders, was arrested. In that same year the strikes included walkouts of stevedores of Callao and telegraph workers and a very bloody walkout of agricultural laborers in Huacho, near Lima.[53]

In 1917 labor activity gathered momentum. The fight of the unions against the rising cost of living continued, and in May 1917 the police closed up most union headquarters in Lima. In the same month, the workers of "El Inca" textile factory went on strike.[54]

Unrest was particularly notable among the agricultural workers near Lima. Early in 1917, Delfín Levano, Adelberto Fonken, and some other anarchists of Lima went to Huacho to do organizing work there. The result was the establishment of a number of unions and the organization of several workers' libraries. The whole movement culminated in June 1917 in a general strike in Huacho, during which a clash between police and strikers cost the lives of several workers.[55]

The workers of the oil fields of northern Peru once more organized and went out on strike in December 1917. Twelve workers were killed, many were wounded, and still others were deported by the government during this walkout.

For the first time, the workers of the Cerro de Pasco mining region were unionized. N. Vera, an indigenous Peruvian, led these workers in a strike, and as a result, the workers won a small wage increase and a reduction of four hours a week in their working time.[56]

The labor movement was obviously beginning to spread beyond Lima and Callao. In the southern coastal town of Ica, a Centro Obrero was organized.[57] In 1918, May Day demonstrations were held in Trujillo, Huacho, Morocha, and elsewhere, as well as in the national capital and its port.[58]

THE 1918–1919 GENERAL STRIKE

There were two important struggles during the immediate post–World War I period, the first for the eight-hour day in December 1918 and January 1919 and the second for the reduction of the high cost of living, later in 1919. The first movement began when the Sociedades Unidas passed a resolution in favor of a campaign against the high cost of living and in favor of an increase in wages and the eight-hour day.

Strikes for the eight-hour day were soon called by the textile workers of El Inca and Vitarte factories, on December 20, 1918. During the next 10 days, the textile workers of La Victoria, La Unión, and El Progreso followed, and a central strike committee was established. On December 30, the members of the Federación de Obreros Panaderos "Estrella del Perú" also quit work, demanding the eight-hour day. The agricultural workers of Huacho sent a delegation to Lima to show their solidarity with the strikers.[59]

A plea from the strike committee to the Students Federation for sympathy and support was answered by Felipe Chueca, then president of the federation, who promised the fullest possible aid from the students. The strike committee then asked to use the federation's headquarters and invited the students to delegate some members to sit on the strike committee. Both propositions were agreed to, and on January 7, the first meeting was held in the federation's office. Three students were named to participate in the strike committee, Víctor Raúl Haya de la Torre, B. Bueno, and V. Quesada.[60]

This was the first appearance of Haya de la Torre in trade union affairs. There has been some controversy as to the part that he played in the struggle for the eight-hour day. In interviews, Haya and Arturo Sabroso, who was already a textile workers' leader in 1918, claimed that Haya immediately took a position of front-rank leadership in the strike. Others denied this.[61] It is certain that Haya and the other student members of the strike committee took a leading part in dealing with public authorities, and it seems likely that Haya had considerable influence on the workingmen who made up the majority of the strike committee.

In a meeting on January 6, 1919, it was decided to rechristen the committee the Comité Pro-Paro General (Committee for a General Strike).[62] Delegates attending this meeting included representatives from textile workers, bakers, leather workers, longshoremen of Callao, trolley car workers, millers, shoemakers, and construction workers. Representatives from unions in Huacho were also present.[63]

The comité sent out a letter asking all unions to strike for an eight-hour day. They received affirmative replies from working-class organizations in Cuzco, Trujillo, and Arequipa, as well as from Huacho, and so the strike movement spread.[64] The miners in the Backus and Johnston mines at Casapalca went out, and troops were called in there.[65] Even the policemen of Lima presented demands and a strike threat to the minister of interior, which the government met by an increase of 10 soles a month in the wages of the policemen.[66]

Members at a meeting of the Asamblea de Sociedades Unidas on January 10 adopted a resolution supporting the strike movement.[67] Two days later, when the police closed the Students Federation headquarters, the Comité Pro Parao General was forced to meet in secret in the building of the Sociedades Hijos de Sol mutual benefit society. In this meeting, the members passed a resolution declaring a 48-hour general strike, demanding unconditional release of all imprisoned workers and expressing solidarity with striking Argentine workers.[68]

During the general strike, there were some clashes with the police, and the leaders of the Callao longshoremen were jailed.[69] The newspaper El Tiempo, which was published by José Carlos Mariátegui and which had given much publicity to the strikers, was suppressed by the police.[70]

The Federación Obrera Maritima y Terrestre de Callao, which had been suppressed by President Billinghurst in 1913, was revived under the leadership of Carlos del Barzo in connection with the 1918–1919 strike wave, and the group led the general walkout in Callao.[71]

There are at least two versions of how the 1918–1919 general strike for the eight-hour day was brought to a successful conclusion. Víctor Raúl Haya de la Torre stressed the role of President Pardo's minister of development and representative of the Liberal Party in the Pardo administration, Manuel A. Vinelli. According to Haya, Vinelli entered into contact, on behalf of the president, with the workers' General Strike Committee and with its student allies, and he was quickly won over to support the idea of having President Pardo issue a general decree establishing the eight-hour day.

Haya also stressed the importance of the General Strike Committee's refusal to call off the walkout, a position that he, Haya, encouraged during meetings of the committee. He also emphasized the division in the councils of the government—which, while negotiating with the workers, was also arresting many of their leaders, and at one point the government ordered soldiers to fire on a building in which the General Strike Committee was meeting. According to Haya, this potential bloodshed was avoided when he first challenged the colonel in charge to shoot him first and then arranged for a peaceful adjournment of that meeting of the General Strike Committee.

Haya de la Torre credited Minister Vinelli with finally convincing the president to issue the eight-hour decree-law. Haya noted that it was Vinelli who sent a meeting of the General Strike Committee a copy of the decree, asking the committee to agree to its conditions. Although some members of the committee wanted to refuse to end the strike until those arrested during the walkout were released, it was finally agreed to accept the decree and to officially end the strike—and as the meeting was breaking up and its members were leaving the building, they met some of the arrested leaders who had just been released from the jail.

On the other hand, Emilio Costilla Larrea and Ricardo Martínez de la Torre told another version of the triumph of the general strike. They claimed that President José Pardo called in the leaders of the Confederación de Artesanos and asked their advice. The secretary-general of the confederación, Federico Ortíz Rodríguez, suggested that Pardo issue a decree establishing the eight-hour day. Following this advice, Pardo issued a decree on January 15 in much the same form suggested by Ortíz, providing an outright grant of the eight-hour day to railroad workers and workers in other government enterprises. In private industry, the decree provided for negotiations between the workers and employers for reaching agreement on the eight-hour day, and in case such agreement was not reached, the eight-hour day should go into effect "until Congress legislates on that matter." It provided that wages should not be reduced with the reduction of working hours and that other points at issue in the strikes then underway should be settled by arbitration.[72]

As a direct result of this eight-hour–day ,movement the Textile Workers Federation was organized at a meeting on January 16. Víctor Raúl Haya de la Torre took part in this meeting, as adviser to the unions participating. Although Martínez de la Torre maintained that "Víctor Raúl" was there only as student representative and was elected president of the meeting only "as a symbolic homage to the university students,"[73] Haya and Arturo Sabroso, who became the principal leader of the Textile Workers Federation, said that Haya was the one who called together the textile union representatives right after the 1919 eight-hour–day strike.[74] In view of their close connection with the event and the fact that the Textile Workers Federation was from then on the stronghold of Haya de la Torre's influence among the workers, it seems reasonable to accept the version of Haya and Sabroso. In any case, the result of this meeting was the organization of the Federación de Trabajadores de Tejidos del Perú.[75]

THE COMITÉ PRO-ABARATAMIENTO DE LAS SUBSISTENCIAS

Only two months after the struggle for the eight-hour day, the Comité Pro-Abaratamiento de las Subsistencias (Committee for Lower Prices) was organized by delegates of the textile workers, bakers, shoemakers, bricklayers, millers, coach drivers, and white-collar workers. The editors of the anarchist periodical *La Protesta* took a leading part in this committee, which decided to meet every Sunday evening to carry out agitation against the high cost of living.[76]

The committee called a general strike to celebrate May Day 1919, which was widely observed. However, there were three rival meetings held on that day in Lima, sponsored by the Comité, the Partido Socialista, and the Partido Obrero, respectively. Those sponsored by the two political parties, both of which were very new organizations, broke up in confusion when anarchist leaders appeared and heckled the speakers, which finally led the demonstrators present at these meetings to join the main anarchosyndicalist parade and meeting sponsored by the comité.[77]

A series of strikes broke out soon after May Day, including walkouts among the textile workers of the Santa Catalina factory, the miners of Ticapampa, the millers and spaghetti-makers of Lima, and trolley-car men. These strikes began to take on the nature of a general movement and were strongly opposed by the newly formed Partido Socialista, which was headed by a well-known historian, Luis Ulloa. As a result of this attitude of the party, Carlos Barba, a young ex-anarchist labor figure, left the group.[78] This experience with the Partido Socialista left a bad taste in the mouths of many workers and is at least a partial explanation for the failure of a Socialist party to develop any major force in Peru.[79]

The Comité Pro-Abaratamiento de Sunsistencias continued its agitation, and on May 27, Gutarra and Carlos Barba were jailed by the police. As a result, the comité proclaimed a general strike. The move was backed hesitantly by the Confederación de Artesanos and the Asamblea de Sociedades Unidas, who asked the government to free the arrested workers and to take some steps to reduce prices. The strike was virtually complete during the first few days in both Lima and Callao, and the government declared martial law in both cities. Street clashes were frequent and machine guns were issued for the police. Almost all the principal labor leaders were either jailed or wounded in the recurring brushes with the police, who made house-to-house searches, confiscating the workers' food reserves. Some 800,000 soles' worth of food was thus seized. An "Urban Guard" was organized to fight the strike. On May 30, a few workers began to trickle back to work, and the walkout was finally called off on May 31 in a secret meeting of the Comité Pro-Abaratamiento.[80] On June 1, things were about normal for a Sunday, and on June 2, the workers were back in full force.[81]

The comité itself was reorganized in July as the Federación Obrera Regional Peruana, the original one having expired some time before. The new FORP was active for some time thereafter. On July 21, 1919, the FORP sponsored jointly with the Partido Socialista a demonstration in favor of the Russian Revolution.[82]

Dissension began to appear in the anarchist labor movement between those who remained loyal to their anarchist ideas and those who were friendly to the Russian Revolution and hence became more interested in party politics. The issue finally came to a head soon after the reformation of the FORP, when Gutarra was offered a candidacy as a deputy by Augusto P. Leguía, who had overthrown José Pardo on July 4, 1919, and become president of Peru once again. Gutarra refused the offer, but a sizable group in the FORP thought that he should accept. This same group, which was also agitating in favor of affiliation of the FORP to the Communist International, finally withdrew from FORP.[83]

There continued to be numerous strikes, particularly in the national capital and in Callao. The most important strike after the general walkout of May 1919 was a general stoppage in Callao in September of the same year, which was successful in getting certain wage increases, particularly for the stevedores.[84] The first major strike in the printing trades was called in October 1919 by the newly formed Federación Gráfica.[85] This walkout continued for about fifteen days and won the members a 5 percent increase in wages. Several leaders of the printers had taken a leading part in the strikes and demonstrations of the early part of 1919, and two of the founders of the Federación Gráfica, Osvaldo Alvarez and Erasmo Sánchez, were jailed during the May events.[86]

THE ESTABLISHMENT OF POPULAR UNIVERSITIES

An important event occurred late in 1919 in the ancient Inca capital of Cuzco when the Students Federation adopted a resolution calling for establishment of "popular universities" by the students in cooperation with trade union leaders. On the initiative of Víctor Raúl Haya de la Torre, this resolution provided that "the Popular Universities will participate officially in all labor conflicts, basing their actions on the principles of social justice." On January 21, 1920, Haya de la Torre, as president of the Students Federation, opened the first Universidad Popular in the headquarters of the Federation in Lima. Similar groups were founded in the years that followed in Vitarte, Trujillo, Huacho, Janja, Arequipa, Cuzco, and Usquil. An attempt to open such a group in Callao was stopped when the police fired on its building on the night of its opening. Among the students who were most active in the popular universities, in addition to Haya de la Torre, were Nestor Díaz, Estéban Pavletich, Luciano Castillo, and Eudocio Rabines.[87]

This was not the first time that attempts had been made to undertake large-scale adult-education programs among the workers. The anarchosyndicalists had had classes on the style of Ferrer's Modern School in Barcelona, Spain, after 1917, and Oscar Miró Quesada (the "black sheep" of one of the richest and most reactionary families in Peru) had been conducting classes for workers. Manuel González Prada had taken an important part in these early workers' education activities.[88]

The popular universities were one phase of the close cooperation during these early years of the 1920s between the group of university students led by Haya de la Torre and the trade union leaders, of whom Arturo Sabroso was the most important. Haya de la Torre, the scion of one of the oldest and most aristocratic Spanish families in Peru, came from the northern city of Trujillo. He first became interested in social problems in 1916–1917 while a student at the University of Cuzco, where he came to realize the need for education and betterment of living conditions among the native Indians. After that year in Cuzco, he became active in the Federación de Estudiantes and was elected its president in 1919.[89]

After Haya became president of the Students Federation, he developed closer connections with the trade unions, and the union leaders came to look to him for leadership in a variety of ways. He took a lead in establishing the "Fiesta de la Planta" ("Factory Celebration") at the Vitarte textile plant, in a move to "support the fetish of Christmas." The first of these celebrations was held on December 25, 1921, when Haya was reported to have made a "moving laical speech."[90] These celebrations were continued throughout the 1920s, for several years after Haya left the country.[91]

The unions remained very active. There was a widespread textile-workers strike in August 1920, and walkouts of millers and railroad workers took place in November of the same year. The chauffeurs of Lima went out in January 1921, the agricultural workers of Chicamo in March of that year. There were lockouts of the El Inca textile-plant workers in September 1921 and of the bakers of Lima in October.[92]

Labor organization spread to white-collar workers. In 1920 the Sociedad Unión de Empleados del Perú was established. It was not characterized by great militancy, and certainly was not of anarchosyndicalist inspiration. Its periodical, *Trabajo y Libertad*, proclaimed,

We are not going to begin struggles between capital and labor ... neither do we intend to raise up with boastful and disgustingly bullying the red banner of revolt.... Our mission is that of protection, of mutual defense, of petition without intemperance, of disagreement without insults or diatribes. We shall search for, by all means at our disposal, the close cooperation between management and *obreros*, directions and *empleados* whose interests are parallel lines reaching to infinity without obstructing without obstructing one another.

However, in spite of the new group's apparent repudiation of militancy, its secretary-general, who had worked for the same firm for more than a quarter of a century, was promptly fired when he assumed leadership of the sociedad.[93]

THE FIRST LOCAL LABOR CONGRESS OF LIMA

The first local labor congress of Lima was held in April 1921. Most labor organizations of the capital were represented, and the principal subject of discussion was whether the congress should pledge support of anarchist Communism. Delfín Levano, who acted as secretary-general, opposed pledging the congress to any particular ideology, although himself an anarchist. The move to declare the labor organizations of Lima to be supporters of anarchist Communism was defeated.[94]

Augustín B. Leguía was by this time president of Peru. He was a man who had mildly opposed the regime of the *civilistas*, as the ruling oligarchy were known, and had therefore built up considerable popularity among the working classes and the advanced intellectuals. Haya de la Torre and most other leaders of the Students Federation were Leguistas before Leguía returned to the presidency for the second time in 1919.[95] However, as president, Leguía tended to fall back on the more conservative groups in the community for support, and by early 1922, he had declared "war without quarter" on the unions and the libertarian organizations. Union leaders were jailed and deported, headquarters were closed, homes were raided, and the books of the unions were seized. Among those exiled was Nicolás Gutarra, who was deported successively from Argentina, Chile, Peru, and Mexico, finally landing in California, where he died in a strike incident.[96]

Early in 1923, Leguía sought to strengthen his position by the gesture of "dedicating" Peru to the Sacred Heart of Jesus. The student leaders and most union leaders resented this draping of a dictatorship in sacred colors. Víctor Raúl Haya de la Torre led a mass protest of workers and students, which was broken up by troops. At the funeral ceremonies for those killed during this demonstration, Haya de la Torre won international attention for his moving oration over their graves, in which he bitterly attacked the government of Leguía. The dictator immediately retaliated by having Haya arrested and incarcerated in the island prison of Frontón. There, in protest against his treatment, Haya went on a hunger strike that soon gained attention throughout the country and finally resulted in his being released from prison and exiled. In a manifesto to the people of Peru upon leaving the country, he made a promise that he would return "when the hour of the great transformation has arrived."[97]

During the years that followed, Haya wandered over Central America, Mexico, the United States, and Europe. After a trip to Russia, he decided against aligning himself with the Communists and instead launched a political movement of his own, the Alianza Popular Revolucionaria Americana (APRA), which had as the basic element of its doctrine the need for an alliance among urban workers, intellectuals, and agrarian workers against the landlords and foreign imperialists.[98]

While he was in exile, Haya de la Torre's memory was kept fresh among the organized workers, particularly the textile workers. On the first anniversary of his exile, in October 1924, there was a front-page picture of him in the textile workers' magazine *El Obrero Textil*.[99] There were articles from time to time in the same magazine about Haya or by him.[100]

THE LABOR MOVEMENT IN THE 1920s

Under the government of Agustín P. Leguía, the Peruvian economy grew and changed. Denis Sulmont outlined these changes:

The government of Leguía displaced the conservative sectors of the civilista oligarchy, to give impulse to the program of modernization based on North American financial capital. Loans and investments permitted the expansion of the state apparatus and economics activities (especially construction), together with urban development, particularly in Lima…. Economic expansion brought with it as a consequence, the increase in wageworkers. In manufacturing activities, employment increased from 20 to 30 thousand workers during the twenties; employment in mining rose from 20 to nearly 30 thousand workers, and in agro-industry from 70 to 90 thousand approximately (a third of them sugar workers).[101]

However, the increase in economic activities and the size of the working class was accompanied by a policy of antipathy toward organized labor on the part of the Leguía government. The attitude of the Leguía government toward the unions was shown by the fact that the textile workers' journal was frequently suppressed. Every time it was closed, it reappeared with a different name and makeup. In September 1923, *El Obrero Textil* was succeeded by *Solidaridad*, which was the organ of the Federación Obrera Local of Lima as well as of the Textile Federation and which included pages devoted to different unions, such as chauffeurs and printing-trades employees, as well as textile workers.[102]

The Federación Obrera Local was the principal labor organization in Peru for some years. It called a general strike in protest against the jailing of Haya de la Torre in October 1923.[103] It carried on a campaign against a new military conscription law during which many leaders were jailed.[104] It cooperated in many strikes, including a stoppage in printing shops of the capital in September 1924, a strike of trolley-car workers in October of the same year, and a walkout of butchers, which was won only after the Federación Obrera Local declared a general strike.[105] Arturo Sabroso of the Textile Workers Federation was secretary-general of the Federación Obrera Local.[106]

The workers' organizations of Peru during the 1920s were aware of their place in the worldwide labor movement. Not only did they celebrate May Day each year, but they also expressed their solidarity with the labor movement in various parts of the world. For instance, there were three general strikes in Lima as demonstrations against the execution of Sacco and Vanzetti, the last of these on the day of their death.[107]

The Second Workers Congress was held in 1927 and was marked by a struggle between the anarchists and their opponents. There were 30 delegations in attendance, including those from six textile unions and two federations of Indians and peasants. Other delegates represented chauffeurs, butchers, printing-trades workers, carpenters, and hat workers. Arturo Sabroso was secretary-general of this congress,[108] which voted to establish the Unión Sindical del Perú,[109] a name reminiscent of the syndicalist Argentine Unión Sindical Argentina. The Second Congress marked the end of anarchist dominance of the Peruvian labor movement.[110]

By this time, there were fairly strong organizations among the railroad workers, which were grouped in the Confederación Obrera Ferrocarrilera, established in 1924. The confederación included workers in Lima, Callao, Guadelupe, and Trujillo and was said to have some 8,000 members. Late in 1925, it split into two groups: the Confederación Obrera Ferrocarrilera, which represented the unskilled workers, and the Confederación de Trabajadores Ferroviarios del Perú, which represented the engineers, firemen, conductors, and white-collar workers.[111]

Some unions appeared among the workers in the agricultural plantations along the coast. The first organizations appeared among the sugar workers, and then unions also were established among laborers on the cotton plantations. In 1921 a Federation of Peasants in the Ica Valley was established in the South, and in 1922 a Federation of Sharecroppers (Federación de Yanaconas) was organized.[112]

In June 1927, the police raided all principal unions, closed the Federación Obrera Local, and assaulted the workers' press. Arturo Sabroso, Felipe Barrientos, and others were jailed.[113] The government at the same time made the claim that there was on foot "a communist plot to assault the banks and divide the lands and goods."[114] Of course, in fact there was as yet no Communist movement in Peru.

THE MARIÁTEGUI GROUP

Soon after this incident, José Carlos Mariátegui took the lead in founding the Comité Pro-Confederación General de Trabajadores del Perú, with the purpose of organizing a new national central labor organization.[115]

Mariátegui was a young man who as a student and newspaperman had expressed various radical ideas. His position was described by one of his biographers as follows:

Mariátegui, Falcón, Valdelomar and other young writers of advanced ideas necessarily had to be on the side of the people, on the side of the left-wing university students in open conflict with the nucleus of plutocratic students and against the "Civilista" faculty members, almost all survivors of the Middle Ages. They were, therefore, Leguistas to a certain degree. Mariátegui and Falcón commenced to move into an area between the classes, and found a periodical to which several workers wrote…. This periodical, *Nuestro Epoca*, had to suspend almost immediately because of economic difficulties. That was the instant in which Alfredo Piedra, Leguía's Minister, offered government scholarships for study in Europe.[116]

While in Europe, Mariátegui became a Marxist. Upon his return to Peru, he did not commit himself in his teaching or writing to any position on the question of Leguía, but Mariátegui gathered around himself a group of young left-wing intellectuals of various political ideologies.

Under Mariátegui's leadership, the periodical *Amauta* was founded. It included among its contributors people who later became Communists and many who did not. These included Haya de la Torre, Carlos Mauel Cox, Magda Portal, Manuel Seoane, Luis Alberto Sánchez, Manuel Vázquez Díaz, and others who became Apristas. Carlos Manuel Cox and Vázquez Díaz were members of the inner group of *Amauta* contributors. César Falcón, Estéban Pavletich, Ricardo Martínez de la Torre , and Eudosio Rabines later became leaders of the Communist Party. Luciano Castillo later became founder and leader of the Peruvian Socialist Party. Finally, *Amauta* published contributions from distinguished foreigners of various ideologies, including Miguel Unamuno, Gabriela Mistral, Alfred Palacios, Tristán Marof, Louis Aragon, and Waldo Frank.

The magazine was both a political periodical with articles on world and local events and a literary and artistic organ. It discussed foreign artistic trends such as the Mexican artistic revolution of the 1920s and gave opportunities to many Peruvian artists and writers to achieve some exhibition of their works.[117]

Members of the Mariátegui group formed the Partido Socialista, to function legally, distribute propaganda, and lay the groundwork for the formation of a Communist Party. This position of the Mariátegui group was severely criticized during the congress of Latin American Communist parties held in Buenos Aires in 1929. Taking a lead in this denunciation was the Argentine Victorio Codovilla, then as later a very important figure in the Communist International in Latin America.[118] The Peruvians were ordered to change their party's name to Partido Comunista and to adopt a program more in line with the Comintern's "Third Period" position.[119]

Mariátegui was said to have opposed the idea of having a strictly Communist party until his death late in 1929, but by the time the final decision was made, he was dead, and only Ricardo Martínez de la Torre and Luciano Castillo opposed the changes ordered by the Communist International.[120] Castillo broke with the Partido Comunista and organized his own Partido Socialista, which continued in existence for more than half a century.

ORGANIZED LABOR IN THE LAST YEARS OF THE LEGUÍA DICTATORSHIP

During the last part of his dictatorship, Leguía severely persecuted the unions. The Federación de Motoristas, Conductores y Anexos del Perú, the trolley-car workers' organization founded in 1921, was first legally recognized by the government early in 1929 and then later in the year was outlawed because of a strike.[121] The Federación de Campesinos y Yanacones (Peasants and Sharecroppers Federation) was outlawed and destroyed by the government in 1929.[122] The Construction Workers Union was virtually annihilated by the government in 1927.[123] Both the Confederación General de Trabajadores del Perú, organized by the followers of Mariátegui, and the mutualist Confederación de Artesanos were officially dissolved by the government.[124] Denis Sulmont concluded that government persecution in this period largely ended anarchosyndicalist influence on Peruvian organized labor. *La Protesta* ceased publication in 1926.[125]

THE OVERTHROW OF LEGUÍA

The year 1930 saw the overthrow of Leguía and the advent of a short period of democratic liberty. This was used to the utmost by the political groups and the labor movement. The exiled Aprista leaders streamed back, and during these months, they took the message of the APRA, or Partido Aprista Peruano as it was now called, far and wide throughout the country. They went into small villages; they went back into the Indian areas. They went into the North and down to the Chilean frontier. With great energy, Haya de la Torre took the message of the Aprista Party to the furthest reaches of the country, as did other Aprista leaders such as Manuel Seoane, Luis Heysen, and Magda Portal.

Never before had such enthusiasm been aroused among the masses. The word "APRA" was chalked on walls in Lima, Callao, and Trujillo and in the smallest Indian villages. The letters were emblazoned on hillsides. Carleton Beales told of seeing a little dog whose hair had been clipped so as to spell out the magic letters APRA.[126] As one of the Aprista leaders wrote later, "A meeting of eight people was converted into an electorate of 110,000."[127]

There were a number of strikes following Leguía's overthrow. One of the most serious of these was a walkout in the U.S.-owned Cerro de Pasco mining enterprise, which resulted in considerable violence. The company demanded the deportation of "labor agitators" whom it blamed for the strike.[128]

In the presidential contest of 1931, Colonel Luis Sánchez Cerro, the mulatto military officer who had overthrown Leguía, and Haya de la Torre were the candidates. *Fortune* magazine reported, "Few people in Lima are so naïve as to believe that Haya de la Torre lost the 1931 election."[129] Although cheated of the presidency, the Apristas did win a number of seats in Congress, and among those elected by APRA was Arturo Sabroso, the textile-union leader, who thus became the first Aprista workingman to be elected to parliament. Other unionists among the Aprista members of the Chamber of Deputies were Manuel Arévalo and Gallegos Zavala.[130]

It was not long before Sánchez Cerro installed his own dictatorship, which lasted for almost two years. During this time, the Apristas, and to a lesser degree other opposition groups, were severely repressed. Haya himself was jailed, as were many other Aprista Party leaders, while still others went into hiding. This period was brought to an end by the assassination of the dictator, supposedly by an Aprista. There then succeeded another short period of democratic liberties under General Oscar Benavides, but within a few months, Benavides also installed a dictatorship.

During the short periods of freedom, there was a considerable impulse given to the trade union movement. Under the leadership of Julio Portocarrero and Avelino Navarro, the Communists were successful in establishing the Confederación General de Trabajadores del Perú (CGTP). It had been launched officially on May Day 1929, but had not been able to operate openly until after the overthrow of Leguía.

The government of Sánchez Cerro at first declared the CGTP illegal and exiled a number of union leaders to the jungle area of Madre de Dios. However, sometime later, when Sánchez Cerro's regime was menaced by an Aprista insurrection, the dictator had the CGTP leaders Avelino Navarro and Simeón Zarate Galarza released from prison, and they spoke to a meeting in support of the government. That constituted de facto recognition of the confederación, and for the rest of the Sánchez Cerro period it functioned more or less legally.[131] The CGTP reportedly held a plenum sometime early in 1931.[132]

The confederación took the lead in organization of national federations. Such organizations of miners, sugar workers, and petroleum workers were among those established during this period.[133] The first of these was organized by the Socialists of Luciano Castillo but then came under Communist control.[134]

There was a great deal of controversy over the origin of the petroleum workers' groups. Eudosio Rabines, who was then the head of the Communist Party, maintained that it was the Communists who organized the Petroleum Federation.[135] Luciano Castillo, on the other hand, claimed that the Socialists had established it.[136] Fernández Stoll, who later headed the government's Labor Directorate, believed that it was the Apristas who first organized both the miners' and petroleum workers' federations. [137] Judging from the political dominance that the Partido Socialista of Luciano Castillo gained in the petroleum area, it seems likely that the Socialists had a major part in organizing these workers.

In Lima, the taxi drivers were among the leaders in this revival of the labor movement. Faced with lack of work, the taxis began to function like small buses, carrying passengers for 10 centavos a head. The bus companies objected, and finally the government prohibited the taxi drivers' change in modus operandi. The result was a strike of all the taxi drivers in the capital, and in the process of the strike, several people were killed. But the strike was finally victorious. As a result of this walkout, the Sindicato de Chóferes del Servicio Público de Lima, made up of taxi men, was formed. The Federación de Chóferes was reorganized in 1934. About the same time, the Sindicato de Autobuses was organized. These groups were controlled by the Apristas.[138]

Another important strike in Lima during the period after the overthrow of Leguía was that of the Federación de Obreros Panaderos "Estrella del Perú," in order to obtain a closed shop.[139]

The labor movement grew in the provinces as well as in the Lima area. The first big strike movement in Cuzco took place in 1930 when there was a general walkout in solidarity with a local textile workers' strike. In spite of being an illegal strike, it won a partial victory for the textile workers. In 1934 there was another general strike in Cuzco, to back up strikers on the Ferrrocarril Cuzco-Santa Ana railroad, which was also successful. The Sindicato de Chóferes, which became the backbone of the labor movement in the ancient Inca capital, was founded in 1932. However, even before the ouster of Leguía, there had been founded an illegal Federación Obrera Departamental, which changed its name to Unión Sindical Obrero de Cuzco in 1934. It was controlled by the Communists.[140]

Probably the most spectacular labor activity during the four years between the Leguía dictatorship and that of General Benavides was the protracted struggle of the miners of the U.S.-owned Cerro de Pasco Company. They went out on a strike in September 1930, which cost six miners their lives. Several months later, the police tried to break up a demonstration of the miners at La Oroya, and the resulting battle brought 22 deaths. Allegedly on the advice of the U.S. ambassador, Sánchez Cerro ordered the dissolution of the unions and arrested their leaders, deporting them to a penal colony. Troops were rushed to the area to deal with a strike of 10,000 miners.[141] Throughout the next year, strikes continued in the mining region, and almost all of them were "crushed with an iron hand."[142]

A SPLIT IN THE CGTP

During the early part of the Benavides regime, the Confederación General de Trabajadores del Perú (CGTP) suffered a schism. It had at first included most of the country's organized workers, of all political tendencies. However, the Communists were in control, and the Apristas broke with the CGTP early in 1934. In January, they established the Reorganizing Committee of the Proletariat, which some months later became the Central Sindical de Trabajadores del Perú (CSTP), of which Segundo P. Black was the secretary-general.

The backbone of the CSTP was the Federation of Textile Workers. However, the Central Sindical had 14 other affiliates, most of them unions in the Lima area, but also including a Regional Federation of the North, the Trade Union Central of the Center, and the National Indigenous Peasant Community. The Federation of Students of the University Reform also belonged to the CSTP.

Understandably, the Communists strongly attacked the new central labor group. One of the principal spokesmen, Ricardo Martínez de la Torre, attacked the CSTP as being anarchosyndicalist. However, in fact, the few remaining anarchists in the labor movement attacked the new Central with as much vigor as did the Communists.[143]

The Central Sindical de Trabajadores del Perú held a national convention, which reportedly was attended by 66 delegates, all of whom were arrested and sent to jail. Then, in December 1934, there was a general strike called by the CSTP, in support of a number of sergeants and other noncoms of the army who were being "persecuted" because of their Aprista sympathies. The government broke this strike and from then on vigorously persecuted the organization, and the CSTP soon ceased to exist. It had lasted some six to seven months.[144]

This split in the labor movement should be judged against the background of the extreme sectarianism, which still characterized the International Communist Line at this time, one aspect of which was the denunciation of all other parties of the left as "social fascists." This is epitomized in the following passage concerning Arturo Sabroso, the leader of the Aprista textile workers' union, which appeared in the pamphlet *Ediciones de Frente,* published by the Communists late in 1934: "Sabroso who, when he was a permanent collaborator in 'our press,' combated those who spoke of making the 'revolution from above,' appears today as the señor deputy of the social-fascists who attempt to make exactly the revolution 'from above,' frightened as he is by the revolutionary intervention of the oppressed masses with arms in their hands."

The pamphlet went on,

To make this "revolution from above" these politicians of matured native fascism, make sure that the workers are not in a position to make it "from below." And there is no better way to prevent this than to destroy their organs of class war. To dissolve the organization of the workers. What better solution than that of Aprista trade unionism! That is, a eunuch trade unionism, effeminate, perverted, deprived of its drive, its spirit, its belligerence, and its intransigence.[145]

This attitude of the Communists, combined with the missionary zeal of the Apristas, probably made this split in the labor movement inevitable. In any case, the Central Sindical and the Confederación General de Trabajadores were both obliterated by the dictatorship after 1934.[146] At that point there was little freedom of action for the unions under Benavides. The only other spurt of labor militancy during that period occurred in 1936 when the Apristas were cheated out of an election victory, and the labor organizations still controlled by them went on a futile protest strike.[147]

BENAVIDES AND ORGANIZED LABOR

After the 1936 strike, Benavides outlawed virtually all unions. For two years or more there were practically no legal labor organizations in the country. Unionism persisted principally among the textile workers, chauffeurs, bakers, printing-trades workers, stevedores, and the railroad workers of Lima-Arequipa Railroad, but most of these organizations were not legally recognized by the government.[148] It was not until Jorge Fernández Stoll became director general of labor in 1938 that the Benavides regime once more began to permit a few legal unions.[149]

Many labor leaders were jailed or driven into hiding during this period. Arturo Sabroso was kept in the notorious Frontón prison for more than four years, where he was one of four hundred Apristas. They organized a popular university in the prison, with courses in Quechua, mathematics, history, algebra, trade unionism, Marxism, German, English, music, shorthand, and Aprista theory. Thus, the morale of the prisoners was maintained, their solidarity was assured, and their time in prison was not a total loss.[150]

Other political groups besides the Apristas also suffered under the Benavides regime. The Socialist Party was driven underground, and its principal leader, Luciano Castillo, spent almost a decade in exile in Mexico, where he worked for the Ministry of Education.[151] The Communists, too, were persecuted during part of this time, although near the end of the Benavides regime, they reached an agreement for limited cooperation with the government.[152]

The selection of Fernández Stoll as director of labor was, a priori, surprising. Fernández was a young writer of somewhat leftist orientation who, upon one occasion, wrote an article quite critical of the regime, which came to Benavides' attention. The dictator demanded to see its author. Fernández Stoll talked with the marshal at length, telling him with as much frankness as seemed diplomatic the faults that he saw in the regime. The next day, he was summoned once more to the presidential palace and to his great amazement was offered the post of director general of labor. After at first protesting that he was too young—and that he wanted to run the Labor Department on very different lines than Benavides would permit—he finally agreed to take the post. The president told Fernández

Stoll that he should do things the way he, Fernández Stoll, wanted to do them and that if Benavides thought that he was mishandling the job, Fernández Stoll would be told quickly enough.

After the new director general of labor took office, there was some loosening up in the government's attitude toward the labor movement. One of the first moves of Fernández Stoll was to grant legal recognition to the Sindicato de Chóferes (chauffeurs) of Lima. Thereafter, other unions were slowly legalized by the government, although the process was a very slow one while Benavides remained in the presidency.[153] However, the Benavides regime inaugurated a procedure that was followed by subsequent dictatorships: having policemen present at all union meetings, with one of the policemen's job being to identify "undesirable" union leaders.[154]

BENAVIDES, PRADO, AND THE COMMUNISTS

In 1939 a presidential election was held. The candidates were Manuel Prado, the government nominee, and Luis E. Flores, leader of the Unión Revolucionaria, the party that had been founded by Sánchez Cerro. The Apristas, still illegal, were not permitted to have a candidate for president or any other office in this election.

Among the supporters of Prado was the Communist Party. The party was not legal, but its leaders were known, and their support was accepted by Prado. The Communists made their claim that the government candidate was the nominee of the "democratic forces," against the avowed fascist totalitarianism of Flores. A successful candidate on the congressional ticket of the Prado forces was Juan P. Luna, at the time the leader of the chauffeurs' union of the capital and a Communist.[155]

Manuel Prado won the election. During the Prado regime, the unions slowly reconstructed. Old organizations revived, such as the Textile Workers Federation, which once again became the most important union in Peru and remained in the hands of the Apristas.[156] A 1940 publication of the federation indicated that it had 18 active unions of textile workers affiliated with it, as well as five unions of hat makers. In addition, it listed four provincial unions, which it classified as "recess with right of defense."[157]

During this period, the Textile Workers Federation submitted a number of proposals to top government officials, including the president and minister of labor. It published at least three of these as pamphlets, under the general title of *Social Question*, dealing with "a just level of wages for the textile workers," "a readjustment of textile remuneration in Peru," and "unevenness of rise in the cost of living and wage improvements."

Union organizations even revived in such areas as the oil and sugar regions of the North and the mining areas of the center of the country.[158] Juan P. Luna estimated that there were a quarter of a million workers in unions by the end of the Prado administration.[159] Perhaps some caution is suggested in accepting this estimate, given that statistics on the subject are at best rudimentary.

Attempts were made to bring the workers together once more in a central labor organization. The Unión Provincial de Trabajadores de Lima, organized in 1942,[160] had the following groups affiliated with it in 1945:

- The Federación Gráfica
- The Sindicato Único de Trabajadores de Autobuses
- The Sindicato de Zapateros (shoemakers)
- The Sindicato de Trabajadores de la Fabrica de Vidrios Fersand (glass workers)
- The Federación de Motoristas y Conductores (trolley car workers)
- The Federación de Panaderos "Estrella del Perú" (bakers)
- The Federación de Trabajadores de Tejidos (textile workers)
- The Sindicato de Trabajadores en Construcción Civil (construction workers)
- The Federación de Sombrereros (hatters)
- The Sindicato de Trabajadores del Mueble (furniture workers)
- The Sindicato de Chóferes del Servicio Público (taxi drivers)

It was said at the time that the "purpose of the Unión Provincial will be to unify the proletariat of the capital, and to help the victory of the United Nations by intensifying production."[161]

There were some other regional federations established, in Cuzco, Callao, Arequipa, and Puno.[162] In Cuzco, the old Unión Sindical Obrera was reorganized in 1939 under the name of Federación de Trabajadores de Cuzco. It was controlled by the Communists.[163] It was claimed that the government paid the salaries of a number of the Cuzco trade union leaders, and it is certain that the government gave the Federación de Trabajadores a new headquarters in 1943.[164]

Numerous new union groups were organized. In 1943 the glass factories were unionized in Lima,[165] and the Agricultural Federation, which had been dormant for several years, was revived.[166] The Federación de Construcción Civil was organized in 1944.[167] After 1942, the Chauffeur's Federation, which had been more or less suspended for many years, was revived and became very active.[168]

LOMBARDO TOLEDANO'S VISIT

A visit to Lima by Vicente Lombardo Toledano, the Mexican labor leader who was head of the Confederación de Trabajadores de América Latina (CTAL), late in 1942 caused some stimulus to the labor movement of Peru. At the same time, it presented a problem for the government. The Prado regime at first refused Lombardo permission to come to Peru, but then when the Aprista and other exiles in Chile publicized this refusal, the government backed down. It decided to allow him to come, but Fernández

Stoll was delegated to accompany him wherever he went. President Prado even allowed the CTAL president to make a public speech and to carry on negotiations looking toward formation of a Confederation of Peruvian Workers.[169]

Lombardo had lunch with President Prado. When first informed of this date with the president, Lombardo was told that "Peruvian labor leaders" would also be there, so he assured the principal Aprista union leaders that they were going to be present. They doubted it, and the morning of the luncheon, Lombardo told them that he had misunderstood the invitation and that they were not invited. Only Communist labor chiefs attended this luncheon.[170]

THE FOUNDING OF THE CONFEDERACIÓN DE TRABAJADORES DEL PERÚ

The next step toward unification of the labor movement of Peru was the visit by several Peruvian labor leaders to the convention of the Confederación de Trabajadores de Chile in 1943. This delegation included the Communists Juan P. Luna, Manuel Ugarte, Valdivia Herrera, and Gallardo and Apristas Arturo Sabroso and Luis Negreiros. While in Chile, the two Aprista delegates issued a statement to the effect that there was no democracy or liberty for the trade unions in Peru, which was countered by a statement by Lombardo Toledano and the Communist Peruvians that the Prado government was "democratic in foreign affairs."[171]

While in Chile, this group of Peruvian labor leaders signed a pact of unity and formed a Comité de Unificación Nacional de los Trabajadores Peruanos to organize a new Confederation of Peruvian Workers.[172] This document was countersigned by Vicente Lombardo Toledano, as head of the CTAL, and Bernardo Ibáñez, secretary-general of the Confederación de Trabajadores de Chile.[173]

This Pact of Unity said that its objective was to create a representative central organization of Peruvian workers. It agreed to aid the government in all democratic acts, to help in the industrialization of the country, to fight for higher wages and better working conditions, to work for freedom of union organization, and to try to bring about an understanding among the political parties working within the unions.[174]

The final step toward unity was taken on May 1944, when a demonstration was held in the General Cemetery of Lima in front of the tombs of Manuel González Prada and José Mariátegui. During the speeches, the Confederación de Trabajadores del Perú was declared to be in existence. Afterward, who was given credit for this proclamation depended on who was recounting what happened. The Apristas maintained that their orator, Luis Negreiros, speaking in front of the grave of González Prada, declared the CTP to be in existence and invited everyone present to sign an official statement attesting to its foundation.[175] The Communists, on the other hand, claimed that the proclamation was made by a Communist in front of the tomb of Mariátegui.[176]

The Confederación de Trabajadores de Peru was dominated by the Communists in its early days, with Juan P. Luna as its secretary-general.[177] The Apristas said later that they allowed the Communists to dominate the organization because that was the only way they could be reasonably sure that the Prado government would not break up the organization.[178]

It is certain that during the Prado regime the Communists worked closely with the administration. The Prado government was a regime without any mass support, and it tried to make the Communists into such a base and thus build up a rival to the Apristas, who were the principal opposition to the government. Whenever the government wanted to make some maneuver against the Apristas, they could count on the support of the Communists.[179] The cooperation between the Communists and Prado seems to have been on an informal plane, and there was never a formal pact between them.[180]

The Communists said later that they regarded the Prado government not as a democratic one, but as a transitional regime. However, they said that they had supported the government in line with the international position of the Confederación de Trabajadores de América Latina, which was to support those regimes in America that were turning toward democracy and that backed the United States in World War II.[181] They claimed that if they had not backed Prado, that would have helped no one but the Axis.[182]

A U.S. observer, Allen Haiden of the *Chicago Daily News,* wrote of the Communists at that time in the following vein: "In the background a small, disciplined, but uninfluential Communist party, financed by the government, watches the game and takes side—if any—with Pardo, who controls the purse strings and has allowed it some freedom of action."[183] The same writer listed the Communists as part of the 10 percent minority that was ruling the country against the wishes of the 90 percent majority. He classed it as part of "the Pradismo" faction of the 10 percent and wrote, "The latter are favored by the president so that it will appear he has the semblance of popular support."[184]

Juan P. Luna was a member of Congress and did yeoman's work for both his party and the labor movement. He was active in getting workers out of jail who had run afoul of the authorities as a result of their union activities, and he succeeded in convincing the administration to push at least some labor legislation. He was said to have fought frequently for the extension of the freedom of unions to organize.[185] In the period before the organization of the CTP, the leaders of the Comité de Unificación Nacional met in Juan P. Luna's house as the only place where they could be reasonably sure that the police would not interfere with them.[186]

The Prado government kept in force its predecessors' laws against the unions. In order to hold a union meeting, it was necessary to have the permission of the police, and every so often, this assent was not forthcoming, in which case it was necessary to hold the meeting surreptitiously.[187] Union headquarters were frequently closed by government decree. For instance, the bakers' union was shut down by the police twice during the Prado administration.[188]

The Aprista trade unionists continued to be persecuted to some degree under Prado, although both Fernández Stoll and the Communists insisted that those individuals were persecuted as Apristas, not as trade union leaders. They pointed to the fact that the Apristas still continued to control a number of the unions, including the Textile Workers Federation, in spite of government hostility. They also pointed out that some Aprista leaders went abroad in government-appointed delegations to the International Labor Organization annual conferences.[189]

THE LIMA GENERAL STRIKE OF SEPTEMBER–OCTOBER 1944

In June 1944, the Apristas won a new power base in the labor movement with the establishment of the Unión Sindical de Trabajadores de Lima (USTL), the central labor organization of the labor movement in the capital city. Although in its "Circular #2," the USTL announced that it had been established "under the single direction of the Confederación de Trabajadores del Perú," this new body, unlike the CTP, was controlled by the Apristas.

In September 1944, the USTL established a Strike Committee, to lay the basis for a general strike in Lima. The avowed purpose of such a walkout was to express solidarity with workers in five different factories in the capital who were in conflict with their employers, as well as to demand "trade union liberty and prompt solution of the demands pending before the Dirección de Trabajo."

Both the Prado government and the Communist leadership of the CTP expressed opposition to the proposed general strike. The Ministry of Justice and Labor claimed that the walkout was being organized by "social agitators who are intervening in the labor organizations." The CTP insisted that "there not being sufficient justification, it is completely inopportune to declare a general strike in Lima."

In spite of the opposition of the government and the Communist leaders of the CTP, the USTL Strike Committee declared a general strike on September 28, 1944. It lasted until October 2, and apparently was widely observed by the workers of the capital. It was finally called off by agreement among the CTP leaders, those of the USTL, and "officials of the labor organizations of Lima and Callao."

Piedad Pareja Pflucker indicated the true significance of this walkout. She said, "The general strike resulted from an open confrontation between the leading organizations of the Peruvian proletariat, the CTP controlled by the Communists, and the USTL by the Apristas. Beginning with it, the latter carried out an offensive to obtain control of the CTP."[190]

LABOR AND THE 1945 ELECTION

The Great Depression and World War II, both making it more difficult for Peru to import manufactured goods from abroad, stimulated what Pareja Pflucker has called "an incipient but active process of industrialization." As she noted,

This process generated rationalization of systems of work and production, altering the character of labor-management relations.... At the same time, this industrial development brought an important increase in the population employed in the industrial sector, providing with that better bases for the more organic development of the Peruvian proletariat. An additional factor of great importance, not only for the factory proletariat, but for all of the popular sectors, was the notable increase in the cost of living during these years, which served to channel all the attempts of organizations of the working class in a framework of greater labor belligerence and conflict.[191]

These developments were encouraged by political events in the immediate postwar period. In 1945 the Prado dictatorship came to an end with the holding of one of the few honest presidential elections in the country's history. Elected was José Bustamante y Rivero, candidate of the Frente Democrático Nacional, who was backed by the Apristas. During the campaign, the Aprista Party was legalized under the name of Partido del Pueblo (People's Party).[192]

Organized labor backed Bustamante. The Confederación de Trabajadores del Perú endorsed his candidacy.[193] It was said that the Communists were opposed to the CTP's officially endorsing Bustamante's candidacy, and it was only after the Communists were threatened with being displaced in the leadership of the Confederación that they acquiesced and the move was made. When *El Comercio*, which was backing Bustamante's rival General Ureta, published a manifesto by 20 textile workers organized in the Unión Patriótica Textil Pro Candidatura Eloy G. Ureta, the Textile Workers Federation sent a letter to the paper *Jornada* denouncing those in this list, saying that the textile workers had passed a resolution condemning the move and reiterating their endorsement of Bustamante.[194]

The Aprista Party was legalized early in 1945, and on May 20, 1945, Haya de la Torre, who had been in hiding for a decade, made his first public appearance in more than ten years. Two hundred fifty thousand people gathered in the Plaza San Martín. All police and soldiers had been withdrawn—in the hope, said the Apristas, that there would be violence, which would have given the government an excuse for calling off the election. Haya spoke for an hour or more to a hushed crowd, a crowd so still, it was said, that one could hear people's breathing.[195]

Haya then went on a tour of the interior. Everywhere he was greeted with cheers and adulation. He was met with "flowers, flowers and more flowers."[196] He demonstrated that in his years of keeping one jump ahead of the police, of living in obscurity in the homes of his lowliest followers, he had lost none of his hold on the masses of his countrymen. He had become a legend, and the astounding thing seemed to be that few of his followers were disillusioned when the legend materialized once more.

The victory of José Bustamante brought a profound change to Peru for a short while. The Apristas gained control of the lower house of Congress, although in the Senate it was said that on rainy days the Apristas had a majority, and when the weather was good, the opposition dominated. The Aprista minority was made up principally of younger men, whereas the opposition was made up of veterans of political life of the era of dictatorship.

Among those elected to Congress in June 1945 on the list of the Frente Democrático Nacional were Aprista trade union leaders. These included Fortunato Jara, a leader of the Lima transport workers and a national secretary of the party; José Sandoval, a textile workers' leader, also elected from Lima; Sóstenas Reynoso, an electrician, from Chiclayo; Alberto Santillana, a barbers' union leader from Arequipa; Andrés Yaraff, an Aprista worker from Trujillo; and Gumercindo Calderón, a textile-union leader from Huancayo, all elected to the Chamber of Deputies. One Aprista textile-union leader, Juan Guerrero Quimper, was elected to the Senate, from Lima.

One other Aprista labor candidate, Santos Reignel, a petroleum worker, was defeated as a candidate for the Chamber of Deputies from Paita by Luciano Castillo, the principal leader of the Socialist Party, which had considerable influence among the country's oil workers. The Socialist Party also won one other seat in the Chamber, as well as two members of the Senate.[197]

The first task of the new regime was to get rid of the dictatorial apparatus. One observer described this process as follows:

The Laws of Exception were killed off with dizzy legislative speed before Dr. Bustamante was installed. The new Congress ... tore right into the job. Veteran Aprista leader Dr. Luis Alberto Sánchez took the floor of the Chamber of Deputies and briefly summarized each decree-law. Each was unanimously repealed as soon as Dr. Sánchez finished. The motion was then sent to the Senate, where Aprista Senator Manuel Seoane read it. The Senate unanimously approved and the packed congressional galleries and excited crowds outside the building roared their approval. The whole business took less than two hours.[198]

The abolition of the dictatorial rule was particularly revolutionary in the trade union field. For the first time in the country's history, the labor movement was able to function without the interference of the police. The necessity for obtaining permission from the police to hold union meetings was abolished. There was no longer any fear that police agents were attending union meetings. Strikes were no longer regarded as an offense against the state. Even the worst enemies of the Apristas admitted that as a result of their electoral victory in 1945, the labor movement experienced a freedom that it had not known before.

ORGANIZED LABOR AFTER 1945 ELECTION

One result of this increased freedom of action of the unions was a very great increase in trade union membership. Juan P. Luna estimated in 1947 that in the two years since the inauguration of Bustamante, union membership had increased from a quarter of a million to more than half a million.[199] Early in 1945 there were 156 recognized unions in the country. At the end of 1946, 106 had been added, and during the first six months of 1947, at least 100 more were legalized.[200]

The Confederación de Trabajadores del Perú absorbed most of the increase in the labor movement. The affiliates of the CTP were of two kinds—(1) the national federations of workers of one trade or profession and (2) the local or provincial organizations. In the middle of 1947, the Confederación claimed 20 industrial federations and 25 regional ones.

Most of these federations were organized before 1945, but there were some new ones. The Federación Minera, the Federación de Azucar (sugar), and the Federación de Petroleros were launched in 1945 and 1946. The first convention of the mine workers in December 1945 was sponsored by the Sindicato Oroya, in perhaps the most embattled mining areas in the country.[201]

The largest and oldest of the national federations was the Federación de Trabajadores en Tejidos del Perú (FTTP), the textile workers' organization. Even before the beginning of the democratic period, the FTTP had affiliated unions in Lima, Cuzco, Arequipa, and Ica. During the late 1944 and early 1945, it organized two wool factories in the Huancayo area.[202]

The railroad workers' Confederación Ferrocarrilera Obrera del Perú, which had existed since 1919, was reorganized in 1945 and was rechristened Federación Nacional de Trabajadores Ferroviarios del Perú. By the middle of 1947, the workers on 14 railroads, both foreign and nationally owned, throughout the country belonged to the Federación. It was estimated that there were some 14,000 members in the organization. The complete freedom of activity existing after 1945 greatly helped the railroad workers' organization.[203]

The Federación de Obreros Panaderos "Estrella del Perú" also prospered under the new freedom. It claimed 15,000 bakers organized in the whole country and some 1,500 in Lima, and it had affiliates in 21 provincial cities. In May 1946, the Federación achieved the abolition of night work in bakeries in direct negotiations with the employers. The federación had a pact with the Sociedad de Industriales en Panadería, which regulated the conditions of work—the worker's task being determined by the value of the bread produced, that is, 53 soles' and 50 centavos' worth in any given day. The bakers worked six days a week, and the federación supplied the relief workers on the seventh day.[204]

The freedom of organization also helped the Federación Gráfica. By 1947 it had a committee in each newspaper and job printing shop in Lima except the daily *El Comercio*, which continued to resist unionization. The federación also had affiliates in Cuzco, Trujillo, Puno, Ica, Huancayo, Chicha, Chiclayo, Piura, Suiana, and Loretto. There were about 1,000 dues-paying members in Lima and about 3,000 printing-trades workers in the provinces affiliated with the federación, although they paid no dues, out of a total of 5,000 printers in the country. The federación membership increased very appreciably between 1945 and 1948.[205]

In 1945 the Federación de Vidrios (glass workers) was formed, with only three unions. By the middle of 1947, nine of the country's 12 glass factories were organized by the federation. The other three plants had paternalistic labor-relations systems that made trade union organization difficult.[206]

ORGANIZATION OF AGRICULTURAL WORKERS

Many peasants and agricultural workers brought their grievances to the Federación de Campesinos y Yanaconas, although by 1948 there were still many parts of the country that had not been reached by the federación. In June 1947, 68 unions were affiliated with the federation, with some 10,000 members.[207]

The single most important rural union group of the 1945–1948 period was the Federation of Sugar Workers, headed by the Aprista Leopoldo Pita. It claimed to have a membership of 50,000 and to have local unions in all of the important sugar plantations. They had collective contracts with all of the companies of importance.[208]

In 1947 the Lima newsmagazine *Presente* noted, "The leaders of that time, in spite of the fact that they knew that the profits of the sugar firms were in the millions with each harvest and that the State participated appreciably in the profits through strong export taxes, kept their demands moderate and prudent."[209]

However, in spite of relatively moderate wage demands, the Federation of Sugar Workers achieved significant gains in working conditions. For instance, they succeeded in getting bags of sugar that workers had to carry limited to 80 pounds, judged to be small enough for a man to carry without straining himself.[210]

Piedad Pareja Pflucker stressed the idea that the rural unions established during the Bustamante period, largely under Aprista leadership, were not, strictly speaking, "anti-feudal" in their orientation. She wrote, "With regard to the categorization of the rural unionism of that epoch, we prefer the adjective 'reformist' expressed in the formula 'economic defense,' from which derive their merely revindicative objectives in a context of democracy and capitalism on the national level. The adjective 'anti-feudal' is not correct to define the rural unionism of this epoch."[211]

More important to many of the agricultural laborers and members of indigenous Indian communities than the activities of the unions—and clearly "anti-feudal" in orientation—was the work of the Indian and Agricultural Worker Secretariat of the Aprista Party. The Buro de Asuntos Indigenas y Campesinos of the party had existed since 1931, but it was not until 1945 that the Apristas effectively penetrated among the Indian communities. After the advent of the Bustamante regime, the party carried on very extensive organization in the countryside, fanning out from Lima, Trujillo, and other urban centers, and it began acting almost like a trade union for the Indians.

The indigenous communities and agricultural workers' groups brought their grievances to the Aprista Party, and the party did what it could to prevent or undo the land-stealing and other abuses to which the Indians had been subjected. The party had enough success in this to be able to extend the party organization into many of the Indian communities, becoming virtually the only political group in the country with a following among the Indians.[212] This growing influence of the Apristas among the Indians was attested to at the time by non-Aprista observers.[213]

UNIONIZATION BY WHITE-COLLAR WORKERS

Considerable progress was also made in organizing white-collar workers during the 1945–1948 period. The old Asociación Empleados was reactivated when an Aprista administration took it over in 1945, and in the next year, it was host to the Second Congress of White-Collar Workers. However, it was January 1947 before the Unión Departamental de Empleados Particulares (UDEP—Regional Union of White-Collar Workers) was organized in Lima. It included employees in both industry and commerce and had at least 25,000 members by June 1947.[214]

Although the Chamber of Commerce and Industry at first refused to have anything to do with the issue, arguing that it was not authorized by its members to do so, the UDEP pressed the demand for a minimum salary for white-collar workers in the Lima-Callao area with the director general of labor.[215]

Finally, the Unión Departamental succeeded in getting the government to establish a minimum salary in the Lima and Callao areas in a decree that established a Tripartite Commission to establish this minimum. The first minimum salary that was established was for 250 soles a month; salaries were as low as 75 soles for women before the decree.

The Federación General de Empleados del Perú was founded in October 1946 and was reported to have 70,000 members six months later. It had affiliates in 16 of the chief cities and towns. National groups affiliated with it included the Federación de Empleados Textiles (white-collar workers in the textile industry), the Federación de Empleados Petroleros (petroleum industry clerks), the Federación de Empleados de la Cerro de Pasco Copper Corporation, Sindicato de Músicos del Perú (musicians), Asociación de Empleados Municipales, the Asociación Nacional de Educación, and the Asociación Nacional de Empleados Públicos.[216] This national white-collar workers' federation was short-lived. James Payne wrote that it "fell apart as soon as it was founded."[217] However, several of its constituent union groups continued to exist.

STRIKE ACTIVITY IN THE 1945–1948 PERIOD

There were a number of strikes accompanying this growth of the labor movement. For instance, the Huascar-Estrella textile plant in Cuzco was strikebound in February 1946 over a demand for a general wage increase.[218] A walkout of glassworkers in Lima brought about a general strike called by the Unión Sindical de Trabajadores de Lima, which was rendered ineffective when the chauffeurs' union, still controlled by the Communists, returned to work.[219] A three-hour printing-trades walkout in Lima in July 1946 brought favorable results,[220] and in October 1946, there was a 17-day bakers' strike.

A nine-day walkout of the railroad workers of the Ferrocarril Central del Perú (Central Railroad of Peru) in March 1947 won a 37 percent average wage increase for the workers on that line belonging to the Sindicato de Trabajadores, Empleados y Obreros. The lower-paid workers got proportionately more. This was the second large strike in the history of the railroad workers federation.[221]

APRISTA CONTROL OF THE LABOR MOVEMENT

The control of the labor movement passed almost completely into the hands of the Apristas. The association of the Communists with the dictatorships—which preceded July 1945 and the great hopes that the Apristas aroused when they were able to come out into the open—and the fact there was in power the Bustamante government that was originally favorably disposed to them combined to sweep out the old anti-Aprista union administrations almost completely and to replace them with Apristas. In the middle of 1947, an estimated 90 percent or more of the labor movement was in the hands of the Apristas.

Shift of control of the Confederación de Trabajadores del Perú from the Communists to the Apristas began three months after the election of June 1945. Soon after the Lima general strike of September–October 1944, the Federation of Textile Workers had demanded that there be new elections within both the CTP and USTL. These took place in the latter in February 1945, but it was at first decided to postpone the selection of a new leadership in the CTP until a congress of the organization, which had been called for December 1945.

However, the Aprista leaders were not willing to wait that long (the Congress in fact did not meet until December 1947), and in September 1945 there was a realignment of the leadership of the CTP. Arturo Sabroso succeeded Juan P. Luna as secretary-general of the Confederación. Another key post, that of secretary of organization, was also given to an Aprista, Luis Negreiros. However, equal numbers of Communists and Apristas were placed in each secretariat, and the APRA was still a minority, with seven out of the fifteen members of the Executive. Subsequently, the other Communists were eliminated one by one in the months that followed, and by the middle of 1947, there were only one or two Communists and a few other non-Apristas on the Executive of the CTP.[222] In fact, one had the impression at that time that the CTP was little more than an adjunct of the Aprista Party.

The manner in which the Apristas took over the unions was a matter of some dispute at the time. The Apristas claimed that their victory was due to a superior organization and to a willingness to provide more reasonable and thorough organization, which made them able to substitute facts and figures on the financial and general situations of the employers for the spellbinding and demagoguery that had sometimes characterized union leadership theretofore.[223] The Apristas said that when they took over unions, it was done by means of peaceful and democratic methods and because they really represented the vast majority of the organized workers of Peru.[224]

The enemies of APRA, on the other hand, maintained that it seized control of the unions through strong-arm methods. They claimed, furthermore, that the union leaders who were put in by APRA were often not really members of the craft or industrial group that they were put in to lead. However, the new secretary-general of the CTP was a living argument against that claim. Arturo Sabroso was still working in the Santa Catalina factory in which he had begun his trade union career several decades before when he was chosen to lead the CTP.[225]

Some anti-Apristas admitted that the Apristas would have gained control of most of the unions without using strong-arm methods, but still maintained that in certain instances, such as with the taxi chauffeurs' union of Lima, the Construction Workers Federation, and the trolley-car workers, the Apristas did use force.[226] One Communist leader gave a somewhat different explanation of the situation when he said that the Apristas were able to seize control of the unions because they worked inside of them in a very disciplined, efficient manner; he said that the Communists, to the contrary, although they worked in an organized way, always tried to form the widest possible united front in the unions, to give their administration the greatest popular support possible.[227]

Luciano Castillo, chief of the Partido Socialista, and a major political leader in the northern petroleum area, argued that the Apristas organized

unions as rivals to the older organizations that were controlled by his followers and that the government and the companies both favored these
Aprista-led unions over the Socialist-controlled ones in the oil region.[228]
Arturo Sabroso denied this charge, claiming that the Aprista-led unions
were the majority groups.[229]

It seems clear that between 1945 and 1948, the great majority of the organized workers were sympathetic to the Apristas. There was a general recognition of the fact that the freedom of organization that existed after 1945 was
directly attributable to the Aprista electoral victory. Further, the workers were
political partisans of the Apristas. Although undoubtedly only a minority
belonged to the Partido del Pueblo, the majority was in sympathy with the
party. This fact would mean that the workers would, if given an opportunity,
put the Apristas in control of their unions. However, it may well be the case
that in some individual instances, the Apristas may have used unorthodox
or undemocratic methods for getting control of particular unions.

In March 1946, the Trade Union Secretariat of the Aprista Party organized
what it called the National Assembly of Unions in the party headquarters
of the Casa del Pueblo. It was addressed by the party chief, Víctor Raúl
Haya de la Torre, and Arturo Sabroso, secretary-general of the CTP, among
others. The assembly pledged the Aprista trade unionists to work for fulfillment of the Aprista program, particularly the establishment of an Economic
Congress—with representatives of all key elements in the economy, including the labor movement—as a companion body with the National Congress
(Chamber of Deputies and Senate) already called for in the Constitution.[230]

DUAL UNIONISM

The attempts of the Apristas' rivals to organize a labor movement to
compete with the Confederación de Trabajadores del Perú were not very
successful. The Federación de Trabajadores de Cuzco and a similar organization in Puno, both under Communist control, withdrew from the CTP
early in 1947. The Cuzco federation affiliated directly to the Confederación
de Trabajadores de América Latina.[231] In Arequipa, too, the labor federation quit the CTP.[232]

In Cuzco the Communist-led group controlled almost all of the organized
workers until early in 1947. Even afterward, it probably continued to be
the most powerful labor group in the city. It launched a popular university,
apparently as a rival to one established by the Apristas. It consisted of a series
of talks on general cultural subjects, as well as classes given by university
professors and others. Subjects included Spanish, history, economics, arith-
metic, and geography, and it had about 100 students in June 1947. The
Federación also maintained a library with several hundred volumes.[233]

The leaders of these splits from the CTP were Communists. However,
there was apparently a difference of opinion among the Communist
leaders. The party's National Trade Union secretary indicated that the

secession of Communist-led unions from the CTP in Cuzco, Puno, and Arequipa was "justified but not approved of" by the national party leadership.[234]

The Apristas organized rivals to the Communist-controlled groups in two cities. In Cuzco they started with the Sociedad Mutual de Empleados, an old mutual benefit society of white-collar workers, and with it as a base, they organized a Federación de Empleados y Obreros de Cuzco, which in July 1947 had 18 affiliates, principally white-collar workers' unions, but including a brewery workers' union and some others. That federation joined the CTP, through the Federación General de Empleados del Perú. However, the Communists claimed that they controlled 90 percent of the organized workers of Cuzco.[235]

In Arequipa the Apristas reorganized the Unión Sindical, which had been founded in the mid-1930s, but had been suspended as a result of government persecution, and then had been succeeded in 1940 by the Confederación de Trabajadores de Arequipa. The Apristas claimed that by mid-1947 their Unión Sindical included most of the important unions of the city, such as the railroad workers, trolley-car men, textile workers, and others.[236]

There was some attempt on a national scale to organize a rival to the Confederación de Trabajadores del Perú. A group of labor leaders affiliated with the Partido Socialista Auténtico—the party organized by Eudosio Rabines, ex-secretary of the Communist Party, after he quit the Communist ranks—established a Frente de Unidad e Independencia Sindical in 1947. The avowed aim of this group was to "free the unions from all political control." The Frente claimed supporters in Chiclayo, Pisco, and Maquena and had friendly relations with anti-Aprista union groups in Arequipa, Cuzco, and Puno.

The leaders of this Frente were mainly ex-Communists.[237] Four of its 17 executive members were members of the Partido Socialista Auténtico. José Benitez, probably the most important member of the group, was at the time unaffiliated politically, although he had been a Communist.[238]

The violence of the Frente's attacks on the Aprista leadership of the CTP was shown in a throwaway the Frente issued entitled "New Aprista Crime Against the Working Class," in which it proclaimed, "The decent and patriotic citizenry of the Republic must say ENOUGH, SERVANTS OF IMPERIALISM! ENOUGH, ENEMIES OF THE PEOPLE AND OF THE FATHERLAND!" It claimed, "The Apristas are pirates, filibusters, sellers of the labor movement."[239]

THE GROWING CRISIS OF DEMOCRACY

By the middle of 1947, the democratic regime that had been elected in June 1945 was entering into crisis. In part, this was due to growing difficulties between President José Bustamante and the Aprista Party. In part, too, it was due to the fact that traditional ruling groups—economic interests connected with the landed aristocracy and those particularly associated with the country's import–export economy and banking—had recovered from the shock administered to them by the 1945 election, and they had begun to mount a major offensive to put an end to the democratic regime.

Relations between President Bustamante and the Apristas grew increasingly difficult, in spite of the fact that his election had been largely due to the backing of the Aprista Party and the fact that Bustamante's election had made it possible for the Apristas to work openly for the first time in a dozen years and even for some months to have ministers in the cabinet. The Apristas found it very hard to collaborate with their partners in the Frente Democrático Nacional.

The situation that developed was an anomalous one. It became as if there were two presidential palaces and two presidents. On the one hand, there was the official chief executive, José Bustamante, and on the other hand, there was Víctor Raúl Haya de la Torre, in the Aprista Party's Casa del Pueblo.

Relations between Bustamante and his closest collaborators on the one hand and the Apristas on the other became increasing strained. By the middle of 1947, this situation was intensified by the launching of a campaign by the opponents of the Frente Democrático Nacional to undermine and destroy the regime.

The right-wing offensive began with a campaign by most of the Lima press—including the newspapers *El Comercio, La Prensa, La Razón,* and *Vanguardia*—accusing the Apristas of being guilty of the January 1947 murder of Francisco Grana Garland, a leading right-wing journalist. This campaign was designed to intensify differences between the president and the Apristas, and its immediate result was to cause the resignation of the cabinet in which the Apristas were represented. Then, in July 1947, the non-Aprista members of the Senate began to boycott meetings of that body, causing a lack of a quorum, as a result of which the Congress virtually ceased to function.

ORGANIZED LABOR AND THE CRISIS OF DEMOCRACY

In the face of the situation, the Bustamante government increasingly ceded to the violently anti-Aprista forces, particularly in its dealings with the labor movement. Piedad Pareja Pflucker noted, "In the middle of 1947, the democratic framework began to be restricted: the number of official recognitions of unions began to be restricted, and the repression of strikes increased." She added, "To the degree that the action of the agro-exporting right began to have results on the government of Bustamante, which had already hardened its labor policy, the period presented an imminent danger of definitive blockade of democratic conditions."[240]

The Aprista leadership of the CTP protested against the situation. Soon after the closing down of Congress, it issued a statement against the closing, noting, "Our first measure to counteract that must be to close ranks around our trade union organizations and our leaders who are those whom we democratically elected. To be silent in the face of the denunciations of our leaders would be to make ourselves accomplices of our enemies."[241]

Pressure grew for organized labor to launch a general strike against the campaign of the political right to destroy the country's democracy. The Textile Workers Federation took the lead in calling for such a walkout to try to force Congress back into action. The CTP and the USTL in Lima finally decided to call a general strike late in August 1947, but instead of launching it as a frankly political walkout, they ostensibly called for it in sympathy with the difficulty that certain unions in Lima were having in negotiations with their employers.

This walkout was a failure. After five days, it was called off by the CTP and USTL. Piedad Pareja Pflucker noted, "The terms of solution of the cases involved did not satisfy the expectations of the workers, or in other words, were not real solutions to the workers' demands. Nor did the strike alter the state of legislative suspension. It left the negative result of numerous detentions and the closing of various workers' headquarters."[242]

The anti-Aprista Frente de Unidad e Independencia Sindical, which was seeking to replace the CTP as the country's central labor organization, used this walkout to attack both the CTP and the USTL. It issued a statement saying, "This strike was launched not to defend the interests of the workers or the solution of a conflict between capital and labor, but to pressure the government and the independent senators and deputies, obliging them to cede to the impositions of the Aprista party."[243]

THE FIRST CONGRESS OF THE CTP

As the future of the Peruvian democracy became more uncertain, the Confederación de Trabajadores finally held its first congress, from December 15 to December 23, 1947. In the period preceding this congress, various regional and national industrial union congresses had been held. For instance, the First Regional Congress of the North had met in October 1946, establishing a regional organization of the CTP in that important petroleum- and sugar-producing area. As a result of that meeting, the National Federation of Sugar Workers of Peru also had been established.[244]

There were 253 delegates at the First Congress of the CTP, of whom 117 were voting members, 134 were observers, and two were fraternal delegates. The only foreign fraternal delegate was from the Socialist faction of the Confederación de Trabajadores de Chile.

In September 1947, the CTP had established an Organizing Commission for the CTP Congress. It had set forth a 12-point agenda, including such subjects as organizational questions, economic and social problems, agrarian issues, international relations, and various others.

It had been expected that the government, in accordance with a budget item that had been introduced by the Aprista labor members of the Congress, would pay for most of the costs of the meeting. However, given the political situation late in 1947, the government refused to make the budgeted funds available. As a result, the CTP and its affiliates had to bear the full cost of the First Congress of the CTP.

There were 44 organizations represented in the Congress. These included local, departmental, and regional groups of the national organization, as well as some national industrial federations and also individual unions that apparently were not affiliated with any regional or national industrial federation. The national federations included those of textile workers, printing-trades workers, chauffeurs, white-collar workers, construction workers, hotel employees, woodworkers, hatters, petroleum workers, railroaders, shoemakers, millers, and the Federation of Peasants and Sharecroppers (Federación de Campesinos y Yanaconas del Perú).

Arturo Sabroso, in his inaugural address to the Congress, discussed a variety of issues facing the meeting and the Peruvian working class in general. These included "the convenience of a democratic attitude toward a democratic state, the need for a labor code, trade union autonomy vis-à-vis the political parties, organization of the National Economic Congress (pushed by APRA), the progressive nationalization of industries to foster industrialization, and the formation of a new fully democratic American regional labor group to replace the CTAL."

The Congress elected a new leadership, presumably to run the CTP until its next congress. Arturo Sabroso was reelected secretary-general, and another Aprista labor leader, Tomás del Piélago of the printing-trades workers, was chosen as first subsecretary of the organization. Four regional subsecretaries were also elected.[245]

PERUVIAN LABOR'S INTERNATIONAL RELATIONS

The question of relations between the Confederación de Trabajadores del Perú and the rest of the Latin American labor movement was an important one dealt with by the First Congress of the CTP. The Apristas had sent an Aprista to substitute for Juan P. Luna on the Executive of the CTAL after taking over the CTP, but Vicente Lombardo Toledano refused to recognize the substitute, saying that Luna had been elected by a congress of the CTAL and therefore could only be removed by the same method. The CTP leaders then "suspended" their relations with the Confederación de Trabajadores de América Latina and joined with the Confederación de Trabajadores de Chile of Bernardo Ibáñez to issue invitations to a congress to launch the new Inter-American Confederation of Workers to rival the CTAL.

The CTP Congress ratified these actions of its Executive. The inter-American labor congress met in Lima in January 1948, a few weeks after the CTP's own congress. Aside from representatives of the American Federation of Labor and the Railroad Brotherhoods of the United States, there were delegates present from Bolivia, Brazil, Colombia, Costa Rica, Cuba, Chile, the Dominican Republic, Ecuador, Dutch Guiana, Mexico, Puerto Rico, El Salvador, and Venezuela, as well as Peru. They voted to establish the Inter-American Confederation of Workers (CIT), with its headquarters in Lima.

However, the government of President José Bustamante soon made clear its opposition to having the seat of the new inter-American labor organization in Peru. As Arturo Jáuregui, the Peruvian trade unionist chosen as secretary of administration and finances of the CIT, explained later, "Soon after the Conference and fifteen days after the CIT was founded with its headquarters in Lima, the Ministry of Police decreed the prohibition of its functioning in Peruvian territory.... It argued that the CIT had a subversive political character that menaced the stability of the duly constituted government, endangered public order and the sovereignty of the nation."[246] As a result of the Bustamante government's decision, the headquarters of the new organization was moved to Santiago, Chile.

THE FALL OF THE DEMOCRATIC REGIME

Meanwhile, Peruvian political conditions went from bad to worse. Early in 1948, an all-military cabinet headed by General Manuel Odría as minister of interior was installed by President José Bustamante.

Then, on October 3, 1948, a naval mutiny, led by dissident members of the Partido Aprista, broke out in Callao. Although the uprising was suppressed with relative ease, President Bustamante responded by outlawing the Partido Aprista. Its leaders—including the principal trade unionists associated with the party—were forced to go into hiding.

Three weeks after the Callao uprising, General Odría led a coup d'état, which overthrew President José Bustamante and installed the general as the new president of Peru. Thus was ended the short experience of Peru with democracy and a period of relative freedom for the organized labor movement.

NOTES

1. Emilio Costilla Larrea, "Apuntes Para la Historia de la Lucha Social en el Perú," manuscript, p. 7.

2. James L. Payne, *Labor and Politics in Peru: The System of Political Bargaining,* Yale University Press, New Haven, 1965, p. 41.

3. Costilla Larrea, op. cit., p. 10.

4. Ibid., p. 8; see also Payne, op. cit., p. 37.

5. Costilla Larrea, op. cit., p. 8.

6. Ibid., p. 9.

7. Moisés Poblete Troncoso, *El Movimiento Obrero Latinoamericano*, Fondo de Cultura Económica, México, D.F., 1946, p. 244.

8. Costilla Larrea, op. cit., p. 8.

9. Ibid., p. 8.

10. Ibid., p. 9.

11. Ibid., p. 9.

12. Poblete Troncoso, op. cit., p. 244.

13. Interview with Augusto Sarmiento, secretary general; Eduardo García, delegate to Federación de Trabajadores de Cuzco; José Lira Rojas, member of defense commission; René Somocurso, president of the cooperative; and Ladisláo Valdivieso, secretary of culture of Sindicato de Chóferes de Cuzco, in Cuzco, June 8, 1947.

14. Costilla Larrea, op. cit., p. 10.

15. Interview with Emilio Vargas, Enríque de la Fuente, Julio Oliveiro, secretary-general, treasurer, and subsecretary, respectively, of Federación Gráfica del Perú, in Lima, June 24, 1947.

16. Costilla Larrea, op. cit., p. 10.

17. Ibid., pp. 10–11; see also Denis Sulmont, *El Movimiento Obrero Peruano (1890–1980), Reseña Histórica,* Tarea, Lima, 1981, p. 18.

18. Poblete Troncoso, op. cit., p. 215.

19. Interviews with Luis Negreiros, secretary-general, Unión Departamental de Empleados Particulares de Lima, former secretary-general of Federación Tranviaria, and A. Hernández, president of Asociación de Empleados del Perú, in Lima, June 22, 1947.

20. Costilla Larrea, op. cit., p. 84; see also Sulmont, op. cit., p. 19.

21. Costilla Larrea, op. cit., pp. 98–102.

22. Interview with Arturo Sabroso, secretary-general of Confederación de Trabajadores del Perú, in Lima, June 17, 1947.

23. *Mother Earth,* anarchist magazine published by Emma Goldman, New York, New York, June 1908.

24. Interview with Arturo Sabroso, op. cit., June 17, 1947.

25. Interview with David Villacorta, secretary of coordination of Federación de Construcción Civil, in Lima, June 23, 1947.

26. *Mother Earth,* September 1907.

27. Costilla Larrea, op. cit., pp. 98–102.

28. *Mother Earth,* op. cit., 1907.

29. Costilla Larrea, op. cit., p. 25; see also Sulmont, op. cit., p. 19.

30. Costilla Larrea, op. cit., p. 28.

31. Ibid., pp. 29–30.

32. Ibid., pp. 35–36.

33. Ibid., p. 36.

34. Ibid., p. 38; see also Sulmont, p. 20.

35. Payne, op. cit., pp. 37–39.

36. Costilla Larrea, op. cit., pp. 38–39.

37. Ibid., pp. 39–40; see also Sulmont, op. cit., p. 20.

38. Costilla Larrea, op. cit., p. 46; see also *The Call,* Socialist Party daily, New York City, November 15, 1913.

39. Costilla Larrea, op. cit., pp. 35–45.
40. Ibid., p. 47.
41. Ibid., pp. 48–53.
42. Ibid., p. 53.
43. Ibid., pp. 53–54.
44. Ibid., pp. 54.
45. Ibid., p. 46.
46. Ibid., p. 62.
47. Ibid., p. 45.
48. Ibid., p. 62.
49. Ibid., pp. 65–67.
50. Ibid., pp. 68–70.
51. Ibid., p. 63.
52. Ibid., pp. 86–87.
53. Ibid., pp. 106–107.
54. Ibid., p. 107.
55. Ibid., p. 112.
56. Ibid., pp. 116–117.
57. Ibid., p. 115.
58. Ibid., p. 118; see also Sulmont, op. cit., pp. 20–21.
59. Ibid., pp. 123–126.
60. Ibid., pp. 127–129.
61. Interviews with Pedro Parra, leader of Frente de Unidad y Independencia Sindical, ex-anarchist, ex-Communist, member of Partido Socialista Auténtico, in Lima, June 25, 1947; and Ricardo Martínez de la Torre, a founder of Communist Party of Peru, leading historian of Peruvian labor movement, in Lima, June 27, 1947.
62. Ricardo Martínez de la Torre, *Apuntes para una Interpretación Marxista de Historia Social del Perú*, Empresa Editora Peruana, S.A., Lima, 1947, Volume 1, p. 424.
63. Costilla Larrea, op. cit., p. 133.
64. Ibid., p. 129.
65. Ibid., p. 132.
66. Martínez de la Torre, op. cit., p. 425.
67. Costilla Larrea, op. cit., p. 134.
68. Ibid., pp. 135–136.
69. Ibid., p. 143.
70. Martínez de la Torre, op. cit., p. 348.
71. Costilla Larrea, op. cit., p. 143.
72. Víctor Raúl Haya de la Torre, *La Jornada de las 8 Horas*, pp. 35–53; Costilla Larrea, op. cit., p. 146; and Martínez de la Torre, op. cit., p. 448; see also Payne, op. cit., pp. 38–39; and Sulmont, op. cit., pp. 21–23.
73. Martínez de la Torre, op. cit., p. 453.
74. Interviews with Arturo Sabroso, op. cit., June 17, 1947, and Víctor Raúl Haya de la Torre, founder and "Jefe" of Partido Aprista Peruano, in Lima, June 18, 1947.
75. Martínez de la Torre, op. cit., p. 451.
76. Costilla Larrea, op. cit., pp. 151–152.
77. Ibid., pp. 153–158.

78. Ibid., p. 165.
79. Interview with Arturo Sabroso, op. cit., June 17, 1947.
80. Ricardo Martínez de la Torre, *El Movimiento Obrero en 1919*, Lima, 1928, p. 33.
81. Costilla Larrea, op. cit., p. 184; see also Payne, op. cit., p. 39.
82. Costilla Larrea, op. cit., p. 194.
83. Ibid., pp. 188–190.
84. Ibid., p. 201.
85. Ibid., p. 202.
86. Interview with Emilio Vargas, Enrique de la Fuenta, and Julio Oliveiro, op. cit., June 24, 1947.
87. Costilla Larrea, op. cit., p. 206.
88. Ibid., p. 206.
89. Interview with Víctor Raúl Haya de la Torre, op. cit., June 18, 1947.
90. Costilla Larrea, op. cit., p. 214.
91. Interview with Arturo Sabroso, op cit., June 17, 1947.
92. Costilla Larrea, op. cit., pp. 207–212.
93. Payne, op. cit., p. 180.
94. Costilla Larrea, op. cit., pp. 209–211.
95. Ibid., p. 128.
96. Ibid., pp. 214–217; see also Payne, op. cit., p. 39.
97. Luis Alberto Sánchez and Alfredo Saco, "Aprista Bibliography," in *Hispanic American Historical Review*, Durham, NC, August 1943.
98. Samuel Guy Inman, *Latin American—Its Place in World Life*, Willet, Clark & Co., New York, 1937, p. 267; and interview with Víctor Raúl Haya de la Torre, op. cit., June 18, 1947.
99. *El Obrero Textil*, official newspaper of Textile Workers Federation, Lima, October 1924.
100. See for example, *Solidaridad*, official organ of Federación Textil and Federación Obrera Local, Lima, September 1925.
101. Sulmont, op. cit., pp. 26–27.
102. *Solidaridad*, op. cit., September 1925.
103. Costilla Larrea, op. cit., p. 219.
104. Ibid., pp. 225–226.
105. Ibid., pp. 221–224.
106. Ibid., p. 227.
107. Interview with Elias García, trade union secretary of Communist Party of Peru, in Lima, June 20, 1947.
108. Costilla Larrea, op. cit., pp. 228–229.
109. Interview with Arturo Sabroso, op. cit., June 17, 1947.
110. Interview with Ricardo Martínez de la Torre, op. cit., June 27, 1947.
111. Poblete Troncoso, op. cit., p. 246.
112. Sulmont, op. cit., p. 27.
113. Costilla Larrea, op. cit., pp. 229–230.
114. *Boletín Diario de Jornada*, Lima, June 21, 1945.
115. Costilla Larrea, op. cit., pp. 229–230.
116. Armando Bazán, *Biografía de José Carlos Mariátegui*, Zig-Zag, Santiago, Chile, 1939, p. 58.

117. The late Ricardo Martínez de la Torre was kind enough to allow me to look through his complete file of *Amauta*.

118. Interview with Ricardo Martínez de la Torre, op. cit., June 27, 1947.

119. Interview with Eudosio Rabines, founder of Peruvian Communist Party, in Lima, June 23, 1947.

120. Interview with Ricardo Martínez de la Torre, op. cit., June 27, 1947.

121. Interview with Luis Negreiros, op. cit., June 22, 1947.

122. Interview with José Navarro, secretary-general, and Juan P. Pérez, press secretary, of Federación de Campesinos y Yanaconas, in Lima, June 23, 1947.

123. Interview with David Villacorta, op. cit., June 23, 1947.

124. Poblete Troncoso, op. cit., p. 246.

125. Sulmont, op. cit., p. 34.

126. Carleton Beales, "Aprismo: The Rise of Haya de la Torre," *Foreign Affairs*, New York, January 1935.

127. "Algunos Datos Biográficos de los Presos Apristas del Perú," in *Claridad*, Buenos Aires, April 1938.

128. *New York Herald Tribune*, November 23, 1930.

129. Survey article on Peru in *Fortune*, New York, January 1938.

130. *Claridad*, op. cit., April 1938.

131. Interview with Eliseo García, op. cit., June 20, 1947; and Martínez de la Torre, op. cit., 1947, p. 259.

132. *RILU Magazine*, organ of Red International of Labor Unions, Moscow, May 15, 1931.

133. Interview with Eudosio Rabines, op. cit., June 23, 1947.

134. Interview with Luciano Castillo, founder of Partido Socialista, in Lima, June 26, 1947.

135. Interview with Eudosio Rabines, op. cit., June 23, 1947.

136. Interview with Luciano Castillo, op. cit., June 26, 1947.

137. Interview with Jorge Fernández Stoll, director general of labor, under Presidents Benavides and Prado, in Lima, June 20, 1947.

138. Interview with Juan Latorre, onetime secretary-general of Sindicato de Chóferes of Lima, in Lima, June 18, 1947.

139. Interview with Eduardo Aspillaga, secretary-general of Federación de Obreros Panaderos "Estrella del Perú," in Lima, June 24, 1947.

140. Interview with Augusto Sarmiento and others, op. cit., June 8, 1947.

141. *American Labor Year Book 1931*, Rand School Press, New York, 1931, p. 290.

142. *American Labor Year Book 1932*, Rand School Press, New York, p. 253.

143. Piedad Pareja Pflucker, *Aprismo y Sindicalismo en el Perú 1943–1948*, Ediciones Rikchay Perú, Lima, 1980, pp. 178–179.

144. Interview with Fortunato Jara, head of Buro Nacional de Sindicatos of Aprista Party, member of Executive Committee of Confederación de Trabajadores del Perú, in Lima, June 19, 1947.

145. Martínez de la Torre, op. cit., 1947, p. 265.

146. Interview with Eliseo García, op. cit., June 20, 1947.

147. Interview with Fortunato Jara, op. cit., June 19, 1947.

148. Interview with Eliseo García, op. cit., June 20, 1947.

149. Interview with Jorge Fernández Stoll, op. cit., June 20, 1947.

150. Interview with Arturo Sabroso, op. cit., June 17, 1947.
151. Interview with Luciano Castillo, op. cit., June 26, 1947.
152. Interview with Víctor Raúl Haya de la Torre, op. cit., June 18, 1947.
153. Interview with Jorge Fernández Stoll, op. cit., June 20, 1947.
154. Pareja Pflucker, op. cit., p. 46.
155. Interview with Juan P. Luna, former secretary-general of Confederación de Trabajadores del Perú, deputy under Prado, in Lima, June 28, 1947.
156. Interview with Arturo Sabroso, op. cit., June 17, 1947.
157. *El Obrero Textil,* official newspaper of Textile Workers Federation, Lima, 1940.
158. Interview with Jorge Fernández Stoll, op. cit., June 20, 1947.
159. Interview with Juan P. Luna, op. cit., June 28, 1947.
160. Interview with Fortunato Jara, op. cit., June 19, 1947.
161. *Democracia y Trabajo,* organ of Communist Party during first Prado administration, Lima, September 11, 1943.
162. *El Popular,* official daily of Confederación de Trabajadores de México, Mexico City, November 10, 1942.
163. Interview with Augusto Sarmiento and others, op. cit., June 8, 1947.
164. Interview with Julio Miguel Mendoza, press secretary, Julio César Abarca, secretary-general, and Alfonso Luna, member of Cuzco Local of Aprista Party, in Cuzco, June 9, 1947.
165. Interview with Raúl Roa, secretary-general of Glass Workers Federation, in Lima, June 23, 1947.
166. Interview with José Navarro and Juan P. Pérez, op. cit., June 23, 1947.
167. Interview with David Villacorta, op. cit., June 23, 1947.
168. Interview with Juan Latorre, op. cit., June 18, 1947.
169. Interview with Jorge Fernández Stoll, op. cit., June 20, 1947.
170. Interview with Fortunato Jarra, op. cit., June 19, 1947.
171. Ibid.
172. Interview with Eliseo García, op. cit., June 20, 1947.
173. Pareja, op. cit., p. 19.
174. "Manifesto de la Confederación de Trabajadores del Perú," Lima, July 15, 1945.
175. Interview with Fortunato Jarra, op. cit., June 19, 1947.
176. Interview Eliseo García, op. cit., June 20, 1947.
177. Interview with Juan P. Luna, op. cit., June 28, 1947.
178. Interview with Fortunato Jarra, op. cit., June 19, 1947.
179. Interview with Jorge Fernández Stoll, op. cit., June 20, 1947.
180. Interview with Eliseo García, op. cit., June 23, 1947.
181. Interview with Juan P. Luna, op. cit., June 28, 1947.
182. Interview with Eliseo García , op. cit., June 23, 1947.
183. Allen Haden, "Peru Capering on Rim of Political Violence," *Chicago Daily News,* September 28, 1944.
184. Allen Hayden, "Only Miracle Can Save Peru from Upheaval," *Chicago Daily News,* September 28, 1944.
185. Interview with Jorge Fernández Stoll, op. cit., June 20, 1947.
186. Interview with Fortunato Jara, op. cit., June 19, 1947.
187. Interview with Juan P. Luna, op. cit., June 28, 1947.
188. Interview with Eduardo Aspillaga, op. cit., June 24, 1947.

189.   Interviews with Juan P. Luna, op. cit., June 28, 1947; and Jorge Fernández Stoll, op. cit., June 20, 1947.

190.   Pareja Pflucker, op. cit., pp. 27–29.

191.   Ibid., p. 9.

192.   *Chicago Daily News*, July 23, 1945.

193.   Juan Antonio Corretjer in *Daily Worker*, daily newspaper of Communist Party of USA, September 18, 1945.

194.   Interview with Fortunato Jara, op. cit., June 19, 1947.

195.   *Boletín Diario de Jornada*, Lima, April 25, 1945.

196.   Interview with Víctor Raúl Haya de la Torre, op. cit., June 18, 1947.

197.   Pareja Pflucker, op. cit., p. 40.

198.   "The New Republic," article in *Inter-American* magazine, New York, September 1945.

199.   Interview with Juan P. Luna, op. cit., June 28, 1947.

200.   Interview with Fortunato Jara, op. cit., June 19, 1947; see also Pareja Pflucker, op. cit., p. 52. Federación Nacional de Trabajadores Ferroviarios, in Lima, June 23, 1947.

201.   Ibid. See also Pareja Pflucker, op. cit., pp. 162–171.

202.   Pareja Pflucker, op. cit., pp. 154–155.

203.   Interview with Máximo Méndez Williams, secretary of press and propaganda, Federación Nacional de Trabajadores Ferroviarios, in Lima, June 23, 1947.

204.   Interview with Eduardo Aspillaga, op. cit., June 24, 1947.

205.   Interview with Emilio Vargas, Enrique de la Fuente, and Julio Oliveiro, op. cit., June 27, 1947.

206.   Interview with Raúl Roa, op. cit., June 23, 1947.

207.   Interview with José Navarro and Juan Pérez, op. cit., June 23, 1947.

208.   Interview with Leopold Pita, former head of Sugar Workers Federation of Peru, in San José, Costa Rica, August 29, 1952.

209.   *Presente*, Lima, June 22, 1957, p. 25.

210.   Interview with Leopold Pita, op. cit., August 29, 1952.

211.   Pareja, op. cit., p. 133.

212.   Interview with Mariano M. Echegaray, national secretary of Indian Affairs, and Cleofe Túpac Yupanque de Sáenz, head of Women and Children's Section of same secretariat of Aprista Party, in Lima, June 21, 1947.

213.   Interview with Alberto Arca Parro, senator, one of founders of Socialist Party of Peru, in Lima, June 27, 1947.

214.   Interview with Luis Negreiros, op. cit., June 22, 1947.

215.   Throwaway of Unión Departamental de Empleados Particulares de Lima, n.d.

216.   Interview with Luis Negreiros, op. cit., June 22, 1947.

217.   Payne, op. cit., p. 181.

218.   Interview with Guillermo Uria, chief of Estrella Section of Fabrica Huascar-Estrella, in Cuzco, June 11, 1947.

219.   Interview with Raúl Roa, op. cit., June 23, 1947.

220.   Interview with Emilio Vargas, Enrique de la Fuente, and Julio Oliveiro, op. cit., June 27, 1947.

221.   Interview with Máximo Méndez Williams, op. cit., June 23, 1947.

222.   Interview with Fortunato Jara, op. cit., June 19, 1947.

223.   Ibid.

224. Interview with Arturo Sabroso, op. cit., June 17, 1947.
225. Ibid., and interview with Eliseo García, op. cit., June 20, 1947.
226. Interview with Pedro Parra, op. cit., June 25, 1947.
227. Interview with Juan P. Luna, op. cit., June 28, 1947.
228. Interview with Luciano Castillo, op. cit., June 26, 1947.
229. Interview with Arturo Sabroso, op. cit., June 17, 1947.
230. Pareja Pflucker, op. cit., pp. 48–52.
231. Interview with Augusto Sarmiento, Eduardo García, and José Lira Rojas, op. cit., June 8, 1947.
232. Interview with Fortunato Jara, op. cit., June 19, 1947.
233. Interview with Augusto Sarmiento, Eduardo García, and Lira Rojas, op. cit., June 8, 1947.
234. Interview with Eliseo García, op. cit., June 20, 1947.
235. Interview with Abraham Vizcarra Rosas, president of Sociedad Mutua de Empleados, organizer of Federación de Empleados y Obreros de Cuzco, in Cuzco, June 11, 1947.
236. Interview with Fortunato Jara, op. cit., June 19, 1947.
237. Interview with Pedro Parra, op. cit., June 27, 1947.
238. Interview with Eudosio Rabines, op. cit, June 23, 1947; see also Pareja Pflucker, op. cit., pp. 59–62.
239. "Nuevo Crimen Aprista Contra la Clase Obrera," throwaway, undated but probably May 1947.
240. Pareja Pflucker, op. cit., p. 52.
241. Ibid., p. 53.
242. Ibid., p. 58.
243. Ibid., p. 60.
244. Ibid., pp. 124–125.
245. Ibid., pp. 86–91.
246. Ibid., p. 99.

CHAPTER 2

Peruvian Organized Labor from 1948 to 1968

The coup d'état of late October 1948 marked the beginning of almost eight years of military rule in Peru. General Manuel Odría presided over the government during that period, first as head of a military junta, and subsequent to elections in 1950 as "constitutional president." In those elections, Odría was the only presidential candidate, and no one who had belonged to the Aprista Party or the Communist Party as of October 1948 was allowed to run for Congress or any other office.

In its first phase, the Odría dictatorship was draconian. On July 1, 1949, it enacted Decree Law 11049, the "Law of Internal Security of the Republic." Among its other provisions, that statute declared guilty of "crimes against the Security and Public Tranquility" anyone who "foments or propagates by any means, individually or as members of associations, institutions, groups or political parties, doctrines or proposals that tend to alter violently the political and social order of the republic," or anyone who "associated with doctrines or international character and tendency declared as such by the Law and those who propagate those doctrines."

Of direct relevance to the labor movement was a provision of the decree outlawing those "who attempt to produce, stimulate or maintain strikes, states of agitation in unions or labor of teaching centers, with the objective of bringing about the ruin of an industry or upsetting public order, pressuring or intimidating authority."[1]

With the "constitutionalization" of the dictatorship, the stringencies of the regime were somewhat relaxed. However, in 1953 the dictatorship clamped down once again, with the allegation that the tiny Trotskyist party, the Partido Obrero Revolucionario (POR), had been fomenting strikes and other disturbances in an effort to overthrow the Odría regime.

As the end of President Odría's constitutional regime approached, new elections were called. There were three principal candidates for president in these 1956 elections. The "official" candidate was Hernando de Lavalle. Running against him were ex-president Manuel Prado and a relatively new figure, Fernando Belaúnde Terry, who had been a member of the Chamber of Deputies for the Frente Nacional Democrático in the 1945–1948 period and who ran a campaign reminiscent of the early years of the Aprista Party.

In preparation for those elections, the underground Aprista Party, forbidden to name its own candidates, negotiated first with the Odriista nominee, Lavelle, and subsequently with its old enemy, Manuel Prado. The major objective of the Apristas, led by Ramiro Prialé, the party's secretary-general, was to assure the re-legalization of the party following the election. Not receiving sufficient guarantees from Odría and Lavelle, the Aprista Party finally threw its support to Manuel Prado, who was elected. The Apristas did not negotiate at all with Belaúnde, feeling that if elected he probably would not be allowed to take office and also seeing Belaúnde as the first real rival for popular support that the party had faced during its quarter-century of existence.

GENERAL LABOR AND SOCIAL POLICIES OF ODRÍA

General Odría was very hostile to the labor movement as he found it when he seized power. Particularly before coming constitutional president in 1950, he was determined to destroy Aprista control of organized labor. To this end, his regime worked with the Communists, particularly the faction led by Juan P. Luna. His government created a Ministry of Labor, to take the place of the labor section of the Interior Ministry.[2]

However, President Odría also had a social policy. He considerably expanded the educational system. His government also built a number of workers' housing projects, which won him some support among the shantytown residents of Lima.

James Payne summed up Odría's social policies in the following commentary:

Odría, like Benavides, was antiunion, but not antiworker. While on the one hand he gave employers what amounted to complete liberty to destroy the unions in their shops, he would give startling wage and social benefits to the workers. He decreed, for example, seven blanket wage increases while in power. Although a study of real earnings during his rule ... shows that real wage gains paralleled, at best, those of the previous government, Odría did leave power with many people convinced that he had done more for the worker than anyone in the history of Peru. Odría's labor policy was, in an elephantine manner, paternalistic. Smashing or incapacitating worker organizations, but using government power to make employers deliver his presents to the workers, he practically destroyed what little existed in the way of conflict-resolving processes. On balance then, the eight years of Odría's rule marked another setback for the labor movement.[3]

However, in spite of his antiunion policies, Odría was able to muster support in the squatter colonies around Lima and other larger cities. Denis Sulmont noted,

These sectors had not been penetrated profoundly by the parties and their griev-ances had not been articulated. With aggressive policies of public expenditures and welfare, the creation of White Collar Workers Social Security, the implementation of works for education and health, support of invasions of urban land and recog-nition of neighborhoods, as well as markedly clientilist distribution of "favors," the regime was able to gain certain popular support to legitimize repression of the more politicized social movement, especially the labor movement.[4]

Odría was to maintain a substantial following among the migrants of the squatter colonies for at least a dozen years after he relinquished control of the government.

PERSECUTION OF ORGANIZED LABOR AFTER THE OCTOBER 1948 COUP

Although General Odría had overthrown the government of President José Bustamante—which had already outlawed the Aprista Party—the new dictator clearly felt that his most significant enemy was Aprismo. He set out to try to destroy the power of the Aprista Party and particularly its control of the labor movement.

Following the October 1948 coup, the headquarters of the Confeder-ación de Trabajadores del Perú was seized, and most of the CTP's principal leaders were arrested. A statement of the Inter-American Confederation of Workers (CIT), with which the CTP was affiliated, sketched the extent of this roundup of Peruvian labor leaders:

There exist thousands of political prisoners in the Peruvian jails, a great percent-age of whom belong to the labor movement, and which include outstanding democratic leaders such as Arturo Sabroso, secretary-general of the CTP and vice president of the CIT; Tomás del Piélago, subsecretary of the CTP and president of the Graphic Workers Federation of Peru; Luis López Aliaga, secretary of press of the CTP and delegate of the Trade Union Center of La Libertad; José Sandoval, defense secretary of the CTP and director of the Textile Federation.... Luis Atencio, secretary-general of the Trade Union Center of Lima.

The same statement also listed provincial union leaders in the provinces of La Libertad, Ancash, Chiclayo, Piura, and Arequipa who had been arrested.[5]

Soon after the coup, General Odría announced his intention of call-ing a "National Labor Congress" to reorganize the labor movement.

The underground organization of the CTP denounced this proposal, saying,

The CTP rejects, from this moment, the proposal of General Odría to attempt to direct from the Palace a "National Labor Congress." A Labor Congress can only be convoked by the workers themselves through their Centrals. No Unión Sindical, no National Federation, no Industrial Union, no base organism can lend itself to a masquerade, an attack on the legitimate authority deposited in the Mother Central as a result of the last Congress of the CTP.[6]

No such labor convention as proposed by General Odría was ever held.

The persecution of the labor movement by the Odría dictatorship was not confined to Lima. This was indicated in a letter from two leaders of the Workers Departmental Trade Union Federation of Junín (USDTJ), based in Huancayo, to President George Meany of the American Federation of Labor in January 1949:

We write you in the name of this organization to acquaint you with the fact that on January 15 our secretary of defense, Martino Palomino, was surprised by an employee of the Secret Police while reading the Boletín of the American Federation of Labor for the first fortnight of the month of December 1948, and was taken to police headquarters. In spite of attempts made to secure his release, he was sent to Lima on the orders of the Prefect of the Department.[7]

This letter went on:

On Wednesday the 19th of January at 6:30 p.m. a meeting of the workers of the 'Sumar' textile union was held to treat with the problem raised by Decree Law #19 of the Military Government committee concerning payment of wages during the regular Sunday day of rest.... But when the meeting had begun, it was raided by the police and those present were detained, men and women. After taking the names of all, the women were released at nine o'clock that evening. The men were not released until the next morning, after they had been taken to the regular police headquarters and then to the office of the Secret Police wished the workers to declare that the secretary general of our USDTJ Julio Faura had called the meeting and that he should have been present at the meeting. The comrades of the Sumar plant refused to do this, because if we had stated that, we are sure that our secretary general would have been jailed and sent to Lima.[8]

During the first two years, the Odría government tried a combination of force and enticement to try to build up a pro-government labor movement, before finally deciding to allow the already-existing unions to function more-or-less openly. On the one hand, between 1948 and 1951, the government jailed and even killed Aprista-inclined labor leaders. The most prominent labor official slain was Luis Negreiros, longtime leader of the trolley-car workers, who was a leader-in-hiding of the CTP at the time he was killed "while resisting arrest" early in 1950. Official protests against Negreiros's murder were sent to the International Labor Office of the United Nations by the American Federation of Labor, the Inter-American Confederation of Workers, and the International Confederation of Free Trade Unions.[9]

While the leaders of the CTP were in jail, the organization's funds were impounded by the government authorities, and all of the CTP press, including its national newspaper *CETEPE*, was forbidden to appear. Hundreds of second-rank leaders were kept in jail, and attempts to strike were ruthlessly surpressed. The most important walkout occurred among sugar workers in the north of Peru, and it was suppressed after several workers had been shot and wounded by the police.[10]

The government's attitude toward the labor movement began to change in 1951. In that year, the founding congress of the inter-American affiliate of the International Confederation of Free Trade Unions, the ORIT (Organización Regional Interamericana de Trabajadores), elected Arturo Sabroso as its president. Most of the principal trade union leaders were released from prison soon after that event.[11]

The principal leaders of the CTP were ultimately brought to trial on charges of being involved in the naval mutiny in Callao on October 3, 1948. There was a certain irony in these allegations being made by a government that had come to power by militarily ousting a regime that the trade union leaders were themselves being accused of having tried to overthrow.[12]

The labor leaders were ultimately cleared of all charges against them. Commenting on this in a May Day 1951 proclamation in the name of the CTP, Arturo Sabroso and José Sandoval noted,

We members of the National Council of the CTP emerged exonerated; but there remain on trial and still continue detained some rank-and-file leaders and delegates to our federation. Some restrictions on the trade union movement persist, in spite of the declarations of the President of the Republic and high Labor authorities promising trade union freedom. These are situations that we must resolve by measures aimed at the primary objective of obtaining full reestablishment of trade union liberties.[13]

Throughout the Odría regime, the police kept as close an eye as possible on the unions. Police permission was necessary to hold union meetings, and police were usually present when they were held. Frequently, the policemen interfered with what was going on, if they deemed it "subversive," and it was not unusual for them to arrest people participating in a meeting.[14]

The police also intervened in bargaining between unions and employers. One U.S. labor periodical wrote, "One of the worst features of the dictatorial decrees was the requirement that a representative of the secret police attend all bargaining sessions between unions and employers. If the police report on the negotiations omitted one of the union's demands, it automatically became illegal to press for it. Strikes had to be approved by the government and such approval was not easily obtained."[15]

EFFORTS TO REESTABLISH THE CONFEDERACIÓN DE TRABAJADORES DEL PERÚ

Although Arturo Sabroso and some others had continued to speak in the name of the Confederación de Trabajadores del Perú, in fact the confederation had been defunct since the coup of October 1948. However, in 1952 serious efforts were made to reestablish the CTP as a functioning organization.

One principal difficulty in reorganizing the CTP was that by 1952 the labor leadership had become quite heterogeneous. The Apristas continued to control the Textile Workers Federation, in which Arturo Sabroso remained the guiding spirit, as he did in the oil workers' union and a number of other important unions. Sabroso and his colleagues were given considerable support when the ORIT in 1951 chose him as its president, and he increased pressure to have the principal CTP leaders freed from prison.[16]

However, the Apristas in the labor movement were being challenged by Communists, Peronistas, and Socialists in the early 1950s. The Communists were divided into different groups, although for certain purposes they continued to work together against the Apristas.

Juan P. Luna, who for long had led the Communist elements in organized labor, had officially resigned from the Communist Party not long before the October 1948 coup d'état because, he said, he had certain disagreements with the party on internal Peruvian matters, although continuing to consider himself a Communist. As a consequence of no longer belonging to the Communist Party, Luna was able in the 1950 election to run for senator from Lima, as head of a Workers' Independent Electoral Committee ticket. He and four candidates for deputy on that ticket were successful. As a senator, Luna was friendly disposed toward the Odría government, labeling the general a "progressive president."

The Communists continued to maintain their strength in organized labor in their traditional strongholds, Cuzco and Arequipa. Juan P. Luna was the principal speaker at the 1952 congress of the Communists' Arequipa union organization.[17] The Communists also succeeded in getting control of the Mineworkers Federation of the Center, based principally on the Cerro de Pasco enterprise.[18]

Followers of Juan Perón were also very active. For several years there were two labor attachés in the Argentine Embassy in Lima who sought to develop relations with the Peruvian labor leaders. Among other things, they offered all-expense-paid trips to Buenos Aires, where the labor leaders were courted by officials of the government-controlled Confederación General del Trabajo.

Most of the Peruvian labor union leaders who were won over by Perón were ex-Communists, apparently people formerly associated with Eudosio Rabines's dissident Communist group. These included some leaders of the dockworkers of Callao, the pastry cooks' union, and the chauffeurs' union of Arequipa.

However, the most important converts to Peronismo were the leaders of the Printing Trades Federation. Tomás del Piélago, who in 1947 had been elected as an Aprista to the second-highest post of the CTP, supported a move in 1951 by the printers to send a delegate to the Latin American labor conference the Argentine Confederación General del Trabajo organized in Asunción, Paraguay, and del Piélago played a key role in that meeting. By 1953, del Piélago was living in Buenos Aires, as an official of the Peronista Latin American labor group, the ATLAS.[19]

Another significant figure among the Peronistas was José Benitez, president of the Printing Trades Federation, who had been associated with Eudosio Rabines and had been the principal figure in the rival to the CTP, which Rabines attempted to organize during the 1945–1948 period. After the coup of October 1948, Benitez had been named to the Lima City Council by General Odría, but subsequently had shifted his loyalty to the Peronistas, whose supposed "anti-imperialism" he liked.[20]

In the beginning, the efforts of the Argentine labor attachés had encouragement from the Odría government, anxious to undermine the influence of the Apristas in the labor movement. However, by 1953, the Odría regime had apparently broken with the Peronistas and forbade them any longer to publish a periodical that they had established in Lima.[21]

The Socialists continued to be a major force among the oil workers in the North. With the approval of the Odría government, the petroleum companies granted recognition to the union controlled by the Socialists, instead of to that led by the Apristas. Although the Socialist leaders claimed to have the support of 90 percent of the oil workers,[22] the labor reporting officer of the U.S. Embassy at that time believed that the Aprista union in fact had a majority of the oil workers in its ranks. The leaders of the Socialist union maintained that they had negotiated contracts with the oil firms without intervention of the Ministry of Labor.[23]

In the early 1950s, the Socialists also claimed to control the Railroad Workers Federation.[24] They certainly were dominant for a while among the workers of the Central Railroad of Peru.[25]

The Socialists likewise claimed to have influence among the agricultural workers and in the Miners' Federation.[26] Some years later, near the end of the second Prado period, a Socialist was president of the Mineworkers Federation of the Center, and eight other members of the party were on its Executive Committee.[27]

The Socialist-controlled unions did not participate in the negotiations in 1952 seeking to reestablish the CTP, claiming that they were a "government maneuver."[28] When the Second Congress of the CTP was finally held in May 1956, the delegation of the Socialist-controlled Oil Workers Federation joined Communist delegates from Cuzco and Arequipa in walking out of the meeting.[29]

Luciano Castillo, the principal leader of the Socialists, was elected to the Senate in 1950. The Socialist Party claimed also to have elected twelve members of the Chamber of Deputies, although the government only recognized the victories of three of these. The Socialists constituted the only consistent opposition element in Congress between 1950 and 1956.[30]

The Odría government itself succeeded in gaining the support of some secondary trade union leaders. Aside from coercion and in some instances bribery, an important instrument used for this purpose was a union-leadership training system established by the Ministry of Labor. Even some union leaders opposed to the government had kind words for the quality of the courses by the ministry.[31]

Among the union leaders who were supporters of the Odría regime were officials of organizations of the port workers of Callao, the white-collar workers of the Lima Light and Power Company, and the Central Railroad Workers Union. They explained their support of the Odría government on the basis of what it had done to expand the education system and to foster workers' housing projects.[32]

Two other efforts to reestablish a functioning Confederación de Trabajadores del Perú had taken place before the efforts undertaken in mid-1952. Juan P. Luna had attempted to use an ad hoc organization dealing with the rent-control law to reorganize the CTP under his leadership, but this failed. Some time later, the Peronistas established a Committee for the Reorganization of the CTP, but this received little support from other elements in the labor movement.

Finally, in mid-1952 the Textile Workers Federation issued an invitation to all of the unions that were formerly members of the CTP to get together again and reorganize the confederación. Most of the union groups that had belonged to the CTP, as well as the Bank Workers Federation, which had not been in the confederation, began a series of Sunday meetings to plan the reestablishment of the Confederación de Trabajadores del Perú.

Among the unions participating in these meetings, aside from the textile workers' union, were the unions of the construction workers, chauffeurs, railroaders, printing-trades workers, miners, bakers, hat workers, transport workers, glass workers, and shoemakers and the Aprista-controlled oil workers' union. However, the CTP's health workers' union no longer existed, and the white-collar workers, woodworkers, millers, and the Union Agricultural Workers and Sharecroppers did not participate in the meetings.

Three meetings worked out the details of the effort to reestablish the CTP. It was agreed to set up a Reorganization Committee, with three delegates from every federation and one from every independent union. The

Reorganization Committee was scheduled to meet to name a Provisional Executive Committee of the CTP.[33]

However, this effort to reestablish the CTP was doomed to fail. When the Reorganization Committee was scheduled to meet at the Printing Trades Workers' Hall, the police broke up the meeting, on the grounds that permission had not been received from the police to hold the session. Attempts by Senator Juan P. Luna to get the Director General of the Investigations to reverse this decision were fruitless.[34]

It was not until April 21–May 1, 1956, shortly before the 1956 election, that the Confederación de Trabajadores del Perú was finally reestablished. According to Arturo Sabroso, President Odría allowed this in the hope of getting the sympathy of the workers for his presidential candidate in the forthcoming election.

A Preparatory Committee, which was established to prepare for the Reorganization Congress of the CTP, was controlled by the orthodox Communists (not Juan P. Luna and his group). The Apristas did not participate very much in the Preparatory Committee, sure that they could make their weight felt in the Congress itself.

At the Congress, the Apristas successfully pushed for representation at the meeting to be by *sindicato* (trade union) instead of by federation. Since the Textile Workers Federation had 75 unions, the Apristas had a majority at the meeting. Aprista control was demonstrated by the fact that only 3 of the 26 members of the National Directorative Council elected by the Congress were members of the Communist Party.

The CTP Congress decided that the confederación would maintain contact with all international labor groups and that the decision as to the CTP's international affiliation would be left up to the next Congress. However, subsequently, the new CTP Executive Committee interpreted "all labor groups" to mean only democratic ones, according to Arturo Sabroso.[35]

Arturo Sabroso was reelected secretary-general of the CTP, and another leader of the textile workers, Santiago Tamariz Sánchez, was named secretary of organization. The subsecretary-general was Rodolfo Galván Montoya of the Federation of Bank Employees. The other members of the National Directive Council included representatives of the major industrial federations, as well as those of some individual unions, including the Union of Domestics.

The new National Directive Council issued a "Manifesto to All of the Republic and General Opinion of the Country," soon after the Congress. It had a subheading "The CTP Cannot Belong to Any Political Party," and the document argued, "To achieve the welfare of the working class, it is necessary to overcome the intestine quarrels which come from the antagonistic ideologies, confusing men and weakening the organization." It also called upon the workers to join their respective unions and for individual unions to join their appropriate federations or form new ones if no relevant one existed.[36]

LABOR CONFLICTS DURING THE ODRÍA PERIOD

In spite of the generally hostile attitude of the Odría regime to such events, a number of strikes did occur during the dictatorship. Most of these were walkouts over strictly economic issues.

One of the earliest and most important exceptions to the economic nature of the strikes of the period was a general walkout that took place in Arequipa in June 1950. During an attempted insurrection in that city, which the government attributed to the Apristas, there was a general walkout there. The walkout collapsed when government troops regained control of the city.[37]

A substantial number of strikes took place in the latter part of 1952 and early 1953. One of the most important of these was a walkout of sugar workers in December 1952. Living and working conditions in the largely foreign-owned sugar plantations were particularly difficult, and in December 1952 workers on a number of them walked out. Many of the union leaders were arrested and sent to jail. Apparently, only three sugar workers' unions were able to survive the government's suppression of that walkout.[38]

Other strikes and threats of strikes in this period included a walkout of workers in 56 textile plants and one walkout of miners. There was a threatened strike of bank employees, which brought the government suddenly to decide that only employees of private banks could form unions, which deprived the Bank Employees Federation of its militant young president, who worked for a government-owned bank.[39]

Late in 1952, there was another general strike in Arequipa, supported by the Aprista and Communist-controlled central labor bodies of the city. The government used that walkout to raise a specter of a revolutionary plot allegedly organized by the Trotskyist party, the Partido Obrero Revolucionario, which in fact consisted mainly of students and had no influence in the labor movement.[40] It also used the Arequipa strike as an excuse for clamping down on organized labor in general.

During the 1953 wave of persecution of the Peruvian labor movement, the Confederación de Trabajadores de América Latina (CTAL) denounced "the detention of the 100 Peruvian trade union leaders and the massive jailing of dozens of students, artisans, professionals and democratic elements who belong to various sectors."[41]

During the 1952–1953 period, there were walkouts in Lima and elsewhere among printers, cement-factory workers, and oil workers of Talara. There were also threats of walkouts among trolley-car drivers and taxi men.[42] In the most important of these walkouts, the workers were able to obtain wage increases.[43]

In mid-1952 there was a threat of a general textile workers' strike. The occasion for this was the arrest and exiling of Rafael Lovet and Lucio Sandoval, secretary-general and secretary of organization, respectively, of the Federation of Textile Workers. They had attended a textile conference of the International Labor Organization in Geneva, where they had been very critical of the labor policies of the Odría government, and they were arrested on returning home. Lovet and Sandoval were finally able to get jobs in the textile plants in Uruguay and remained in exile until near the end of the Odría regime.

The exile of these two leaders of the textile workers aroused wide protests in Peru and abroad. After first contemplating a general strike of protest, the leaders of the Textile Workers Federation decided against the idea, fearing that the Odría government would use a walkout as an excuse to crush the federation entirely.[44]

Among the foreign protests was one by the Congress of Industrial Organizations of the United States. It published a letter against the exile of the two textile-union leaders, sent to the minister of government by Lovet and Sandoval.[45]

In 1954, as the Odría regime was entering its last years, a strike wave developed. Early in that year there were walkouts in the textile industry, on the Lima trolley cars, and among municipal workers and petroleum workers. Of particular importance was a successful strike of the workers of the Central Railroad of Peru, which won a 10 percent increase in wages.[46]

Of considerable importance, too, was a walkout of the Bank Employees Federation, seeking salary increases and augmentation of family allowances and other fringe benefits, as well as employment stability. Although the government declared the work stoppage illegal, it was at least partially successful.[47]

Strikes continued in 1955. One of the most important of these was a 24-hour general strike declared by bank employees and white-collar workers in industry and commerce in protest against passage of a law altering the social security system made without any consultation with the labor movement.[48]

In some cases, the relative liberalization of the Odría regime's treatment of organized labor as a new election approached led important employers to seek to improve their relations with their unions. Such was the case with the W. R. Grace & Company's handling of the workers in its four textile plants in the Lima area. This change came about after a visit to the United States on a foreign aid grant of one of the principal leaders of one of those unions, during which he conferred with officials in Grace headquarters, explaining to them the Peruvian textile workers' complaints. Thereafter, Grace appointed a director of labor relations for the four textile plants and began to confer with the unions on all significant aspects of labor–management relations.[49]

THE ADVENT OF THE SECOND PRADO ADMINISTRATION

At the end of Odría's "constitutional" regime in 1956, there were once again elections. However, unlike the situation in 1945, the Aprista Party was not legalized before the poll. Although it was able to run a handful of candidates, including some union leaders, as "independents," its principal objective was to assure that the new president would legalize the party.

Negotiations to this end were conducted by Ramairo Prialé, who returned from exile to be secretary-general of the Aprista Party. He succeeded in rebuilding the party organization and proved to be a skillful negotiator with the competing candidates.

President Odría was anxious to get the Apristas to back his candidate, Hernando de Lavalle, who was not a professional politician and who was a onetime friend of Víctor Raúl Haya de la Torre. During negotiations with Odría, the Apristas published a periodical, *Impacto*, which had kind things to say about Lavalle. However, when Odría refused to legalize the Aprista Party or to guarantee that Lavalle would do so if elected, the Apristas threw their support to ex-president Manuel Prado, who was willing to agree to legalize the party. The Apristas did so only two weeks before the election, but their party network was sufficiently widespread that Aprista support guaranteed Prado's election.[50]

This time, the Apristas were more careful in their relations with the Prado administration than they had been with the government of José Bustamante. They sought to avoid confrontations with the president and his administration. They realized that the possibility of their party's ultimately coming to power depended on the maintenance of the Prado regime, culminating in elections at the end of the Prado government in 1962, which they hoped they would win.

For their part, President Prado and his administration clearly recognized that their advent to power and remaining in office depended very much on continuing to enjoy the support of the Apristas. As a result, they too were anxious to avoid any kind of showdown with the Aprista Party.[51]

This situation had a strong impact on the labor movement between 1956 and 1962. The Apristas, who were clearly dominant in organized labor during that period, were anxious not to have organized labor generate a crisis that would imperil the continuation of President Prado's government. For its part, the Prado administration was willing to make concessions that would favor the continuation of Aprista control of the great majority of the labor movement.

The relative stability of labor relations and freedom of the labor movement during the second Prado period was indicated by the fact that many important labor organizations held congresses during those years. James Payne noted that "as a result of the past history of repression, there are few organizations which had held even one congress." However, the Textile Workers Federation, founded in 1919, held its first congress in 1958, the National Union of Primary School Teachers, dating from 1936, held its first congress in 1956; and the Lima Regional Labor Federation, established in 1940, had its first congress in 1959. Payne noted, "The dates for other organizations are similar."[52]

GROWTH OF THE LABOR MOVEMENT DURING
THE SECOND PRADO GOVERNMENT

One characteristic of the Peruvian labor movement in the second administration of President Manuel Prado was its considerable growth. Old union groups came back into activity, and a considerable number of new ones were established.

Although no total figures are available regarding the increase in the size of the labor movement during the second Prado period, James Payne calculated the rise in the number of legally recognized unions in the last two years of the period. He noted that the Ministry of Labor reported that on January 1, 1960, there were 712 legally recognized unions, of which he calculated 30 were either federations or "nonexistent" organizations, leaving 682 functioning local unions. In 1960 there were 52 additional unions recognized, and in 1961 another 70 received recognition, for a total of 805 on January 1, 1962.[53]

Payne also gave information on the growth of three federations. The Textile Workers, which in 1950 had 60 member unions, had 82 in 1961, with a total of 21,000 members. The Federation of Metallurgical Workers, which was only established in 1957, with five unions, had 63 local unions in 1961, with a membership of about 3,000. Only two of the federation's member unions had been established before 1954. Finally, the Federation of Hotel and Restaurant Workers had had 12 member unions in 1950, with 2,000 members, but by 1961 had 25 affiliates with about 5,000 members.[54]

By the end of the Prado administration, according to Payne, all firms with more than 50 workers were unionized. However, only about 15 percent of the nonagricultural workers were organized, which compared to about 30 percent at that time in the United States.[55] Payne estimated that at the end of the Prado period, there were about 329,000 "effective members" of Peruvian organized labor. He defined "effective" as being "that muster of workers who will obey a strike order when given under suitable conditions by the organization to which the worker immediately belongs." Payne estimated the "dues-paying membership" at 50–60 percent of the effective membership.

Of the 329,000 effective members of organized labor in 1962, some 45,000 were in manufacturing, with textiles accounting for almost half of these; about 12,000 were in the food and beverage field; and some 52,000 were in the extractive industries, with 30,000 being in the central mining area. Payne estimated that organized agricultural workers numbered about 55,000, of whom 35,000 were in the sugar plantations. Commerce accounted for about 13,000 effective union members, and transportation had some 37,000 members, including truck and taxi drivers, bus drivers, trolley-car men, railroaders, dockworkers, and aviation and maritime workers. Some 11,000 organized workers were in communications, almost half of these in the postal service. In the service trades, there were an estimated 99,000 organized workers, with the public school teachers accounting for almost half of these, and with construction workers, market vendors, hotel and restaurant workers, the electric light and power industry, street cleaners, and hospital workers making up the other half.[56]

One part of the labor movement that expanded particularly rapidly during the second Prado period was that of white-collar workers. Shortly before the end of the Odría dictatorship, in September 1955, the Central Sindical de Empleados Particulares (Confederation of Private White-Collar Workers—CSEPP) had been established. By September 1961, it had 24,040 members, of which 19,000 were employees of industrial firms. Other affiliates of CESPP included the Arequipa Regional Union of Telephone Workers and the Federation of Petroleum White-Collar Workers. All in all, the CSEPP had 92 affiliated organizations.[57]

Unlike most Peruvian labor organizations, the CSEPP carried out "a moderately firm policy toward organizations which do not pay dues," according to James Payne. The CSEPP constitution provided that an affiliate that did not pay its dues for a period of six months was to be dropped from membership, and in some instances this rule was actually applied—seven affiliates were dropped for this reason in 1960.[58]

Throughout the Prado period, the Central Sindical de Empleados Particulares del Perú was controlled by Apristas or elements sympathetic to Aprismo. As a consequence, when the National Federation of Bank Employees was captured in 1958 by far-left elements, it withdrew from the Central.[59] In its congress of December 1961, the CSEPP voted to affiliate with the Confederación de Trabajadores del Perú.[60]

ORGANIZATION OF GOVERNMENT WORKERS

Some efforts were made during the 1956–1962 period to organize government employees. For many years there had existed social organizations among these workers, but as James Payne noted, "associations formerly devoted exclusively to hold dances are beginning to take up fundamental issues."

Government employees were faced with the fact that they were legally prohibited from striking. A walkout of the telegraph and postal workers in 1959 was broken when all of the leaders of the walkout were dismissed, after which organization remained "incapacitated."

In 1959 a national organization of government workers was established, the Asociación National de Servidores Civiles del Estado (ANSCE), including 21 different groups of employees of ministries and other government dependencies. It got off on the wrong foot, however, when shortly after its establishment, its president, Victor Checa, who belonged to an opposition party, called a general strike of all government employees, supposedly in sympathy with the postal workers' walkout. This was, according to James

Payne, "a political maneuver designed to weaken the government," and the administration reacted strongly, dismissing 74 leaders of "the few organizations which had obeyed the strike order."

The ANSCE was revived a year after the strike and was given legal recognition. However, it remained "in a state of relative inactivity, confining attention to occasional attempts to codify the operations of the public employees' pension system."[61]

The one area of public employment in which workers formed a strong organization–one that was to become one of the most powerful segments of Peruvian organized labor—was education. Four different groups of teachers—primary, secondary, physical education, and manual training—had established mutual benefit organizations and an overall group, the Asociación Mutualista Magesterial (AMM), during the Odría period. When the AMM had sought to go beyond mutual benefit activities and begin to assume the functions of a trade union, the Odría government had intervened, removing the leadership and imposing its own people to head the organization.

However, during the second Prado administration, the AMM converted into the Federación Nacional de Educadores del Perú (FENEP), composed of unions of the four different kinds of teachers. It became one of the best-financed segments of the labor movement.

According to James Payne, the FENEP succeeded in making substantial gains for the teachers during the Prado years. It largely eliminated the use of teaching jobs as political patronage, succeeded in getting preferential treatment for normal school graduates as opposed to untrained teachers, and won wage increases for teachers in the provinces to bring them up to the standards of the schools in Lima. It also won a system of job–salary classification for the whole national school system.

The FENEP carried out two strikes, in 1960 and in 1961, which succeeded in winning substantial salary increases for the teachers.[62] There were then about 43,000 members in FENEP, of whom 30,000 were in the National Union of Primary Teachers.[63]

ORGANIZATION OF AGRICULTURAL WORKERS

One area in which trade unionism was revived and expanded during the second Prado administration was the countryside, particularly the coastal areas, where plantation agriculture was extensive. The number of legally recognized rural workers' unions grew from three in 1956 to 33 by 1960. These groups rose from 4 percent of all unions in 1956 to 14 percent in 1960.[64]

The sugar workers' unions were among the first to be reestablished. However, there had been considerable mechanization of the sugar industry since 1948. As a result, the number of sugar workers had decreased from 100,000 to 40,000. Also, wages had fallen drastically during the Odría period and were reported by 1957 to be lower than the wages in dictator Rafael Trujillo's Dominican Republic, according to the International Labor Organization.[65]

With the advent of the new Prado regime, Aprista trade unionists set out to reorganize the local unions on the sugar plantations. Finally, on June 20, 1957, a congress reestablished the Federación de Trabajadores Azucareros del Perú.[66]

By the end of the Prado administration, there were 13 sugar workers' unions in operation. James Payne noted in 1965 that these unions "operate[d] like any other organization of industrial workers, and most ... obtained for their workers wage and conditions benefits comparable to those of urban workers."

Payne also noted that the other unions had been set up on large cotton plantations and that they were "becoming strong enough to present and enforce demands for better living conditions, school facilities, and occasionally, higher wages." However, he added, "The impediments to organized activity in the coastal region are many. Ownership usually opposes the formation of a union, and often effects reprisals on workers who lead organization attempts.... Also, the lower cultural level of workers on such haciendas makes it difficult to take collective decisions, to collect dues, and carry on sustained, coordinated activities."[67]

Rural union organization also expanded in the mountain region. During the Prado period, two rival organizations sought to represent the largely Indian workers and peasants of the highlands. These were the Confederación de Campesinos del Perú (CCP) and the Federación Nacional de Campesinos del Perú (FENCAP).

The CCP was controlled by the far left, with Trotskyists and members of the Leftist offshoot of the Apristas, APRA Rebelde (subsequently renamed Movimiento de Izquierda Revolucionaria—MIR), among its leaders. James Payne noted, "The extremist CCP is not an organization in the sense that it has its own finances, an organic structure, or a coherent, representative decision-making process. It lacks all three. Rather it is a group of agitators in Lima and in certain agricultural areas, and includes members of opposition parties."[68]

In Cuzco in January 1961, there was founded the Federación Departamental de Campesinos del Cuzco, affiliated with the Communist Party–controlled Federation of Workers of Cuzco. However, this peasant group was not controlled by the Stalinist party, but rather by Trotskyists of the faction headed by Hugo Blanco, who for some time had been active in organizing peasant unions, particularly in the area of the La Convención valley. Sometime later, Blanco was to lead a peasant insurrection in the La Convención area.[69]

The FENCAP was the renamed Federación de Campesinos y Yanaconas of the earlier period and, like it, was controlled by the Apristas. It was finally established in January 1959. Payne described it as "a rather interesting combination of politics, altruism, and chaos." At its "founding congress" there were present representatives of 29 indigenous communities, 8 unions of tenants, 6 organizations of sharecroppers, 11 unions of day laborers, and 5 small owners' groups. However, Payne wrote, "these 59 organizations that sent representatives to the congress represent only a small part of the number of groups with which FENCAP has contact."

The FENCAP was involved in "organizing regional congresses and assisting in the resolution of known collective conflicts." It also, according to Payne, had before the end of the Prado regime begun "to serve as a productive national lobby for agricultural workers."[70]

Some rural employers were very resistant to attempts to organize their workers, and this resistance sometimes led to violence. For example, in July 1957 the CTP issued a communiqué denouncing the efforts of two haciendas to break a strike of their employees, which had been in progress for 29 days, and the cooperation the employers received from local police officials, who provided armed escorts for strikebreakers. Several people were wounded in this case.[71]

THE ROLE OF THE CTP

The Confederación de Trabajadores del Perú (CTP) largely dominated the labor movement during the 1956–1962 period. It had within it s ranks in 1961 some 240,000 workers, which amounted to about 75 percent of the total number of organized workers.[72]

There were several attempts during the second Prado administration to organize a rival to the CTP, although none were successful. James Payne noted that the most important of these, launched by the Bank Workers Federation after it fell into anti-Aprista hands, was the Frente Único de Trabajadores (FUT). But "like several other attempts the extremists made to form a national center, the FUT had quickly collapsed."[73]

During this period, the CTP was dominated by the Aprista Party. Because the party had been largely responsible for bringing the Prado regime to power and was anxious to have it remain in power until the 1962 election, this put the leadership of the CTP in a somewhat anomalous position.

James Payne argued that the CTP leadership engaged in what he called "political bargaining" with the Prado regime. He explained, "The power of the CTP lies in its potential ability to call a nationwide general strike which would paralyze the country and provoke widespread violence. Such a general strike, combined with the agitation of opposition and extremist parties, would probably sound the death knell for the incumbent regime."

However, "the general strike is finite, limited weapon. The more it is used, the less effective it is likely to be. The leaders of the national center must attempt to use the *threat* of a strike as much as possible, avoiding the actual strike itself."

As a result of this and because of the Aprista support of the Prado government, "from 1956 to 1962 the APRA-led CTP played an unnerving game of 'chicken' with the Prado regime. The CTP attempted to frighten the executive as much as possible with threats of a general strike while making every attempt to postpone such a strike, thus giving the executive ample opportunity to move out of the way before a collision occurred."[74]

In fact, the CTP called only one general strike during this period, on May 13, 1960. It was a protest against "police brutality" in several strike situations. It was not officially aimed at the government, but at "assassins at the service of imperialistic companies." Called for only one day, it was almost totally effective, with even the left wing–controlled unions adhering to it. As James Payne commented, "Through this strike the CTP demonstrated, apparently, that it could command the labor movement. And it was able to demonstrate this without seriously threatening the Prado government."[75]

The potential power of the CTP to disrupt the economy and put the government itself in danger provided the CTP leadership with extensive power to bargain with the Ministry of Labor and the administration generally, on behalf of its affiliates. As Payne wrote, "When the secretary-general, for example, came to the Ministry of Labor to complain about something, government officials listened. The visits of confederation officers were not just occasional; scarcely a day went by when one of the top leaders did not walk straight into the minister's office with a problem."

As a result, said Payne, "Utilizing its position of access and power, the CTP became, in many cases, the link between worker organizations and the ministry. The leaders took up the problems of the smallest unions and resolved them personally with ministry officials. The CTP was, in practice, a body to which disappointed leaders could appeal for aid. When their cases were taken up by confederation officers, these lesser leaders usually obtained a satisfactory solution."[76]

Payne noted that even the anti-Aprista extremist-led unions sometimes sought the help of the CTP. He noted, "Of course, extremists attacked the CTP because it was an APRA-controlled organization which tended to support the Prado government. But when they found themselves in difficulty, extremist leaders frequently turned to the CTP for help."[77]

According to James Payne, the system of "political bargaining, largely involving the CTP and its affiliates functioned well during the second Prado period." He wrote, "During the years 1956–1961, the system of political bargaining was successful in the following senses: inflation was kept at a reasonable level (about 8 per cent yearly); employers were not brutally mistreated and the investment climate was considered 'promising'; organized labor made significant gains in wages and working conditions."[78]

THE STRUCTURE OF THE CTP

Ideally, the CTP should have been composed of national industrial federations and regional bodies bringing together all of the CTP-affiliated unions in a particular area. However, at the CTP Congress of 1958, there were 10 regional federations and 18 industrial federations, but also 25 individual unions represented. Some of these individual unions were important organizations for which no federation existed, but others were quite small with less than 100 members.

This persistence of a large number of unions directly affiliated to the CTP created a situation in which the actual functioning of the confederation was quite different from what was provided for in its constitution. In theory, an assembly of delegates from each affiliate was to serve as the interim highest body of the CTP between congresses. However, given the allocation of delegates in this assembly as provided in the constitution, the assembly would have been dominated by the representatives of small and relatively weak organizations, who could dictate to the larger and more powerful CTP affiliates how they should behave.

As a consequence, the delegates' assembly in fact lost its role as a guiding body of the CTP. James Payne noted that there was "degradation of the assembly of delegates to the point where it became practically function-less. The assembly, instead of being representative of the power distribution in the labor movement, is nothing more than a gathering of labor leaders."[79]

Payne added, "The meeting time is spent largely reading minutes, letters, reports, or exposition of problems. The votes are usually unanimous ratifications of leadership proposals. Very little time is spent on productive discussions or exchange of views. In fact, an assembly of delegates of the CTP is one of the sleepiest affairs in organized labor in Peru."

Given this situation, Payne raised the question, "How does the CTP continue as a relatively cohesive and surprisingly effective organization? For it is both."[80]

It was effective in large part because its leadership was mostly in the hands of members of the Aprista Party. Dissident unions or federations established by anti-Aprista left-wing elements were not admitted to the CTP. The few unions in the CTP that were under left-wing leadership constituted a "very tiny minority."

Payne explained, "Consequently, the parallel views on goals, means and enemies, and the feeling of responsibility and loyalty to fellow party members, tend to reduce conflict among the many APRA leaders in the CTP. On important issues, delegates and officers may reach a decision either informally or at the *buro sindical*, the labor office of the APRA party, thus rendering the assembly a public body which only manifests decisions already taken elsewhere."[81]

At the end of the second Prado period, all 25 members of the Executive of the Confederación de Trabajadores del Perú were members of the Aprista Party. However, in the leading bodies of the principal federations affiliated with the CTP, Aprista domination was less complete. In the White-Collar Workers' Federation, for instance, although the secretary-general was an

Aprista, there were also Christian Democrats, members of Belaúnde's Acción Popular, and independents in the Executive Committee.[82]

In addition, the relatively conservative strike policy of the CTP tended to strengthen its cohesion. Had the CTP called frequent general strikes, James Payne believed, these walkouts might have given rise to great dissidence within the organization. Finally, the top leadership of the CTP being chiefly in the hands of the confederation's larger and more powerful unions, 21 of the 26 positions on its National Executive being held by representatives of "important organizations," provided cohesion to the CTP leadership.[83]

The Aprista Party was very well organized within the CTP and its various unions, as well as within opposition elements in unions controlled by the "extremists." On a national level, the party worked through its union bureau, or *buro sindical.*

In July 1957, the *buro sindical* organized a national meeting of its trade unionists, which it labeled the National Assembly of Unions (Asamblea Nacional de Sindicatos). Its opening session was addressed by party secretary-general Ramiro Prialé, and the Asamblea was presided over by José Sandoval of the Textile Workers Federation. Among the things discussed were the party organization within the labor movement, participation of trade unionists in the National Executive of the party, labor-leadership training programs run by the party, and relations with international organizations, as well as a wide range of economic and social problems.[84]

OUTSIDE FINANCING OF ORGANIZED LABOR IN THE SECOND PRADO PERIOD

The internally generated financial resources of Peruvian organized labor were for the most part scanty during the 1956–1962 period. But internally generated funds were supplemented by financial resources from outside of the Peruvian labor movement. This fact provided both benefits and difficulties.

Undoubtedly, several factors accounted for the relatively scarce internal financial resources of the Peruvian unions, particularly the national industrial federations and the CTP. Of some importance, certainly, were the low wages of the average Peruvian worker, although this was not the most crucial factor. Undoubtedly of more significance was the general cultural lack of a tradition of paying regular sums to private voluntary organizations. Also, James Payne noted that in the case of the textile workers' organizations, there was a persistence of the traditional anarchist suspicion of the idea of paid union officials, who were often seen as "exploiting" their members.

The industrial federations were particularly lacking in what might be considered adequate funding from their rank-and-file unions. Even in the Textile Workers Federation, the country's oldest and relatively best-financed federation, only 13 percent of the local union dues were passed on to the federation. At the other extreme, the Lima taxi drivers' union passed nothing on to its federation.

This lack of adequate financing had a number of effects. For one thing, there were few full-time union officials, or even office secretaries. Payne estimated that not more than 30 unions had either of these. Also, there were virtually no unions that had strike funds, although from time to time money was raised in other unions to finance a particular organization's walkout. This partly reflected the fact that strikes generally tended to be of short duration.[85]

During the period under discussion, however, funds generated from within the Peruvian unions were substantially supplemented by income from outside the labor movement. This was true of both the CTP and the Aprista-controlled unions, and those dominated by left-wing parties.

The CTP and unions associated with it received funds from three different outside sources: the international trade secretaries, the Organización Interamericana de Trabajadores (ORIT), and the Aprista Party. In each case, these funds were used for specific purposes.

The international trade secretariats are international federations of national unions of a particular branch of the economy—transport, mining, textiles, and so on. The secretariats are associated with the International Confederation of Free Trade Unions. According to James Payne, "The international trade secretariats spend their funds entirely in maintaining the regional office and advisor, holding schools for leaders, arranging congresses and conferences, and supporting key organizational drives. Little, if any, money is spent for permanent subsidy of either organizations or leaders."[86]

The ORIT was the American regional organization of the International Confederation of Free Trade Unions. In general, during the period under discussion, it was a channel for funds from the United States and Canadian unions to the unions of Latin America and the Caribbean.

The ORIT money, which went to the CTP and some of its regional and national industrial federations, went as outright subsidies to the organizations involved. Payne estimated that between $500 and $600 a month was going to the CTP, and smaller sums were being sent to the Arequipa and Lima regional federations of the CTP and the CTP federations of construction workers and taxi drivers, among others.

James Payne had serious criticisms of the ORIT type of direct subsidies. He argued that they tended to make union leaders receiving them "independent" of their memberships, discouraged the union leaders from trying to get their own members to financially support their unions, and gave rise to jealously between those getting subsidies and those not getting them. He also argued that these subsidies, because they were not publicly reported, tended to generate false rumors about their coming from the government or from large employers.

Aprista party funds given to the labor movement were reported by Payne as being "not particularly large." He added, "The party does operate its own labor leadership training and indoctrination courses, and probably finances the trips of APRA labor leaders when they serve a semipolitical function."

The anti-Aprista left-wing unions also received external financial support during the 1956–1962 period. Payne observed,

Given the diversity of the extremist left in Peru, it seems certain that there is more than one source for the outside funds received by extremist-led organizations. Exactly what these sources are remains in doubt. The Soviet bloc, Communist China, other Latin American extremist movements, and local sources are all possibilities. The last source may be more important than at first imagined. Extremist parties have wealthy members, and a devotion to the "cause" might well lead them to part with some of their income. In addition, with very few exceptions, extremist-led labor organizations are usually turned over to new leadership in a bankrupt condition.

Payne gave some details on the finances of the Communist-controlled Union of Construction Workers, as one group that clearly obtained outside funding. He indicated that dues payments declined steadily after 1956, and by 1961 the union was receiving virtually no dues from its members. Based on partial figures published by the union, he estimated that its monthly deficit by 1961 was 10,000 soles. In addition, over the years the union had had extraordinary expenses, including those of a congress in 1958 to organize a national construction workers' federation rival to that belonging to the CTP, which he estimated to have cost at least 25,000 soles. Another 10,000 soles went toward financing a trip to the interior by six delegates from the Lima union, to drum up attendance at the congress. Payne wrote, "It is not unreasonable to conclude that the Lima Union and its offspring, the extremist Federation of Construction Workers, receive a minimum of 15,000 soles monthly from outside sources."[87]

FAR-LEFT ORGANIZED LABOR IN SECOND PRADO PERIOD

Although the Apristas largely dominated the labor movement during the second Prado administration, there was a continuing anti-Aprista far-left minority in organized labor during that period. Payne identified seven groups that he called "extremist," which operated within the labor movement. These were two Trotskyist groups, the so-called Leninist Committee, the Rebel APRA Party, the Communist Party, the Progressive Socialist Party, and the Socialist Party of Luciano Castillo.[88]

I would not put Luciano Castillo's party in that company. Although it was in the opposition to the Prado government, was anti-Aprista, and controlled the petroleum workers' union, which dealt with employers in at least part of the period, it had little in common with the other six far-left groups. In ideology it was democratic Socialist, and it seldom if ever cooperated with the "extremists."

Payne also noted that although the major opposition parties—the Popular Action Party of Fernando Belaúnde, the Unión Nacional Odriista, and the Christian Democrats—had little influenced in organized labor, they tended to side publicly with the far-left faction of the labor movement. He noted, "These three moderate parties were quite weak in the labor movement; they usually depended on genuine extremist elements to call strikes and organize roots and then publicized these events as proof of the 'nefarious policy of the government.' " [89]

Payne argued that although what he dubbed the "extremist" parties probably had between 20,000 and 41,000 members, only about 1,000 of these participated in the labor movement. But he added that "the power of this small group of individuals lay in its ability to gain the support of unconcerned or unaware rank and file. The total number of workers controlled by extremists was about 25,000 to 30,000 in 1961, a figure considerably lower than in 1957. The figure represented about ten per cent of the entire number of organized workers." [90]

Payne also noted, "The most significant feature of extremist activity in the Peruvian labor movement during the period under study was its lack of success. Once in control of a body of workers through a labor organization, extremists demonstrated a marked inability to maintain that control. They were either voted out of office, or, more frequently, their organization lost members or member unions." [91]

Payne listed 11 "important" worker groups that the "extremists" controlled during all or part of this period and indicated that the total number of workers in them had declined from an estimated 53,000 members in 1957 to 21,000 in 1961. This decline took place in the face of an overall increase of 20 percent in the number of unionists in Peru. [92]

The major conquest the far-left made in the labor movement during the second Prado period was to win control of the Bank Workers Federation. This occurred as a result of a strike of the bank clerks that lasted from April to August 1959. The minister of labor at the time, Antonio Pinilla, procrastinated in issuing a resolution about the walkout, and during this interim, the extremists in the union forced the union's Aprista leadership to resign. [93] The leaders of the CTP thereafter refused to support the strike, which was settled on conditions unfavorable to the workers. [94]

The group that took control was far from monolithic. Payne noted that "aside from their desire to weaken the government, the only point of unity was their common opposition to the APRA. For the extremists this antipathy was a useful tool for maintaining themselves in power."

When new elections for bank union officers occurred in 1950, the extremist leadership split, running two different candidates. However, one of these won, with the man backed by the Apristas coming in second. In the following year, the anti-Aprista elements united once again. By the end of the period, the union was "an extremist-led organization with moderate forces in control of two fifths of the assembly of delegates."[95]

The strongest center of Communist Party support in the labor movement was in the Cuzco region. However, even there, there was a certain degree of decline in the Communists' position during the second Prado period.

Communist strength in Cuzco dated from the early 1930s. In that period, Eudosio Rabines, who was then secretary-general of the Communist Party, had considerable success in proselytizing among the Indians there the idea that the Communists were the legitimate heirs of the communal society of the Incas, an unorthodox but effective message, of which some other Communist Party leaders did not approve.[96]

Whereas in most of the country the Prado government largely ignored the "extremist" unions, which were unable to mount actions that were a danger to the stability of the regime, Cuzco was the exception. There, the government struck a deal with the leaders of the Communist-controlled Cuzco Regional Federation of Workers, a deal that lasted the better part of three years.

The occasion for this deal was a sympathy strike called by the Cuzco Federation in April 1958. Payne has described what happened:

The Federation willingly supported the April 1958 extremist effort and succeeded not only in paralyzing the city, but in controlling it as well. The FTC called upon students from the local university ... and numbers of totally ignorant Indians. The mobs overturned trucks, smashed car and store windows, and even captured the general of the army division stationed in the city. The armed forces held back, realizing that an attempt to establish order might, in view of the state of agitation, result in a massacre of enormous proportions.

As a result, the Prado government made a bargain with the local Communist labor leaders. It appointed a mayor of Cuzco who was sympathetic to the Communists, if not an actual party member, and he in turn gave the FTC "freedom to carry on its activities." For their part, the FTC leaders agreed to eschew violence. This agreement persisted until late 1961.

At that time, the pro-Communist mayor was removed and was replaced by one who was instructed to "maintain law and order." However, when the FTC called a general strike in protest of Prime Minister Pedro Beltrán's presence in the city, stating that the strike would last until he left Cuzco, the strike largely failed. On the urging of Beltrán, who said he would not leave until the strike was over, merchants kept their stores open, transportation kept moving, and Aprista-led workers, whose numbers had increased considerably, reported to work. The police successfully confronted university students who tried to close down the city. As a consequence of all of this, the FTC announced that the strike was not of unlimited duration, but was to last only one day.

About two weeks after this incident, the Apristas succeeded in organizing a rival to the Federación de Trabajadores de Cuzco: the Unión Sindical de Trabajadores de Cuzco. Although this rival organization was relatively weak, it did gain some strength during the last year of the Prado regime.[97]

Another center of strength for the Communists and other far-leftists during the Prado years was the Lima Union of Construction Workers. It owned the largest trade union headquarters in the capital, built with funds provided by the Odría government from money accumulated for "indemnity" for workers laid off from their jobs, but not collected by temporary workers who came in from the countryside for short-term employment in construction. The Union of Construction Workers rented rooms in its building as headquarters for other unions for meetings of various kinds.[98]

The importance of this union to the far left in the labor movement declined during the second Prado period. On the one hand, according to James Payne, the leaders of the organization did not spend the time and effort required to maintain organization among a group of laborers whose workplaces shifted frequently. In addition, there was a decline in the construction industry during the period in question.[99]

The "extremists" had several other regional labor groups in addition to the one in Cuzco, including groups in Huancayo, Puno, Ica, Arequipa, and Callao. However, Payne said that these were "so weak that is difficult to ascertain their existence."[100]

The Aprista-controlled unions in the construction field formed their own Federación de Trabajadores de la Construcción Civil del Perú, which claimed to have a majority of workers in this category in its ranks. It was affiliated with the CTP. Although the Communist-controlled federation succeeded in holding on to the headquarters given to it by the Odría administration, the CTP-affiliated federation established its own headquarters.[101]

THE LIMA TRANSPORT WORKERS FEDERATION

The Lima union group with the longest history of Communist control was that of the transport workers. It had been the base of Juan P. Luna, onetime head of the CTP, and Luna had continued to have influence among those workers after officially quitting the Communist Party. During the Odría period, he had been Odría's staunchest ally in the labor movement.

The Odría government had given the Lima chauffeurs' union a headquarters that occupied a whole city block. There they established a restaurant and a cooperative. The Federation of Chauffeurs also imported cars, which it sold to its members, and maintained a legal service to help taxi men and others who got in trouble with the police.[102]

The Federation of Chauffeurs consisted of seven unions in Lima—taxi men, bus drivers, intercity truckers, and so on—as well as affiliates in some of the provincial cities. Although the federation participated in the preliminary negotiations leading to the reestablishment of the CTP at the end of the Odría administration, they did not join the reorganized Confederación de Trabajadores del Perú.[103]

Left-wing control of the chauffeurs was seriously undermined during the second Prado administration. The Apristas first gained control of the Bus Drivers' Union and subsequently of the Taxi Drivers' Union, which had been the original base of Juan P. Luna.[104]

When the Prado government decreed an increase in the price of gasoline, with part of the increase going to a road-building program and part to the International Petroleum Company, the chauffeurs protested. The Taxi Drivers' Union (Sindicato de Servicios Públicos) agreed to support that part of the price increase to be used for road-building, but opposed paying anything more to the petroleum company, and the government accepted this modification of the price increase. When the group associated with Juan P. Luna tried to launch a nationwide general strike on the gas price–increase issue, it failed, receiving virtually no support in Lima and lasting in a few provincial cities for only a day or two.

Finally, in December 1958, the Sindicato de Servicios Públicos called a congress to reorganize the Federación de Trabajadores Chóferes, the chauffeurs' national federation. However, the elements associated with Juan P. Luna called their own congress at the same time. As a result, thereafter there were two chauffeurs' federations.[105]

STRIKES AND OTHER ACTIVITIES DURING THE SECOND PRADO PERIOD

Strikes were rather frequent during the 1956–1963 period. The number of strikes increased each year. There were 161 in 1957, 213 in 1958, 233 in 1959, 285 in 1960, and 339 in 1961.[106]

However, most strikes were of short duration. Fully 46 percent of them were over in a day, another 25 percent did not last longer then 3 days, 18 percent were of 4 to 10 days' duration, and only 11 percent lasted 11 days or more.[107]

This was in sharp contrast to the United States in the same period, where over 37 percent of all strikes lasted two weeks or more.

The causes of strikes in Peru were also markedly different from those in the United States. Only 16 percent of the Peruvian strikes of 1960 were over wage issues, compared with almost half of the walkouts in the United States in the same year. The largest single issue in Peru was "failure to comply with norms and contracts," whereas 22 percent of strikes were listed as being due to "poor worker–management relations." Strikingly, 16 percent of all Peruvian strikes in 1960 were sympathy walkouts with other union groups, in contrast to only 1 percent being provoked by that cause in the United States.[108]

The motivations for and nature of strikes involving unions under "extremist" leadership and Aprista leadership were clearly different in this period. The former were eager to use any excuse to embarrass and even, if possible, bring down the Prado government. The Aprista trade union leaders, in contrast, were anxious to be sure that walkouts they led did not put the Prado regime in peril. Thus, the Federation of Hospital Workers called off a strike of their members on April 9, 1958, when far-left unions were seeking to launch a sympathetic general strike.

James Payne said of the Aprista trade union leaders' use of the strike,

> Although they refrained from overt attacks upon the government in such moments of crisis, the Apristas certainly did not relinquish the use of the strike and its related tactics. The Federation of Textile Workers, the National Union of Bank Clerks before 1958, the Federation of Metallurgical Workers, and many other organizations where APRA had a controlling position, all engaged in strikes—but always for limited worker objectives. In fact, in the period 1956–1961, APRA labor leaders were strict trade unionists, and largely for this reason they were successful.[109]

The Ministry of Labor not infrequently intervened in cases involving CTP-affiliated unions to avoid strikes by forcing concessions on the employers. Sometimes, when the Ministry of Labor was unable to bring about compliance with such decisions, the Ministry of Interior, in charge of the police, stepped in. Thus, in the case of a strike on the buses of Lima, where the government ordered wage increases, but refused to grant concurrent fare rises, and the employers refused to make any wage concession, the Ministry of Interior stepped in to collect and count all fares, while the government temporarily paid for the wage rises out of its own funds.

In another instance, the Santa Maria textile company dismissed 13 workers, including 8 officers of the union, and the Ministry of Labor ordered the reemployment of the workers involved. When the employer refused, the Federation of Textile Workers declared a solidarity strike. The Ministry of Interior then ordered the employer to obey the Labor Ministry's order and provided police escorts to the dismissed workers as they went back to their jobs.[110]

In the case of the textile industry, the Ministry of Labor sponsored formation of a bipartisan Permanent Board of the Textile Industry, the objective of which was to head off disputes before they reached the strike stage. The organization of textile employers and the Federation of Textile Workers named the members of this body. Payne noted, "Even before the board was created, the textile industry had been subject to a number of special regulations which together form the *regimen textil*. The board has become the official decision-making center for expansion and modification of these regulations."[111]

In some cases, there was a modification of union representation in dealing with the employers. This was the case in the petroleum industry, where there were two different unions, one controlled by the Apristas and one by the Socialist Party. In the 1945–1948 period, the Aprista union was the bargaining agent with the International Petroleum Company (IPC), but during the Odría administration it was the Socialist union that negotiated with the company. With the advent of the second Prado administration, the two unions negotiated jointly with the IPC. Although there were negotiations to merge the two workers' organizations, these were not successful.[112]

The existence of industry-wide employers and workers' organizations was sometimes helpful in disciplining particularly recalcitrant employers. James Payne noted, "The ownership organization is especially likely to support the workers if the one firm where the problem has arisen has precipitated the conflict by violating accepted norms which the other producers respect."[113]

In the case of the hotel workers of Lima, there was a two-week strike of employees of the Savoy Hotel over dismissal of a union officer. At the end of that time, the federation declared a general hotel strike in the capital, and the union leader was restored to his job after two days. James Payne noted that the influence of the organization of hotel owners "was instrumental in the speedy solution to the strike." In another instance, when the Federation of Metallurgical Workers struck over dismissal of four workers who were trying to form a union in their plant, the issue was settled when other firms agreed to employ the workers involved.[114]

END OF THE SECOND PRADO REGIME

As the second administration of President Manuel Prado was drawing to an end, there were new elections in 1962. Fernando Belaúnde Terry and ex-president Manuel Odría early proclaimed their candidacies.

The Apristas moved more slowly. There was apparently some interest in the party in supporting a non-Aprista as their candidate. One possibility would have been the newspaper publisher and businessman Pedro Beltrán, who, although much more conservative than the Apristas, had served some time as prime minister under Prado and had gotten along reasonably well with the Apristas in that capacity.[115]

However, the Apristas finally named Víctor Raúl Haya de la Torre as their nominee. He was, perhaps, the Aprista candidate against whom the forces of the political right, including specific elements of the armed forces, were most strongly opposed. However, as founder and ideologue of the party, he was the candidate upon whom all elements of Aprismo could agree.

Elsewhere, I have written,

When the election of 1962 finally approached, the Apristas nominated Haya de la Torre for president. This was a risky decision on the party's part. The old Army-Aprista enmity continued and, by this time, had come to concentrate largely on the personality of Haya de la Torre. There was doubt in the minds of many Apristas whether if Haya won, he would be allowed to take office. However, the rank and file of the party was exceedingly anxious that the wrong done to Haya thirty-one years before be rectified in 1962, and that their leader become the constitutional president of Peru.

I continued, "If Haya had won by a very strong majority, he perhaps might have been able to take office. The United States Government, through President John Kennedy and Ambassador James Loeb, made it clear that they felt strongly that the military should recognize the election of whoever was victorious in the poll."[116]

However, Haya did not win a strong victory. In fact, although he got the most votes of any of the candidates, he did not receive the required 33 1/3 percent of the total vote, coming in only slightly ahead of Belaúnde and Odría. As a consequence, there were extended negotiations in Congress, which had to make the final decision. The Apristas reportedly controlled 114 members of Congress, but needed 120 in order to elect Haya, with the Belaundistas having 76, the Odriistas having about 50, and independents making up 8 of the members.[117]

While negotiations were in progress, Fernando Belaúnde insisted that the elections had been fraudulent. Also, some leaders of the armed forces, who were absolutely opposed to the election of Haya de la Torre, demanded that the election results be canceled and new elections be held.[118]

An agreement was finally reached between the Aprista congressmen and those of Odría, to support Odría's election. Within 24 hours of that decision, the armed forces carried out yet another coup, installing a military junta.

Some leading figures in the Aprista Party, in retrospect, felt that that coup was a godsend for the Aprista Party. Had the Aprista congressmen gone through with their agreement to vote for Odría, that action, they felt, would have seriously split the party, the opposition to Odría within the Aprista ranks being so strong.[119]

However, the Aprista-controlled Confederación de Trabajadores del Perú called a general strike in protest against the coup d'état. An agreement had been reached a month before the election to take such action if any move was made to interfere with the election or its results.[120]

The strike failed. James Payne commented, "The military junta had a considerable amount of support including extremists and Acción Popular, and rank and file sentiment for the strike was not sufficiently aroused."[121]

About a year after this coup, new elections were held. The same three men—Víctor Raúl de la Torre, Fernando Belaúnde, and Manuel Odría—were the principal nominees. However, this time, Belaúnde won a clear victory, although his supporters won only a minority in Congress. During the almost six years of Belaúnde's administration, the legislature was controlled by an alliance of the Apristas and Odriistas.

These events were destined to bring about substantial changes within Peruvian organized labor.

LABOR UNDER THE 1962–1963 MILITARY REGIME

The impact of the thwarted 1962 election and situation began to be felt during the 1962–1963 military regime. Although there were no major changes in the labor movement as a whole during that period, some individual unions did feel the impact of the coup.

One U.S. Labor Department source wrote shortly before the end of the period about the military regime's general impact on the labor movement. This individual reported, "Although the Communists secured some minor benefits from Junta support in the initial days, no major effort has yet been made by the Junta to intervene in CTP affairs or administration."[122]

However, some particular unions had problems during the military regime. For example, in the case of the government-owned Santa Steel plant, where relations between the union and the management had been quite amicable preceding the coup, the military junta named a new administration of the enterprise, which refused to negotiate directly with the union, the result being that most issues that arose had to be dealt with in the Ministry of Labor.[123]

At least one serious labor dispute erupted during this period, at the Cerro de Pasco mining enterprise, in December 1962. The union demanded a 20 percent wage increase, but the company offered only 8 percent. When negotiations broke down, the union called a strike.

An organ of the International Metalworkers' Federation described what happened next: "The authorities branded the strike illegal. On December 17, the police fired on the strikers, killing two and seriously wounding several others. Violence broke out, instigated naturally by totalitarian elements, and the company warehouses were burned and sacked."

Subsequently, the police charged three representatives of the International Metalworkers' Federation with "being agents of international Communism, responsible for acts of sabotage which occurred in the installations of the Cerro de Pasco Corporation ... and charged they were instigators of present plans of Communist agitation in various parts of Peru.[124]

Understandably, the international group protested strongly to the Peruvian government, not only about the attacks on its representatives, but also about the way authorities had handled the Cerro de Pasco strike. Among the other international labor groups that also protested the handling of this strike was the Catholic-oriented regional labor organization, the Confederación Latinoamericana de Sindicalistas Cristianos (CLASC), which accused the Peruvian regime of violating the fundamental right to strike, guaranteed not only by agreements of the International Labor Organization but also by the Universal Declaration of the Rights of Man of the United Nations, to both of which Peru was officially committed.[125]

One other labor event of considerable future importance in this period was the establishment in Peru of the Centro de Estudios Laborales del Perú (Peruvian Center of Labor Studies—CELP), an organization for training labor leaders, which launched its first course for 29 students on March 25, 1963. The CELP was set up as a result of an agreement among the U.S. government's Agency for International Development, the Peruvian Ministry of Labor, the Confederación de Trabajadores del Perú, and the American Institute for Free Labor Development (AIFLD), run by the American Federation of Labor-Congress of Industrial Organizations. The CELP was financed and administered by the AIFLD.[126]

FIRST ADMINISTRATION OF FERNANDO BELAÚNDE TERRY

Fernando Belaúnde served as constitutional president from mid-1963, when he assumed office, until his overthrow by the armed forces in October 1968. During those years, his party, Acción Popular (AP), had a minority in Congress, which was dominated by a coalition of the Apristas and the party of ex-dictator Manuel Odría, the UNO.

Belaúnde's government can be best described as reformist. It gave legal recognition to several hundred indigenous Indian communities,[127] sponsored passage of a modest agrarian reform law, which exempted the commercial plantations of the Pacific coastal area, gave Indian tenants proprietorship of the small plots of land their landlords had traditionally allowed them to have to grow their own food, and had somewhat vague— and largely not applied—provisions for a more widespread expropriation of large landholdings in the mountainous part of the country. Among the properties expropriated were a large agricultural holding of the Cerro de Pasco mining company and properties in the La Convención Valley in the Cuzco area, where Trotskyists had led a peasant insurrection.[128]

Belaúnde also pushed expansion of the educational system, as well as his favorite project: beginning to construct a road from north to south on the eastern side of the Andes. He likewise established Cooperación Popu-lar, a program to organize local citizenry to undertake and agitate for proj-ects to improve their villages or urban communities—the program most strongly opposed by the Apristas, who saw it as a tool for establishing a system of local patronage to benefit Acción Popular.[129]

Belaúnde was faced in 1965with the phenomenon of rural insurrection, which was to presage a much more serious uprising when he returned to power in 1980. Although this insurrection was put down with relative ease, probably its most important impact was on the military, who for the first time were forced to raise the question of why largely Indian peasants were willing to revolt against a supposedly democratically elected and reformist regime.

Bu the latter part of the Belaúnde administration, the administration was facing serious economic difficulties, the solution to which required some unpopular measures. The Apristas were not anxious to take the responsibility for having Congress authorize those policies. However, apparently faced with fear of a military coup that would cancel the 1969 election, which they hoped to win, they finally agreed to have Congress give a new cabinet special powers for 60 days to legislate on the financial crisis. Belaúnde thereafter issued about 20 decrees, including increases in income taxes, a new property tax on both urban and rural property, and a gas-tax increase, particularly unpopular because it raised the retail price of gas.[130]

Insofar as the labor movement was concerned, undoubtedly the most significant development during President Belaúnde's first administration was the beginning of the decline of the influence of the Aprista Party in organized labor. At least in part, this was due to the alienation of many workers by the partnership between APRA and the party of ex-dictator Manuel Odría during most of the Belaúnde administration.[131] The two parties not only worked together in Congress, but also ran joint tickets in municipal elections on two occasions, in spite of the strong opposition within the Aprista Party to that coalition and the passive resistance to it by some of the important leaders of the Partido Aprista.[132]

By the end of the Belaúnde period, the Communists had succeeded for the first time in organizing a rival to the CTP.

THE CTP IN THE FIRST BELAÚNDE ADMINISTRATION

The Aprista-controlled Confederación de Trabajadores del Perú continued throughout the 1963–1968 period to be the country's largest central labor organization. It held two national congresses in those years, in 1964 and 1967.

The process of establishing new national industrial federations was continued during the 1960s. By 1967, the CTP had 73 industrial and regional federations in its ranks. Between the 1964 and 1967 congresses, 15 new industrial federations and nationwide unions had joined the CTP. These included two maritime organizations, which had rejoined the organizations, as well as the national unions of primary and secondary school teachers and two federations of fishermen. "Many other unions that lack Federation" had also joined the CTP.[133]

One union federation that was significant during the 1963–1968 period and that was to play a major role in the labor movement in the following decade was that of the miners. The various mine workers' unions had been joined into regional federations in the North, the South, and the nation's center. But in the early 1960s, these were loosely joined to form the Federación Nacional de Trabajadores Mineros, Metalúrgicos y Similares. For some time, this organization was under Communist control, but the Apristas regained leadership in 1966, and the federation remained affiliated with the CTP until after the military coup of October 1968.[134]

After Arturo Sabroso finally retired as head of the confederación, he was succeeded by Julio Cruzado, who, like Sabroso, was a leader of the Textile Workers Federation and Aprista.

Under Cruzado, the organizational structure of the confederación was strengthened. It developed a register of all of its affiliates, both federations and individual unions, which it had never had in the past. It also established much closer contact than in the past with its local groups. For the first time, its periodical, *CETEPE*, appeared fairly regularly, and the CTP established a regular television program, which appeared 40 times during 1966. It also had regular radio broadcasts of news and opinion.

The CTP carried out an extensive leadership-training program, not only through the Centro de Estudios Laborales del Perú, which had been established in collaboration with the American Institute for Free Labor Development near the end of the 1962–1963 military regime, but also through its own Institute of Trade Union Education and Research, organized in conjunction with ORIT. A substantial number of higher-ranking Peruvian trade unionists were also sent abroad for training in institutions maintained by the ORIT, the International Trade Secretariats, and the International Confederation of Free Trade Unions.

The CTP also maintained an active Secretariat of Economic Affairs, which established an Institute of Economic and Social Studies to study the country's economic and social problems. It likewise organized a number of seminars, lectures, and other public meetings on these issues.

The CTP maintained a Juridical Office, which provided legal advice not only to leaders of affiliated unions, but also to individual workers. Also, unlike the situation in earlier years, the CTP carried on extensive lobbying with the administration and Congress and succeeded in obtaining passage of a substantial number of new laws and administrative decrees favorable to the workers.

Finances continued to be a major problem for the CTP. Regular dues payment by its affiliates tended as before to be inadequate for the needs of the confederación. These were supplemented by special donations from the financially stronger affiliates and by sale of "Bonds of Trade Union Cooperation" to union members and others.[135]

Unions affiliated with the CTP carried out strikes from time to time during the first Belaúnde period. Inflation continued to be a serious problem, and union leaders were under considerable pressure to gain wage increases sufficient to offset the rise in prices.

Until October 1967, none of the walkouts constituted a danger to the elected government. However, in that month, a series of walkouts occurred in the southern cities, in which CTP and Aprista influence was least, against the high cost of living. Even after the government offered wage increases varying from 10 percent to 20 percent, depending on the wage category of the particular worker, strikes in Cuzco, Arequipa, Juliaca, and Puno became virtually universal. A number of CTP-affiliated unions participated in these walkouts.

In the face of this situation, Julio Cruzado, secretary-general of the CTP, called on the workers to accept the increases offered by the government. He added, "We have contributed patriotically to a decorous solution, which saves the country from the danger of economic, political and social chaos," and urged the workers not to follow themselves to be misled by "demagogic promises."[136]

LEFT-WING UNIONS DURING THE FIRST BELAÚNDE PERIOD

By no means did all of the labor movement belong to the Confederación de Trabajadores del Perú during the 1963–1968 period. The original Federation of Chauffeurs of Peru—from which the Aprista-controlled chauffeurs' unions had split by 1958 to form a rival federation that affiliated with the CTP—continued outside of the confederación. It also continued to be controlled by Juan P. Luna, who maintained a close personal relationship with General Odría, although claiming not to belong to his political party.

The Communists split into two rival parties during the early 1960s, with the traditional party remaining loyal to Moscow and a dissident one using the same name but supporting Mao Tse-tung and the Chinese. According to Juan P. Luna, although the pro-Moscow party controlled most of the Communist-influenced unions, the pro-Peking group had some support among the metal and construction workers.[137]

The pro-Moscow Communists remained the principal far-left group active in organized labor. Although their fortunes within the labor movement oscillated in various periods and in various segments of the movement, they made overall gains and were able for the first time in a decade and a half to establish a central labor under their control.

One field in which the Communists were particularly active was that of the miners. Under the overall Federación Nacional Minera, there were regional federations in the North, the South, and the country's center. The Apristas maintained firm control of the northern federation, but the Communists and their allies captured the central federation, although the Apristas recaptured that group in 1966. The Communists won and maintained control of the Southern Mining Federation.[138]

Throughout the period, the pro-Moscow Communist Party worked to establish a viable rival to the Confederación de Trabajadores del Perú. As early as 1961, they had set up the Comité Reorganizador de la CTP (Reorganizing Committee of the CTP). It lasted through 1964.[139] During the early years of the Belaúnde regime, the government was seen by the Apristas as being favorably disposed toward this committee, given that Belaúnde's Acción Popular had little following of its own in organized labor and was anxious to break the hold of the Apristas on the labor movement.[140]

However, with the outbreak of rural guerilla fighting, led by elements to the left of the pro-Moscow Communist Party, the Belaúnde government turned strongly against all of the far-left parties. One casualty of this change of policy was the Comité Reorganizador de la CTP.

It was not until 1966 that the pro-Soviet Communists were able to renew their effort to establish a rival to the CTP. They organized the Comité de Defensa y Unificación de la Clase Trabajadora (Committee of Defense and Unification of the Working Class) to try to bring together that part of the labor movement outside of the Confederación de Trabajadores del Perú. According to Gustavo Espinoza, one of the principal leaders of that group, the committee had 10 federations and 52 unions affiliated with it, with a membership of some 70,000 workers.[141]

Finally, in June 1968 the committee organized the First Congress of the Confederación General de Trabajadores del Perú (CGTP). It claimed that 19 federations and 76 unions, with about 110,000 members, were represented at that founding meeting of the CGTP. However, Aprista union leaders claimed that the CGTP in 1968 had only scattered unions among construction workers, chauffeurs, and fishermen.[142] Even one of the principal founders of the CGTP conceded several years later that the CGTP had had only "a few unions" at its inception.[143]

The CGTP elected Gustavo Espinoza, a member of the Political Bureau of the pro-Soviet Communist Party, as its secretary-general. The pro-Soviet union leaders had invited Juan P. Luna's Chauffeurs' Federation to participate in founding the CGTP and had offered him the secretary generalship of the organization. But he refused to have his federation participate, apparently feeling that the new central labor group would be stillborn, and it did not then become part of the CGTP.[144]

By 1968, the Aprista Party and the pro-Moscow Communists continued to be the parties with the most influence in organized labor. Fernando Belaúnde's Acción Popular and the Christian Democrats both had sought to develop some following in the labor movement, but neither of them had had any appreciable success.[145]

ECONOMIC CHANGES IN PERU FROM 1948 TO 1968

The evolution of the labor movement, which we have been sketching, took place against the background of major changes in the Peruvian economy. Denis Sulmont noted,

The process of capitalist expansion and diversification [that] started during the period of Odría continued in the following years, with the growing importance of the multinational corporations. The Law of Industrial Promotion of 1959 stimulated the installation of a series of assembly plants, especially in the automobile, domestic electric artifacts, and pharmaceuticals industries. The metal-mechanic and chemical industries grew. There occurred the "boom" of fishing for the production of fishmeal, stimulating the industrial development of the coastal ports. Steel production and some industrial parks developed in the provinces. Parallel with this, civil construction activities, transport, finances and urban services expanded. Thus there developed around the urban industrial centers and on a national level a web of inter-related activities requiring a larger number of wage workers.[146]

The number of industrial workers grew to 200,000 by the late 1960s. Employment also grew in the decades following 1948, by 20,000 in fishing and by 150,000 in construction, while the number of bank employees expanded by 30,000, and there were 100,000 more teachers. Commercial employment increased even more rapidly than strictly productive activities. Commerce had 400,000 more employees, and there were 260,000 more government workers.

As a result of these economic developments, new trade union groups came into existence. Among these were the Federación de Trabajadores Metalúrgicos del Perú, the Federación de Trabajadores de las Industrias Quimicas y Afines (chemical workers), and the Federación de Trabajadores en Laboratorios, Droguerías y Afines (pharmaceutical and drugstore employees). Others were the Federación Nacional de Educadores del Perú, set up by the teachers in 1959, and the Federación Nacional de Trabajadores Mineros, Metalúrgicos y Similares, the national miners' union, which was also established in 1959.[147]

There was also expansion of organizations of peasants. New groups included the Confederación Campesina del Perú, set up under Communist leadership in 1956; the Federación Nacional de Campesinos del Perú, organized under Aprista leadership in 1960; and the Frente Sindical Campesino, founded under Christian Democratic sponsorship, also in 1960.[148]

However, in the last two years of the first Belaúnde administration, the country suffered a substantial economic crisis. Inflation reached the level of 50 percent a year, the Peruvian currency was devalued, and Belaúnde cut government expenditures. This situation provoked a political crisis in 1967, as already noted.

CONCLUSION

There were no fundamental changes in the Peruvian labor movement during the first administration of President Fernando Belaúnde Terry from 1963 to 1968. The Confederación de Trabajadores del Perú continued to have within it the considerable majority of the country's unions, and the CTP continued to be controlled by the Partido Aprista Peruano. Under the leadership of a new secretary-general, Julio Cruzado, the CTP developed a more efficient organization and a closer relationship with its rank-and-file unions. It also expanded its leadership-training activities, as well as its participation in a wide variety of governmental and semi-governmental bodies dealing with the country's economic and social problems.

Relations between the leadership of the CTP and the Belaúnde government changed during the Belaúnde administration. At first, the president encouraged efforts to undermine Aprista control of the labor movement, including Communist efforts to split the CTP. However, after the guerrilla uprising of 1965, Belaúnde turned against the far left, and relations between the CTP leadership and the administration substantially improved. Collective bargaining was standard during this period, with relatively few crises putting the elected government in jeopardy.

However, there were certain trends within organized labor during this period that were to be very significant in the years that followed. There was considerable disillusionment in the labor rank and file over the Aprista Party's alliance with the party of General Odría, not only in Congress, but also in municipal elections. Also, at the end of the Belaúnde period, the Communists were able for the first time to organize a rival to the CTP, in the form of the Confederación General de Trabajadores del Perú (CGTP). Although the CGTP remained quite weak during the Belaúnde administration, it was in place to take advantage of the situation that followed the overthrow of President Belaúnde by the military in October 1968.

NOTES

1. "Ley de Seguridad Interior de la República," Lima, July 1, 1949.

2. James L. Payne, *Labor and Politics in Peru: The System of Political Bargaining,* Yale University Press, New Haven, 1965, p. 46.

3. Ibid., p. 51.

4. Denis Sulmont, *El Movimiento Obrero Peruano (1890–1980) Reseña Histórico,* Tarea, Lima, 1981, p. 65.

5. "The Interamerican Confederation of Labor Refutes the Junta Militar de Gobierno of Peru," Santiago, Chile, December 28, 1948, signed by Arturo Jáuregui and Isidoro Godoy.

6. "Manifesto de la Confederación de Trabajadores del Perú," Lima, November 20, 1948 (mimeographed).

7. Letter of Víctor Carrión and Manuel España of Workers' Departmental Trade Union Federation of Junín to George Meany, January 20, 1949.

8. Ibid.

9. *Inter-American Labor News,* periodical of Confederación Interamericana de Trabajadores, Washington, DC, February 1950.

10. *New York Times,* January 18, 1949.

11. Interview with Sandy Pringle, second secretary and labor reporting officer, U.S. Embassy, in Lima, August 18, 1952.

12. *Inter-American Labor News,* op. cit., September 1950.

13. "Confederación de Trabajadores del Perú," supplement of *Obrero Textil,* 1st fortnight of May 1951.

14. Interview with Carlos Aramburu, secretario de hacienda, Confederación de Trabajadores del Perú, in Lima, August 29, 1956.

15. "Peruvian Unions Lead Reconstruction Drive," in *AFL-CIO News,* Washington, DC, December 1, 1956.

16. Interview with Arturo Jáuregui, exiled Peruvian labor leader, in Montevideo, Uruguay, July 29, 1952.

17. Interview with Juan P. Luna, pro-Odría Communist union leader, in Lima, August 19, 1952.

18. Interview with Arturo Sabroso, former and future president of Confederación de Trabajadores del Perú, in Lima, August 18, 1952.

19. Interviews with Tomás del Piélago, ex-Aprista, pro-Peronista leader of Graphic Workers Federation, in Lima, August 18, 1952; Arturo Sabroso, op. cit., July 12, 1953; Sandy Pringle, op. cit., August 18, 1952; and Humberto Cano Sánchez, secretary of hygiene of Federación de Panaderos "Estrella del Perú," in Lima, August 18, 1952.

20. Interview with José Benitez, president of Confederación Gráfica del Perú, in Lima, August 18, 1952.

21. Interview with Arturo Sabroso, op. cit., July 12, 1953.

22. Interview with Francisco Viale, a leader of Socialist-controlled Petroleum Workers Federation, Socialist member of Chamber of Deputies, in Lima, August 18, 1952.

23. Interviews with Sandy Pringle, op. cit., August 18, 1952; and Víctor Zavala V., a leader of Socialist-controlled Petroleum Workers Federation, Socialist member of Chamber of Deputies, in Lima, August 19, 1952.

24. Interview with Luciano Castillo, leader of Partido Socialist del Perú, in Lima, August 18, 1952.

25. Interview with Octavio R. Dulanto, founder and ex-president of Sindicato de Trabajadores del Ferrocarril Central del Perú, in Lima, August 29, 1956.

26. Interview with Luciano Castillo, op. cit., August 18, 1952.

27. Interview with Mary Castillo, member of National Executive of Partido Socialista, wife of Luciano Castillo, in Lima, April 6, 1962.

28. Interview with Luciano Castillo, op. cit., August 18, 1952.

29. Interviews with Serafino Romualdi, assistant secretary of ORIT, in Santiago, Chile, July 30, 1956; and Luciano Castillo, op. cit., August 29, 1956.

30. Interviews with Luciano Castillo, op. cit., August 18, 1952, August 29, 1956.

31. Interview with Alberto Lizarzaburu, a leader of Textile Workers Federation, in Lima, July 31, 1954.

32. Interviews with Juan Andrés Sime Rivadeneira, director of Maritime Workers Hour, head of Dock Watchmen's Union of Callao, in New Brunswick, NJ, March 12, 1954; Héctor Petrovich Aguero, secretary of organization, Lima Light and Power Company *sindicato,* in New Brunswick, NJ, February 24, 1954; and Antonio Alcazar Sarmiento, secretary of defense of Sindicato Ferrocarril Central del Perú, in New Brunswick, NJ, February 24, 1954.

33. Interview with Arturo Sabroso, op. cit., August 18, 1952.

34. *La Prensa,* Lima, August 25, 1952, p. 1.

35.   Interviews with Arturo Sabroso, op. cit., August 30, 1956; John C. Amott, labor reporting officer, U.S. Embassy, in Lima, August 29, 1956; and Serafino Romualdi, op. cit., July 30, 1956.

36.   Confederación de Trabajadores del Perú, "Manifesto a Todos Los Trabajadores de la República y Opinión General del País," Lima, n.d. (but circa May 1956).

37.   *New York Times,* June 17, 1950.

38.   Interviews with Arturo Sabroso, op. cit., July 12, 1953.

39.   Interviews with Carl Brauer, first secretary, U.S. Embassy, in Lima, July 13, 1953; and Arturo Sabroso, op. cit., July 12, 1953.

40.   Interview with Luciano Castillo, op. cit., July 13, 1953.

41.   *El Siglo,* newspaper of Communist Party of Chile, Santiago, March 20, 1953.

42.   Interview with Ricardo Martínez de la Torre, historian of early Peruvian labor movement, in Lima, July 13, 1953.

43.   Interview with Eugene Gilmore, economic counselor of U.S. Embassy, in Lima, August 2, 1954.

44.   Interviews with Arturo Sabroso, op. cit., July 12, 1953; and Alberto Lizarzaburu, op. cit., March 3, 1954.

45.   *Boletín Latino Americano del CIO,* Washington, DC, September–October 1953.

46.   *Noticiario Obrero Norteamericano,* publication of American Federation of Labor, Washington, DC, March 1, 1954.

47.   Interview with Eugene Gilmore, op. cit., August 2, 1954; see also *ORIT Notes 1954: "Huelga General de Bancarios."*

48.   *ORIT Notes December 1955: "Huelga de Empleados."*

49.   Interview with Alberto Lizarzaburu, op. cit., September 3, 1956.

50.   Interview with Arturo Sabroso, op. cit., August 30, 1956.

51.   Harry Kantor, *Patterns of Politics and Political Systems in Latin America,* Rand McNally & Company, Chicago, 1969, p. 476.

52.   Payne, op. cit., p. 55.

53.   Ibid., p. 134.

54.   Ibid., p. 35.

55.   Ibid., p. 131.

56.   Ibid., pp. 129–131.

57.   Ibid., pp. 181–182.

58.   Ibid., p. 184.

59.   Ibid., p. 184.

60.   Ibid., p. 186.

61.   Ibid., pp. 233–237.

62.   Ibid., pp. 235–240.

63.   Ibid., p. 238.

64.   Ibid., p. 225.

65.   *Presente,* Lima, June 22, 1957, p. 25.

66.   Interview with Leopoldo Pita, secretary, secretary-general, Federación de Trabajadores Azucareros del Perú, in Lima, July 6, 1957; see also *Presente,* op. cit., June 22, 1957, p. 25.

67.   Payne, op. cit., p. 225.

68. Ibid., p. 230.
69. Gonzalo Añi Castillo, *Historia Secreta de las Guerrillas*, Ediciones "Mas Alla," Lima, 1967, p. 59.
70. Payne, op. cit., pp. 231–232.
71. *La Tribuna*, Lima, July 6, 1957.
72. Payne, op. cit., p. 167.
73. Ibid., p. 170.
74. Ibid., pp. 167–168.
75. Ibid., p. 169.
76. Ibid., pp. 169–170.
77. Ibid., p. 170.
78. Ibid., p. 73.
79. Ibid., p. 171.
80. Ibid., p. 173.
81. Ibid., pp. 174–175.
82. Interview with Arturo Jáuregui, op. cit., in Mexico, D.F., August 16, 1963.
83. Payne, op. cit., pp. 174–175.
84. *La Tribuna*, Lima, July 5, 1957.
85. Payne, op. cit., pp. 192–199.
86. Ibid., pp. 199–200.
87. Ibid., pp. 200–205.
88. Ibid., p. 94.
89. Ibid., pp. 95–96.
90. Ibid., pp. 96–97.
91. Ibid., p. 100.
92. Ibid., pp. 100–101.
93. Ibid., p. 70.
94. Ibid., p. 170.
95. Ibid., pp. 106–108.
96. Interviews with Abelardo Salazar, a leader of Communist Party in Cuzco, in Cuzco, June 12, 1947; and Juan P. Luna, op. cit., September 3, 1956.
97. Payne, op. cit., pp. 110–112.
98. *Vanguardia*, Lima, May 7, 1957, p. 24.
99. Payne, op. cit., pp. 112–114.
100. Ibid., p. 158.
101. Interview with Celestino Bastidas C., member of Executive of Aprista-controlled Federción de Trabajadores de la Construcción Civil del Perú, in Rios Piedras, Puerto Rico, July 29, 1959.
102. Interview with Augusto López, secretary of economy of Federación de Chóferes del Perú, in Lima, September 1, 1956.
103. Interview with Pedro Parra, secretary-general of Federación de Chóferes del Perú, in Lima, September 3, 1956.
104. Interview with Fortunato Jara, member of Buro Sindical of Aprista Party, in Lima, September 3, 1956.
105. Interview with Medaro Gomero Gomero, member of Executive of Sindicato de Chóferes de Servicio Público de Lima, in Rio Piedras, Puerto Rico, July 29, 1959.
106. Payne, op. cit., p. 265.
107. Ibid., p. 266.

108. Ibid., pp. 264–265.

109. Ibid., p. 122.

110. Ibid., pp. 65–66.

111. Ibid., pp. 73–74.

112. Interviews with Leobardo Zavala Núñez, official of Sindicato Unido de Obreros y Empleados de la International Petroleum Company of Callao, in Rio Piedras, Puerto Rico, June 5, 1958; and Juan Tabada, secretary-general of Sindicato Petrolero de Talara #1, in Washington, DC, November 26, 1967.

113. Payne, op. cit., p. 63.

114. Ibid., p. 63.

115. Interview with James Payne, scholar of Peruvian labor movement, in New Brunswick, NJ, January 20, 1962.

116. Robert J. Alexander, *Aprismo: The Ideas and Doctrines of Víctor Raúl Haya de la Torre,* the Kent State University Press, Kent, OH, 1973, p. 16.

117. Interview with Armando Arévalo Silva, northern secretary of Confederación de Trabajadores del Perú, in Rio Piedras, Puerto Rico, July 9, 1962.

118. Payne, op. cit., p. 52.

119. Interview with Luis Alberto Sánchez, one of the principal leaders of Partido Aprista, in Salvador, Brazil, August 9, 1962.

120. Interview with Armando Arévalo Silva, op. cit., July 9, 1962.

121. Payne, op. cit., p. 53.

122. United States Department of Labor, "Peru: Guide to Program Officers, Tam Managers and Lecturers," n.d. (circa 1963), p. 4 (mimeographed).

123. Interview with Rogelio Cotillo, member of Executive of Santa Corporation Workers Union of Peru, in Annapolis, MD, September 28, 1963.

124. *Metal,* periodical of International Metalworkers Federation, September–October 1963, pp. 1–2.

125. Confederación Latinoamericana de Sindicalistas Cristianos, "Manifesto de la CLASC en Torno al Problema Laboral del Perú," Santiago, Chile, December 22, 1962.

126. United States Department of Labor, "Peru," op. cit., p. 11.

127. Interview with James Green, official of United States Agency for International Development in Peru, in Lima, June 30, 1966.

128. Interviews with David Brown, adviser to the Ministry of Agriculture, economist from Iowa State University, in Lima, July 1, 1966; and Gerald de Santillana, political officer of U.S. Embassy, in Lima, June 30, 1966.

129. Interviews with James Green, op. cit., June 30, 1966; and Carlos Manuel Cox, Aprista member of the Senate, in Lima, June 29, 1966.

130. Interview with David Greene, economist of United States Agency for International Development Peru, Lima, July 24, 1968.

131. Interview with Mike Vela, former representative in Peru of Clerical Office Workers Trade Secretariat, in New York City, January 25, 1965.

132. Interview with Virginia Yzaguirre, member of National Executive of Partido Aprista Peruano, in New York City, May 11, 1964.

133. Confederación de Trabajadores del Perú, *Memoria 1964–1967: Un esfuerzo permanente por la dignificación del Trabajador,* Lima, 1967, p. 5.

134. William Bollinger in Gerald Michael Greenfield and Sheldon L. Maram (editors), *Latin American Labor Organizations,* Greenwood Press, Westport, CT, 1987, p. 654.

135. Foregoing from Confederación de Trabajadores del Perú, *Memoria 1964–1967 etc.*, op. cit., pp. 10–16.

136. *La Prensa,* Buenos Aires, October 27, 1967.

137. Interview with Juan P. Luna, op. cit., July 25, 1968.

138. Interview with Pompeyo Mendoza Benavides, delegate of Unión Sindical de Pasco to Confederación de Trabajadores del Perú, in Lima, July 24, 1968.

139. Interview with Gustavo Espinoza, secretary-general, Confederación General de Trabajadores del Perú, in Lima, July 12, 1972.

140. Interviews with José Sandoval Morales, adviser to Confederación de Trabajadores del Perú, former head of Textile Workers Federation, in Lima, June 29, 1966; Alberto Pérez, secretary of Grievance Committee, Sindicato Municipal de Transportes, in New Brunswick, NJ, September 13, 1963; and Lucio D'Angles, secretary of organization of Federation of Private Employees in La Libertad, Peru, in Annapolis, MD, September 28, 1963.

141. Interview with Gustavo Espinoza, op. cit., July 12, 1972.

142. Interview with José Sandoval Morales, op. cit., July 25, 1968.

143. Interview with Isidoro Gamarra Ramírez, president of Confederación General de Trabajadores del Perú, in Lima, July 17, 1975.

144. Ibid; see also Sulmont, op. cit., p. 95.

145. Sulmont, op. cit., p. 88

146. Ibid., pp. 72–73.

147. Ibid., pp. 73–76.

148. Ibid., p. 79.

CHAPTER 3

Unionism under the Reformist Military Regime of General Velasco

On October 3, 1968, President Fernando Belaúnde Terry was overthrown by a military coup that made General Juan Velasco Alvarado the chief executive. There were undoubtedly both short-range and long-term reasons for the establishment of still another government of the armed forces, which proved to be the longest such Peruvian regime in the twentieth century.

For one thing, the Peruvian military was faced with two situations that it found unacceptable. One was a growing corruption scandal, particularly involving Navy people associated with administration of the country's ports, a scandal that was being investigated by Congress. The other was the increasingly likely prospect that the Aprista Party would win the elections scheduled for May 1969, a possibility that still encountered very strong opposition within the armed forces.[1]

However, there was another kind of motivation for the October 1968 coup. The Peruvian military, particularly much of the army leadership, had experienced a major change in its view of its role in Peruvian society. Traditionally, aside from protecting the nation's frontiers, it had seen its task to be maintaining internal stability and the status quo. This meant, in practice, that it was an ally of the dominant rural and commercial oligarchy, which had its roots in the colony and early decades of independence.

At least two factors in post–World War II changed the military's view of itself. One was the establishment of the Center of Higher Military Studies in 1947, where mid-career officers spent a year studying such subjects as economics, sociology, and politics, rather than strictly military matters. A number of their instructors were civilians of advanced ideas.

The second element in the Peruvian military's change of outlook and attitude was undoubtedly the military's experience in the 1960s of having to put down rural guerrilla activities. During the 1962–1963 military government, armed forces had been faced with the Trotskyist-led uprising in the La Convención Valley near Cuzco, which was followed by the government's distribution of most of the large estates in that area to the Indian peasants. Then in 1965, a more widespread revolt led by Castroite elements also required a significant effort on the Army's part to overcome it. The experiences convinced many of the officers that the root of the willingness of peasants to undertake revolt was the vastly unequal distribution of land and the grinding poverty in the countryside and that something should be done about these conditions, which inevitably meant putting an end to the traditional alliance of the armed forces with the rural–commercial oligarchy.[2]

NATURE OF THE NEW MILITARY REGIME

The regime established by General Velasco was markedly different from the military governments of the past. It proclaimed itself revolutionary, nationalistic, and seeking to establish a society which was neither capitalist nor Communist. It brought about one fundamental change that was irreversible—an agrarian reform—and attempted several others, which proved of relatively short duration.

Most long-range was the military government's agrarian reform program. It provided for taking over virtually all large landholdings in the country. Nancy Johnson reprinted a semiofficial statement of the "basic principles" of the 1969 agrarian reform law:

(a) to regulate and limit the right to land ownership in harmony with the social interest; (b) to redistribute the land to small and medium size proprietors who work it themselves; (c) to guarantee communal rights of ownership of the farming communities ... (d) to organize and regulate cooperatives for exploiting the land; (e) to regulate agrarian contracts and to eliminate indirect forms of exploitation in order that the land may belong o those who work it; (f) to regulate rural labor and social security, abolishing any relationship between granting use of the land and the rendering of personal services; and (g) to promote agricultural and livestock development.[3]

The 1969 agrarian reform law was considerably different from the one that had been enacted under President Belaúnde. It provided for rapid takeover of virtually all of the country's private landholdings, including the modern sugar, cotton, and other plantations of the coast, which had been exempted from the earlier law. It also included reorganization on a new basis of the Indian communities, which also had not been included in the agrarian reform of the Belaúnde period.

The Velasco government's agrarian reform program definitively took the rural land away from the large private landowners, many of whose families had held those lands since colonial times. However, the agricultural workers and peasants were by no means happy with the results of the agrarian reform. We note later in the text how this unhappiness influenced the labor movement.

The Velasco government's reform in urban areas involved two different programs. On the one hand, it provided for nationalization of a number of key parts of the economy. On the other, it initiated a new institutional form of ownership and control of much of the urban economy, the so-called industrial community.

The first spectacular move of the Velasco government when it seized power was to nationalize the holdings of the International Petroleum Company (IPC), a subsidiary of what was then the Standard Oil Company of New Jersey. Indeed, the alleged connivance of the Belaúnde government with IPC was used as an excuse for the October 1968 coup.

Subsequently, other important segments of the economy were nationalized by the Velasco government. These included the U.S.-owned Cerro de Pasco Corporation mining and grazing enterprises in Central Peru, and the U.S. Marcona Mining Company, as well as the relatively new anchovy fishing industry, which had become an important source of exports.

The military regime also established a government firm, SIDERPERU, "to control, develop, and market steel, iron and related products, and give control of the state-operated Chimbote steel plant to SIDERPERU." In the case of the auto industry, it was provided that the foreign-owned operations had to be converted into "joint enterprises," with the government as a partner.[4]

Similarly, the Velasco government established ELECTROPERU "to operate and build all future generating plants and to regulate both private and public electric power utilities." It seemed likely to "ultimately be the sole supplier for the country."[5]

The Velasco government also adopted a general law providing that any foreign-owned firm that had been in Peru before June 30, 1971, had to become a mixed or national firm within 15 years. A time schedule for transferring control was established. Any foreign firms established after July 1, 1971 also had to transfer ownership to Peruvians within 15 years.[6]

Seeming to run against this nationalization trend was the treatment of two substantial foreign concessions by the Velasco regime. One was a grant to the Occidental Petroleum Company to seek for and exploit oil in the area east of the Andes, and the other was the protection of the large concession of the Southern Peru Copper Corporation (a subsidiary of the American Smelting and Refining Company), which became the country's largest source of copper exports.

On July 26, 1974, the Velasco administration expropriated the country's most important newspapers, as well as its broadcasting stations, which had been critical of the regime. One principal newspaper, *La Prensa*, which had belonged to Pedro Beltrán, became the "Daily of the Labor Communities of Peru."[7]

Previous to this, the military government had passed a so-called "freedom of the press" law. Among other things, it forbade criticism of government leaders and government institutions. Among other cases prosecuted under this law was that of a lawyer who had published a magazine article criticizing the lack of training of the police—he was fined 20,000 soles and was sent to jail for six months.[8]

The Velasco regime also substantially modified Peru's foreign policy. It made explicit its desire to free Peru of "dependence" on the United States. It recognized the Castro government in Cuba. Most importantly, it bought substantial quantities of military equipment, particularly for the air force, from the Soviet Union, running up a debt to the USSR of over half a billion dollars in the process.[9]

THE INDUSTRIAL COMMUNITIES

Of particular concern to the labor movement was the Velasco government's establishment of "industrial communities." This was provided for in the General Law of Industries of July 1970.

Nancy Johnson outlined the principal provisions of this law:

Under this law, an "industrial community" was established in an enterprise by the Ministry of Industry and Trade at the request of any worker. All permanent employees—those who had successfully passed the three-month probationary period and worked at least a four-hour day—constituted an industrial community and were entitled to share in its management, profits and ownership. Membership was limited to one community per individual.

Johnson continued,

Industries were compelled to distribute 25 percent of their pretax income in the following manner: 15 percent for the "industrial community" (comprising all the workers of any firm having more than six workers) in the form of equity in the enterprise (some communities were permitted to purchase up to 50 percent ownership in the firm) and 10 percent in cash to individuals workers. Worker participation in essential industries, however, was subject to the state's discretion.... Under the law, a worker with veto rights had to be a member of the board of directors.[10]

Understandably, the owners and managers of most firms to which the law applied were very unhappy with it. To the degree possible, they sought to sabotage its application. One pro-government periodical described some of the means used to do so:

The enterprises undertook a systematic destruction of the essence of the Industrial community.... The procedures for that were multiple, from impeding the formation of the Community, failing to summon representatives of it to meetings of the Board of Directors, carrying on sessions in English, privately, dividing the firms into industrial and commercial ones, reducing the profits and falsifying the accounts, and in some extreme cases, even promoting the deliberate and fraudulent bankruptcy of the firms.[11]

Nancy Johnson confirmed the use of these dodges by Peruvian firms to avoid application of the General Law of Industries. However, she argued that foreign-owned companies were not able to use such procedures "because of their tenuous positions."[12]

The industrial communities, which were set up in the mining and fishing industries and in a number of manufacturing firms, also presented serious problems for the organized labor movement. The government was equivocal concerning the role of the trade unions in those sectors of the economy in which industrial communities came into existence, and this led to a number of controversies between segments of the labor movement and the government.

The Socialist Party leader Luciano Castillo saw the industrial communities as a means of getting rid of the trade unions, on the theory that if the workers ran their firms, there would be no need for unions. However, he added that in most cases it would take 20 to 30 years before the industrial communities would control 50 percent of the stock of their respective companies.[13] Some foreign observers agreed with Castillo—that one objective of the industrial-community legislation was the ultimate liquidation of the labor movement.[14]

The Velasco military government and its industrial-community law did not last long enough to know what impact it ultimately would have had on the labor movement. However, so long as it did exist, this law presented a challenge to organized labor, to determine just what the relationship between the trade unions and the industrial communities would be.

Luis Pasara and Jorge Santistevan noted the reactions of a few of the unions to the advent of the industrial community. In the case of a large bottling plant in Lima with a strong union, the union carried out a 48-hour strike to force the firm to admit a member of the industrial community to the company's board of directors, as the law prescribed. Subsequently, the union took the lead in having the industrial community challenge the accounting procedures of the firm, which the managers claimed showed the enterprise as losing money—as a result of which there was no profit to share with the industrial community.

In other cases cited by these two authors, where relations between the union and employer had been more or less cordial, no such conflicts arose. In some instances, the establishment of the industrial community stimulated the founding of a union where none had previously existed.[15]

THE SINAMOS

One of the principal problems of the Velasco military government was that it was seeking to carry out a species of social revolution from the top, from the leadership of the armed forces. Most of the ministers and other leading figures in the regime were military officers, principally of the army.

The military leaders wanted popular support. They pictured their revolution as being one of "Armed Forces and the People," but the fact was that they had great suspicion of the civilians, particularly the politicians, trade unionists, peasant leaders, and others who had a mass base of their own.

To try to deal with this situation, in mid-1971 the Velasco regime established what they called the Sistema Nacional de Apoyo a la Movilización Social (National System of Support of Social Mobilization—SINAMOS). Named to head it was General Leonidas Rodríguez, but as his "sub-chief" a civilian was named, Carlos Delgado, a onetime leader of the Aprista Party Youth who had left the Apristas in the early 1960s.

SINAMOS brought together 10 branches of the government that had "been dealing with social problems, and coordinate[d] their efforts." Carlos Delgado stressed that SINAMOS was not to become a political party, and in fact, he largely ruled out any role for political parties in the future revolutionary Peru.[16]

The decree establishing SINAMOS set forth that its objectives would be "1. Training, orientation and organization of the national population. 2. Development of entities of social interest. 3. Communications and particularly the dialogue between the Government and the national population."[17]

Among the other "social" areas in which SINAMOS intervened was the area of organized labor. In August 1972, General Leónidas Rodríguez announced that SINAMOS would "promote the formation of labor unions where needed." Although he promised that "this activity would be carried on chiefly in the field of diffusion and training," that statement did not allay the fears of the existing labor organizations that the government would seek to organize its own trade union movement.[18]

In fact, ultimately a new trade union central organization was established, largely through the efforts of SINAMOS. However, the work of that group proved to be largely unsuccessful.

THE ECONOMIC CRISIS OF THE VELASCO REGIME

During the first years of the Velasco regime, the country experienced an "economic reactivization," which Denis Sulmont attributed largely to "the dynamism of the export mining sector and the association between international capital and the State."[19] Most notable were the investments of the Southern Peru Mining Company in opening up a new copper-mining operation, the search for oil in the trans-Andean region by Occidental Petroleum, and the growth of anchovy fishing and fishmeal industry along the coast.

However, by the mid-1970s, the country was facing an exceedingly serious economic crisis. There were several factors leading to this. For one thing, the Velasco administration's policies largely discouraged private investment, whether domestic or foreign—with the major exceptions of investments of the Occidental Petroleum Company and the Southern Peru Copper Corporation. For another, the government borrowed abroad heavily in the early 1970s, particularly on a short-term basis, with many of the loans falling due by the latter part of the decade. Very extensive government expenditures, not only on international projects but also on purchases of Soviet arms, contributed to the crisis also.

Factors not under the Peruvian government's control that led to the economic crisis included the onslaught of "El Niño," the change in ocean currents that deprived the country of most of the anchovies that it had become accustomed to catching and exporting. Another such event was the worldwide inflation which seriously raised the cost of the country's imports.

There were three principal effects of this situation. One was the beginning of a high level of inflation in 1973. The rate of price increases by 1975 was 24 percent. The second result was a large foreign exchange deficit of $405 million in 1974 and $1,099.3 million in 1975. In the third place, there was an overall decline in the rate of growth of the gross national product, with a 0.4 percent decline in 1975–1976.[20]

Another aspect of the Velasco regime came under increasing criticism from the opposition. This was the corruption of the military government. As previously noted, a corruption scandal within the military was a contributing cause of the October 1948 coup. Under the Velasco regime, with no functioning parliament, restrictions on the functioning of the political parties, and growing infringement on the freedom of the press, that situation did not improve.

The corruption took various forms. One was that of the military men holding more than one job—their armed forces rank and positions in the civilian government—from both of which they drew income. Another was corruption involved in the granting of contracts and other benefits at the disposal of the armed forces regime.[21]

Although at one point a subsecretary of interior was officially charged with looking into rumors of corruption, whatever efforts he made were not fruitful. Of course, reports of corruption could not get beyond the rumor stage, considering that the press was not free to report them. When President Velasco was succeeded by General Morales Bermudez, several important figures from the Velasco administration were indicted for corruption.[22]

THE CTP DURING THE VELASCO REGIME

During the administration of President Velasco Alvarado, there were major shifts of power and influence within the organized labor movement. The principal loser in this situation was the Confederación de Trabajadores del Perú.

Although the CTP clearly dominated the Peruvian labor movement until the October 1968 military coup, with the advent of the Velasco government, this was no longer the case. The revolutionary military regime was strongly opposed to the Aprista Party, the influence of which was dominant in the CTP. Therefore, the Velasco government was clearly hostile to the CTP and sought actively not only to undermine its influence, but also to support the development of rivals to it.

The leadership of the CTP adopted a cautious approach to the government in the face of this situation. They sought basically to maintain their forces intact, insofar as possible, awaiting a more favorable shift in the political situation, which they knew was inevitable.

The cautious attitude of the CTP and its affiliates was reflected in strike statistics for the Velasco period. For example, in 1973 the CTP-aligned unions engaged in only 7 percent of all strikes, compared with 48 percent attributed to unions of the Communist-controlled CGTP and 39 percent to far-leftist unions outside of any central labor group. Comparable figures for 1974 and 1975 showed the CTP unions accounting for only about 1 percent of all walkouts.[23]

The CTP was also plagued with some internal dissension in this period. Some fellow Aprista trade unionists objected to what they conceived to be the somewhat high-handed policy of Julio Cruzado, who some years before had succeeded Arturo Sabroso as secretary-general of the CTP.[24]

In a number of cases, federations or individual unions withdrew from the CTP, either to remain independent or to join a rival confederation. In some instances, these actions resulted from unhappiness with the lack of militancy of the confederation, as in the case of the Cerro de Pasco mine workers. But in many cases, withdrawal was forced by pressure from the Velasco government. In a number of other instances, although the leadership of the CTP affiliate concerned remained in the hands of Apristas, it was decided that the best way to preserve the organization was to leave the CTP, hoping to be able to have it rejoin the confederación when changing political circumstances permitted.[25]

Nancy Johnson presented an example of such government-forced withdrawal from the CTP. She wrote, "The contract negotiations of a CTP-affiliated dockworkers' union with the Port Authority in the early 1970's afford a good illustration. Each time that the CTP affiliate was scheduled to negotiate, the meeting was canceled at the last moment. The union was advised that it would have no opportunity to negotiate until it affiliated with the CTRP," the confederation established under government patronage.[26]

The government used its influence in other ways to undermine some of the unions that remained in the CTP. In the case of the Federación de Trabajadores de Hospitales, the Velasco regime decreed that because government employees could not form legal unions, the Federation of Hospital Workers could not have legal recognition. As a consequence of this, although the federation continued to exist, it no longer enjoyed the check off of union dues, which it had won earlier through collective bargaining. In addition, the government's hospital management began dismissing and transferring workers who were particularly active in union affairs.[27]

The CTP was the second-largest central labor organization during most of the Velasco period. It maintained the textile workers, sugar workers, miners in the North, some maritime workers, some railroaders, metal-workers, chauffeurs, food workers, and general agricultural workers in its ranks.[28]

In the case of the chauffeurs, long a scene of rivalry between the federation affiliated with the CTP and the independent one led by Juan P. Luna, the two federations continued to exist. The CTP group was dominant in the cities in the northern part of the country, and Luna's federation held strong in the southern cities. In the Lima-Callao area, the principal chauffeurs' union in Callao continued to be affiliated with the CTP federation, whereas in Lima there were internal problems within the CTP federation's union, and the Luna union continued to have considerable backing.[29]

In 1972 Gustavo Espinoza, secretary-general of the Communist Party–controlled Confederación General de Trabajadores del Perú, credited the CTP with a membership of about 200,000, compared with the 420,000 he claimed for his own organization.[30] However, Nancy Johnson several years later claimed that the CTP "is ineffective in organization and lacks a full-time staff."[31]

Some sense of the scope that the CTP was able to maintain during the Velasco period can perhaps be determined from looking at the membership of the National Directive Council elected to serve from 1973 to 1976. Of the 60 members, there were six from the textile workers, including Secretary-General Julio Cruzado; three from the White-Collar Workers' Confederation, including a CTP assistant secretary-general; two from the Federation of Mining and Metal Workers, including an assistant general secretary; and two from the sugar workers, also including an assistant secretary-general.

In addition, the hospital workers had three members, the railroaders two, the Commercial Workers' Federation two, and the pharmaceutical workers two. The miners' federation had three members of the CTP Executive. In addition, the municipal workers, petrochemical workers, glass workers, and Federación Nacional Campesinos had one each. The rest of the members came from either individual unions or regional organizations of the CTP.[32] Presumably, representation in the National Council reflected at least to some degree the importance that the groups represented in the total CTP membership.

Among the activities that the CTP pursued during the Velasco period was leadership training, which it had been conducting since the Apristas took control in the mid-1940s. In this program, the CTP received aid from several of the International Trade Secretariats and from the AFL-CIO through the American Institute for Free Labor Development.

However, in 1971 the Velasco government refused to renew the contract by which the AIFLD operated in Peru, and the AIFLD office was closed down. Nevertheless, Charles Wheeler, who was officially country program director of the AIFLD in both Bolivia and Peru, continued to aid the CTP, with advice and financing. It was reported that in 1975, the AIFLD was still contributing about $25,000 a year to the CTP. There was also certain tension between Wheeler and the U.S. Embassy in Peru.[33]

One problem with which the CTP unions, as well as other segments of the labor movement, had to deal was that of the "industrial communities" organized under the Velasco regime. The industrial communities were organized into federations, with a Confederación Nacional de Comunidades Industriales as an overall body.

The CTP unionists, like those of other affiliations, were afraid that the industrial communities would be used as a weapon to weaken or destroy the trade unions. A meeting of the Federation of Textile Industrial Communities protested against the prohibition of union officials holding office in the industrial communities, saying that the government was seeking "to confuse the interests of the industrial community with those of the enterprise." It also condemned the sanctions, which were provided against the industrial communities' disclosing "improper" information about the firms involved, posing the question of whether information disclosed about firms' double bookkeeping would be "improper."[34] The textile workers, of course, remained members of the Federation of Textile Workers, the most important single affiliate of the CTP.

There were a few showdowns between the CTP and the Velasco government. One of these was a one-day general strike called by the confederación in May 1973, the results of which were modest.[35]

THE CASE OF THE SUGAR WORKERS' UNION

One showdown between the Velasco government and the Confederación de Trabajadores del Perú in which the CTP was victorious was that of the sugar workers' unions of the northern coastal area. It was a struggle over the "cooperatives" established in the sugar area under the Velasco government's agrarian reform program.

The Agrarian Reform Law (Decree Law No. 17716) provided for expropriation of the sugar plantations, which were to be reorganized as workers' "cooperatives." A subsequent statute, Decree Law No. 18299, specified the way in which such cooperatives would be established, and there were parts of this law to which the sugar workers' unions strongly objected.

Even the pro-government and Communist-influenced newspaper *Expreso* admitted that one of the objectives of Decree Law No. 18299 was "to preclude control over the governing bodies by partisan union members," meaning control by the Aprista leaders of the sugar workers.[36] Joseph Novitski of the *New York Times* noted with regard to one Aprista sugar union leader, Roger Aguilar, "For three years the government tried to keep Mr. Aguilar and other union leaders like him from coming to power in the sugar cooperatives. It objected to their loyalty to the APRA, a populist, anti-military political party."[37]

The "cooperatives" were supposed to have as their highest authority an "assembly of delegates" representing the workers. However, the assembly that was established for one plantation was typical of the situations that resulted: in this case in point, of the 120 "delegates," 77 were named by the government, and they included many people who had just been brought in to work on the plantation as well as bureaucratic people appointed by the governmental authorities. Anyone who had held office in a union or a party was declared ineligible to be a member of the assembly. Actually in charge of each cooperative was a military officer, appointed to the post by the government.

The new management of the plantations refused to have anything to do with the workers' unions. Furthermore, management began to violate provisions of existing collective bargaining contracts—for example, giving sick workers only 80 percent of their regular wage during their illness, as provided by law, instead of 100 percent, which had been provided for in the collective bargaining agreement.[38]

The Federation of Sugar Workers strongly protested these arrangements. It adopted and presented to the government a document setting forth its objections to the agrarian reform law insofar as the sugar industry was concerned. It claimed, "The Decree-Law does not provide for the cooperativization of the sugar industry but for the statization of the sugar business.... In the statized entities, which are to be organized, the workers will not be the proprietors, but rather according to article 75 the proprietors will be these entities."[39] The document also demanded that the government "guarantee the survival of the Sugar Workers Unions of Peru."[40]

The agrarian reform law had also prohibited strikes or even protests against the law or its administration. It provided for

a sentence of not less than six months, nor more than 5 years in prison, in addition to exclusion from the benefits of agrarian reform, for anyone who, by means of pamphlets, flyers, speeches or any other means of communication, spreads false rumors concerning the acts that are carried out in the implementation of agrarian reform, or concerning the substance or manner in which the law is being enforced. It also applies to anyone who takes advantage of his status as a member of a managing entity of the agrarian cooperatives, federations, unions or peasant communities, to interfere with the constitution or organization of the cooperative or to obstruct its functioning.[41]

In the period following the enactment of the agrarian reform decree, there were some protest strikes among the sugar workers. The government cracked down very hard on these, arresting their leaders and having them tried in military courts for "sabotaging the agrarian reform."[42]

In July 1971, the leaders of the Federation of Sugar Workers sought an audience with President Juan Velasco, to present their grievances, but he refused to meet with them. In a press conference held in the headquarters of the Confederación de Trabajadores del Perú, the sugar workers' leaders threatened that if something was not done to right the abuses in the so-called cooperatives, the federation would call a general strike of sugar workers.[43]

The workers ultimately won out in this struggle. Early in 1972 the government enacted Decree No. 19312, which provided for the direct election by the sugar workers of the members of the delegate assemblies. These elections were held on April 16, 1972. At the installation of the new assemblies of delegates—although several of them were addressed by General Rudecindo Zaveleta, director of the Cooperative Advisory and Supervision System, who brought greetings from President Velasco and from General Lorenzo Rodríguez, head of SINAMOS[44]—these ceremonies were clearly a victory for the Aprista-controlled and CTP-affiliated Federation of Sugar Workers.[45]

Two years later, the British publication *Latin America* pointed out that only in the Cayalti sugar cooperative in the Lambayeque department was a far-left union group dominant. It added that "in the neighboring department of La Libertad, where all cutting is mechanized, the government has reached a comfortable accommodation with the Apra-dominated unions."[46]

PROBLEMS OF THE FEDERACIÓN NACIONAL DE CAMPESINOS DEL PERÚ (FENCAP)

The more general peasants' organization of the CTP, the FENCAP, did not fare as well as the Federation of Sugar Workers during the Velasco period. During the late 1950s and the 1960s, the FENCAP had been very active in organizing all kinds of rural workers. Rural wage earners were brought together in trade unions. In the case of the "feudatories," peasants who worked for landlords in return for use of small plots for their homes and gardens, FENCAP worked to get the Indian peasants titles to those small plots, as provided for in the agrarian reform law passed under Belaúnde, and claimed to have gotten some 60,000 such titles for the feudatories. The federation worked to get credit and technical assistance for the Indian communities that were affiliated with it. Small landholders belonging to FENCAP were organized into selling and credit cooperatives. Finally, in the case of peasant squatters on the eastern side of the Andes, the federation worked to get them titles to the land, which they had developed, although in many cases they suddenly found that large landholders had hastened to claim that the land in question belonged to them.[47]

FENCAP and its members were very unhappy about the functioning of the agrarian reform law enacted by the Velasco government. For one thing, it provided for conversion of the self-serving Indian communities into "cooperatives," and the agrarian reform authorities themselves appointed the officials to run those cooperatives, in the place of the leaders who had traditionally been chosen by members of the communities.[48]

In the case of the selling and credit cooperatives established by FENCAP, the members were instructed by the agrarian reform authorities to convert these into full-scale production cooperatives. When FENCAP protested against this to authorities in Lima, they were told that the order had been a "mistake" by local agrarian reform authorities, but the process continued.[49]

The "ex-feudatories" were also adversely affected by the Velasco regime's agrarian reform law, according to FENCAP. They were deprived of the small plots of land that they had acquired under the Belaúnde period of agrarian reform, and these plots became a part of "cooperatives" that were established when the haciendas where these plots were located were taken over by the government. Henceforward, agrarian reform officials in charge of these so-called cooperatives indicated what should be planted where on the ex-haciendas as a whole.[50]

For several years, FENCAP sought to fight against these policies of the Velasco regime. SINAMOS began to organize rival organizations to those of FENCAP.[51] The federation was under tremendous pressure from the government. Nancy Johnson indicated what happened as a consequence of these pressures: "The regime pressed for support and created internal conflict by advocating nonpayment of federation dues by members. When the FENCAP finally admitted defeat and gave its support to government policies, the regime proclaimed the fact in national headlines. As a result, the FENCAP immediately was alienated from the CTP.... To date [1979], relations remained strained between the federation and the confederation."

Johnson added, "By 1976 ... the past difficulties of the FENCAP had led to its reorganization and a dramatic drop in membership (from a claimed 1,000,000 in 1965 through 1971 to 25,000 in 1976). In any case, the 1976 figure is probably closer to reality than the original."[52]

THE CONFEDERACIÓN GENERAL DE TRABAJADORES DEL PERÚ UNDER VELASCO

During the regime of General Juan Velasco Alvarado, the Confederación General de Trabajadores del Perú became the country's largest central labor organization. It also certainly was the most militant one.

At the time of the CGTP's Second Congress in December 1971, it claimed to have 44 federations and 150 other unions not affiliated with any federation within its ranks.[53] At the time of its Third Congress in March 1974, it reported that there were 1,350 unions in it, of which about 1,000 were in 43 federations and over 300 were affiliated directly with the confederación. In all, it claimed to have 400,000 workers as members.[54]

As in the case of the CTP, some idea of the sectors in which the CGTP had its principal support can be obtained from the makeup of its National Council elected at the 1974 congress. Of the 39 members of that body, there were three each from the construction workers, metalworkers, and peasants; two each from the bank clerks, shoe workers, teachers, commercial employees, and clothing workers; and one each from the soft-drink workers, millers, fishermen, textile workers, pharmaceutical employees, plastic workers, bakers, telephone employees, laundry workers, and market employees. The rest of the council members represented regional organizations of the CGTP.[55] In fact, the CGTP had only very scattered membership among the textile workers, and between the Second and Third Congresses had lost most of the mine unions (including their federation), which had previously belonged.

Meetings of the CGTP were held frequently during the period of the reformist military regime. There was an Extraordinary Congress in December 1969, the Second Congress was held two years later, the Third National Congress took place in March 1974, and what was labeled the Fifth Congress met in September 1978.

The National Assembly of Delegates, supposedly the highest body of the CGTP between congresses, was very active. For instance, it was reported to the Third Congress that the assembly had met 17 times in the year 1973 alone.[56] There were also numerous congresses of the various federations affiliated with the confederación.

The CGTP frequently lent its support to individual affiliates in their disputes with the employers. The National Council reported to the CGTP Third Congress, "Practically all those who had conflicts experienced to a greater or lesser degree our warm solidarity. In some cases, those who struggled received our moral and material support, in others, received our class encouragement, our stimulus to continue in the struggle. There were not lacking either those who receive from us opportune counsel, clarification, a fruitful gesture, a positive contact."

The Council then listed 36 different cases in which, in one way or another, it had intervened to support the negotiations of specific individual unions. It also listed nine federations that it had aided in their conflicts with employers.[57]

The CGTP also was active in lobbying with the military government. The same report of the National Council to the Third Congress, after citing several cases of success in such lobbying, commented, "Thus one could cite numerous other cases, in which the vigorous action of the proletariat has succeeded in obtaining real modifications in the labor policy of the Government."[58]

The CGTP also conducted an active program of leadership training during the period of the military regime. Isidoro Gamarra, the president of the CGTP, said in 1975 that one of the principal problems of the organization was its lack of experienced leadership. He commented that most of the leaders were "very young, revolutionary in spirit, but untrained."[59]

To remedy this situation, the CGTP established the National Trade Union School. The National Council reported to the 1971 Congress that in that year the school had carried out four successive programs "on a basic level on trade unionism." Each of these had consisted of courses in trade union organization, labor administration and defense, elementary mathematics, theory and tactics of the labor movement, history of organized labor, the industrial community, and accounting.[60]

By the time of the Third Congress in March 1974, the CGTP leadership training activities had expanded considerably. It had mounted regional courses in nine different provincial cities, had had courses with two Lima universities on the study of pre-Hispanic Peru and the Commune of Paris, and had had special courses for several of its federations. It had also had the collaboration of the local representative of the International Labor Organization in preparation of a seminar on social security.

The National Council reported that the Trade Union School had handled 200 students in 1970, 580 in 1971, 600 in 1972, and 680 in 1973. In addition, it had had 40 students in special courses for workers in the Banco de Lima, 100 in the Bata shoe firm, and 60 for construction workers.[61]

Like the CTP, the CGTP professed to have financial problems. Isidoro Gamarra blamed this situation in part on the tradition established by the CTP that dues payments were not really necessary, an idea that workers belonging to the CGTP found it hard to shake.[62]

The National Council reported to the Third Congress of the CGTP, "The economic aspect has always been the most notable weakness of the CGTP. The finances have never marched to the rhythm of the organic growth or to the rhythm of trade union and political needs. Many factors have influenced this: dilatory payment of dues, little interest on the part of some in financial campaigns of the Central, and the small amount raised by the delegates."[63]

COMMUNIST PARTY CONTROL OF THE CGTP

From its inception, the Confederación General de Trabajadores del Perú was controlled by the pro-Soviet Communist Party of Peru. This profoundly influenced the attitude of the CGTP toward both the government of General Juan Velasco and that of his successor, headed by General Morales Bermudez.

The degree of Communist Party control of the CGTP was clear. Gustavo Espinoza, the confederation's secretary-general during the Velasco period, was a member of the Political Bureau of the Communist Party, and as he commented, there were "other Communists" in the CGTP leadership.[64] The editor of the Communist newspaper Unidad noted modestly that the Communists were "an important element" in the leadership of the CGTP, although there were some other groups that had representation, including the Christian Democrats, the anti-Belaúnde faction of the Acción Popular, and the Socialist Party.[65]

Control of the confederation by the pro-Soviet Communists was also clear in the operation of the CGTP itself. The confederation played an active part in the affairs of the Soviet-controlled World Federation of Trade Unions and its Latin American regional grouping, and there was heavy representation of "fraternal" delegates at the CGTP congresses from Communist-controlled trade union groups in Europe and Latin America. At the 1971 Congress of the CGTP, a joint declaration was issued by the CGTP and the visiting Soviet delegation, which said, among other things, "The Peruvian trade union delegation greet with great enthusiasm the success achieved by the Soviet workers in the construction of the Socialist and Communist Society, in the task of raising very high the material conditions of the Soviet people."[66] The 1974 Congress passed a resolution "saluting and supporting the conclusions adopted in the World Congress of the Forces for Peace held in October 1972 in Moscow, to support the strengthening of the Socialist System, as a fundamental guarantee to assure a lasting peace."[67]

Clear evidence of the role of the role of pro-Soviet Communist in the CGTP was also provided by what happened to the CGTP's Miners' Federation. When the three top leaders of that group were expelled from the Communist Party, they took the federation out of the CGTP.[68]

The degree of party control over the CGTP during the early years of the Velasco regime was also indicated by the claim of the National Council of the confederation that less than 10 percent of the delegates to the 1971 congress had opposed the line laid down there.[69]

CGTP SUPPORT OF THE VELASCO REGIME

Communist control of the CGTP assured that the confederation would support the government of General Juan Velasco. The pro-Soviet Communist Party clearly backed the regime. The editor of the party's paper *Unidad* stated frankly in 1975 that the party supported the Velasco government, saying that the regime was "democratic and progressive," adding that it was the only one that had given the Communist Party perfect freedom to operate, which was enough to prove that it was democratic and enough for the Communists to support it.[70]

A previous editor of *Unidad* indicated that the government's attitude toward the pro-Soviet Communists was one of officially ignoring them, but accepting the support that the party offered, without any public recognition of gratitude. He added that there were a few party leaders who had "more or less close relationship with elements in the regime."[71]

There were undoubtedly at least two major reasons that the pro-Soviet Communist Party—and therefore the CGTP—supported the reformist military regime. One was certainly the fact that they believed that a profound revolutionary change—albeit under military direction—was underway in Peru. They usually talked about "the revolutionary process," implying that country would not always remain under the control of the generals and sooner or later would become "socialist" under the leadership of the Partido Comunista del Perú.

The other determinant of the attitude of the PCP-CGTP was the very friendly relationship between the military regime under General Velasco with the Soviet Union. The very extensive purchase (on credit) of arms from the Soviet Union has been noted already. In addition, the USSR and East European countries provided modest aid to economic development, including the construction of a new fishing port. On the principle that "any friend of the Soviet Union is a friend of ours," the pro-Soviet Communists had little alternative but to support the reformist military regime.

The CGTP support of the Velasco government was made clear on numerous occasions. For instance, in his May Day 1972 speech, Secretary-General Gustavo Espinoza said, "We have to say clearly that we develop a class policy, and that this political line—and we must say this now—and the line brings us to support resolutely, frankly, loyally the Peruvian revolutionary process."[72] Later in the speech he added,

In fixing our positions toward the Revolution we must say that nothing ties us to the Government, that we have no agreement, public or private, with the Revolutionary Government, but that we recognize that this Government has men who are making a great effort to construct a new Peru. We want to recognize in this meeting of masses the now legendary figure for our country, General Juan Velasco Alvarado, the Chief of the Peruvian Revolution.[73]

Aside from the frequent public statements of support for various actions of the Velasco government, the CGTP on many occasions organized public meetings and demonstrations of support for the regime. Some of these were noted by the National Council of the confederation in its report to the Third Congress. They wrote,

We have to mention particularly the great popular and trade union parade carried out in Lima on March 18, 1973 in backing and support of President Velasco. Similarly, we must mention the concentration of June 7, which also counted with the presence of the CGTP, the meeting of January 1 in the Plaza San Martin in support of the nationalization of Cerro de Pasco and the great popular meetings in Trujillo, Arequipa, Huancayo, Cuzco and many other cities in the country.[74]

Throughout the military period, the CGTP leadership was under constant fire from the elements to its left for its support of the regime. The National Council of the confederation noted in its report to the 1971 Congress, "The groups of adventures of the ultra-Left also attack us due to the support we give the process. They also do not tire of filling the ears of the workers with charges against us, saying that we discount the revindicative struggle of the workers, that we are under the leash of the Ministry of Labor, that we applaud without reserve any law promulgated by the Government."

In reply to these charges, the National Council said, "Naturally our support does not compromise the class independence of the federation, since in the legitimate use of our right to dissent, we have criticized the Cuajone contract, the recent petroleum agreement, the detention of the miners' union leaders and their advisers, the deportation of the teachers' leaders, the use of reactionary violence against the people, etc."[75]

However, the CGTP support of the military regime caused the confederación's leadership a certain degree of embarrassment. This was reflected in the report of the National Council to the Third Congress of the confederación in March 1974, in its discussion of the question of the use of the general strike.

After a discussion of the ways in which the CGTP had shown its solidarity with particular unions having difficulties with employers, the National Council commented, "For us, it is clear that replacing this conduct of solidarity with an explosive moment of solidarity ... is not characteristic of our class, but a reflection of bourgeois influence within the labor movement. Those who have slipped into the ears of combatants ideas with a profound opportunist content have appealed to this influence."

The National Council continued,

From the beginning, from the initiation of the activities of the CGTP ... there have not been lacking those who have approached the fighters to whisper in their ears the phrase as well known as it is discredited: "IF the CGTP really supports us, ask them to declare a General Strike." Thus, they have asked for a General Strike in solidarity with the workers of Sider Peru, another to back the comrades of Cuajone, another in support of the comrades of the JJ Camet, another for the workers of Paramonga, another against the CTP, another to combat SINAMOS, thus one after another.

Finally, said the National Council, "In the height of their desperation they have demanded that the CGTP call a General Strike for nothing less than to achieve 'the overthrow of the dictatorship and convoking of election,' so that through these could be installed 'a Communist Government with a socialist program.' "

The National Council replied that to demand such general strikes was to think that the CGTP and the workers in general were stupid. "Only being so is it possible to conceive that in this country the job of the working class is to overthrow what they call 'Fascist dictatorship' and convoke the bourgeois carnival which the electoral farces have always signified in our country, as a means of nothing less than bringing the Communist Party to Power with a socialist program."

Such demands, the National Council said, could only serve

imperialism, which does not accept social transformations in Latin America or any change that damages its interests…. The overthrow of the Government through a General Strike of a generalized action of the working class, would free to act directly the most reactionary forces, which, however, would not for a minute permit in the country a workers' government (even less, naturally, a Communist one) and which would take advantage of the situation to take control of the country and launch against the working class the most brutal repression that has ever been known in the history of our fatherland.[76]

The National Council accused the "ultra Left" of launching such demands and said that many of them were not in fact of the left at all, but of the right. It added that there were also some people who were "sincerely misled or mistaken" and said that "we call upon those people to reflect that they are digging their own graves and at the same time digging a grave in which to bury for many years the classist trade union movement of our fatherland."[77]

THE VELASCO GOVERNMENT'S ATTITUDE TOWARD THE CGTP

Generally, the government of General Velasco was friendly disposed to the Confederación General de Trabajadores del Perú. The regime was strongly opposed to the Aprista Party and was happy to see, and to encourage, a strong rival to the Aprista-controlled Confederación de Trabajadores del Perú.

Certainly, the Aprista trade unionists saw the Velasco regime as supporting the CGTP. As one of the leaders of the CTP reported in 1972, when strikes were called by CGTP unions, the regime usually rushed to settle them on terms favorable to those unions—in sharp contrast to its attitude toward walkouts of the CTP unions.[78]

However, there was much more concrete evidence than only CTP leaders' claims of the favorable attitude toward the CGTP by the Velasco regime. For one thing, the government legally recognized the CGTP in January 1971, an event that the National Council of the CGTP said "was the result … of the evolution of the political situation."[79]

The legal recognition of the CGTP had been the subject of dispute within the military regime. The general who was minister of interior in the Velasco government strongly insisted on such recognition if the CGTP had the legally required number of affiliates, but refused to do so if those requirements were not fulfilled. When the minister of interior insisted on legalizing the confederation even though it did not have the requisite number of affiliates, the minister of labor resigned. Legal recognition was extended soon afterward, and with its legalization, the CGTP in fact did soon have the number of subordinate groups that the law required.[80]

Clear evidence, too, of government encouragement of the CGTP was the relatively easy access of its leaders to high officials of the Velasco regime. As we shall see, on many occasions the CGTP leaders had entrée to the minister of labor, to the minister of interior, even to local military officials, and occasionally to the president himself, to deal with problems facing their confederation and its affiliates.

Also, it was to the CGTP that the Velasco government turned to choose people to fill the relatively few posts in the administration that were reserved for representatives of organized labor. Thus, they were chosen for labor representatives to the governing boards of the social security system.[81] They were the Peruvian representatives to the Fourth Interamericana Conference of Ministers of Labor in November 1972 and to the meeting of the ministers of labor of the Andean Pact in October 1973.[82]

Starting in 1972, the government chose CGTP leaders to represent labor in the tripartite delegation to the annual conference of the International Labor Organization. In that year, after the ILO meeting in Geneva, the CGTP representatives, together with those of the Confederación de Trabajadores de la Revolución Peruana, accompanied the minister of labor on a trip to Hungary, Poland, and Czechoslovakia.[83]

Sometimes this support of the CGTP paid off handsomely, insofar as the government was concerned. Thus, in 1972, when Gustavo Espinoza was the Peruvian worker delegate to the ILO Conference, he gave a speech lauding the Velasco regime. He said, among other things, "We may dissent, and in fact dissent, from some measures adopted by the Government, or from some ideological concepts expressed by it. We must, however, indicate the honor, the abnegation and patriotism that characterizes the Peruvian military team, which under the correct leadership of General Juan Velasco Alvarado, seeks to displace from power the traditional sectors that have always held it, to create a meritorious, free and sovereign fatherland."[84]

Not infrequently, during the early years of the Velasco regime, leading figures in the government intervened personally in labor disputes involving CGTP unions to help force a settlement favorable to the unions involved. There was one incident in which two cabinet members left a cabinet to rush to the scene of a CGTP miners' strike and forced a settlement involving a considerable wage increase.[85]

FOUR CRISES OF THE CGTP DURING THE VELASCO REGIME

During the Velasco period, the CGTP faced at least four situations of crisis, which embarrassed its relations with the government. These involved the unions of the Cerro de Pasco mining region, the national teachers' union, the labor movement in Arequipa, and the workers of the government steel plant, Sider Peru.

In the La Oroya branch of the miners' federation in June 1971, two "agents" of the Cerro de Pasco firm were seized by their fellow workers and were intensively "interrogated," reportedly confessing that they were guilty of being agents of the CIA and of other "crimes." In the face of the capture of these two, the police engaged in "violent Aggression" against the union, with the arrest of various union leaders.

Gustavo Espinoza, secretary-general of the CGTP, then went to La Oroya, and upon his return to Lima, he told the minister of interior, "In our opinion, police violence must disappear to give way to a new attitude in which discussion, dialogue, becomes the rule." He demanded punishment of the police officers involved. In a press conference, he defended the "respectful and democratic" nature of the interrogation of the two individuals involved. The union leaders were subsequently released.

However, soon after this, the 15 unions in the Cerro de Pasco complex declared a general strike in the enterprise. The CGTP officially opposed the walkout.

In November 1971, a new aspect of the crisis in Cerro de Pasco developed. The 15 unions there had presented a series of demands to the company some months earlier. The CGTP leaders judged that these demands were excessive. The National Council later reported to the confederation's Second Congress, "We thought that the characteristics of the demand, which included a wage increase of 297.95 soles in basic wages, contributed to strengthening the positions of the most reactionary groups of the country."

The CGTP leadership, headed by Secretary-General Gustavo Espinoza, presented their judgment to representatives of the 15 unions late in August. As the National Council reported, "Unfortunately, we were not listened to, and they maintained the previously stated criteria, seriously damaging relations between the union leaders and the CGTP."

Subsequently, the Cerro de Pasco union leaders forbade any participation of representatives of the CGTP in collective bargaining negotiations. However, both Espinoza and CGTP president Isidoro Gamarra, as well as other CGTP leaders, were permitted to appear before and speak to union meetings.[86]

Their intervention was fruitless. A general strike began early in November at Cerro de Pasco. It quickly turned violent. The workers at the Cobriza mining camp seized hostages. This was followed with an attack by specialized police on the Cobriza area, and in this clash with the miners, more than 20 people were killed. Fifty-nine union leaders were arrested.[87]

Although the CGTP tried to bring about the release of the arrested union leaders, the result of this series of incidents was that the CGTP lost control of the unions in the Cerro de Pasco mining complex, which some time later was expropriated by the Velasco regime.

The second crisis facing the CGTP was a general strike of teachers on August 31, 1951. The Federación Nacional de Enseñanza del Perú, an affiliate of the CGTP, was involved. According to the National Council of the CGTP, this union "starting with just demands, marched by a tortuous way toward a confrontation form which no one was to emerge more defeated than the teachers of the Republic."

At the beginning of the conflict, the CGTP indicated its support for the teachers. It intervened in their negotiations, with CGTP representatives meeting with the minister of education, the minister of economy, and President Velasco himself, on their behalf.

Subsequently, the CGTP leadership claimed that in neither of these cases did the leadership of the FENEP submit the government's offer to the membership. The CGTP National Council said, "The intransigence of the leadership, motivated perhaps by youth, inexperience and immaturity, brought failure of what had been a serious consultation and finally gave rise to breaking of the Teachers Strike Committee."

On September 10, there were extensive riots by students, ostensibly in support of their teachers. The CGTP denounced these: "On the night of the 10th there took place many events, which had nothing in common with the just revindicative struggle of the teachers, but much with open organized counterrevolutionary sedition, organized and promoted with the deliberate purpose of overthrowing the government and replacing it with a reactionary fascist, repressive and antiworker one."[88]

Some of the leaders of the FENEP called off the teachers' strike on September 14, 1971. Subsequently, the National Council of the CGTP reported, "Now, with some time having passed and many of the problems raised then having been resolved, the facts confirm the justice of the line put forth by the CGTP and the tragic error committed by those who launched the teachers' trade union movement precipitously in a stupid counterrevolutionary effort."[89]

This observation was more optimistic than the facts deserved. Following this strike, the FENEP was replaced as the principal teachers' organization by the Sindicato Unido de Trabajadores de la Educación del Perú (SUTEP), which was not affiliated with the CGTP. It was to become one of the key unions that constituted the far-left opposition to the CGTP.

The third crisis of the CGTP was a series of events in the southern city of Arequipa. The first of these took place in April 1972, when the Federación Departamental de Trabajadores de Arequipa (FDTA), the regional affiliate of the CGTP, declared a general strike in the department. The FDTA demanded the return home of teacher-union leaders who had been deported and demanded that workers at the Cuajone mine area of the Southern Peru Copper Company, who had been dismissed following completion of construction work on which they had been employed, be returned to their jobs. The CGTP intervened directly in this situation, sending assistant general secretary José Chávez to Arequipa. The CGTP won both a promise to allow the teachers' leaders to return and a reemployment of the Cuajone workers.

However, the labor situation in the Department of Arequipa remained disturbed. Not all of the Cuajone workers were reinstated, and there were various other labor conflicts pending to which a favorable solution was not found. So in May 1973 the FDTA declared another general strike, which lasted eight days. The National Council of the CGTP subsequently reported, "The conflict was resolved after various emergencies, and the workers of Cuajone kept their jobs, their wages and their labor conditions. The other problems were resolved." Once again, the CGTP had publicly backed up the actions of its Arequipa affiliate.[90]

However, in November 1973 there was another outbreak of violence in Arequipa that was a great embarrassment to the CGTP. It began with a teachers' strike in October, called by the SUTEP, in which the CGTP claimed that only 15 percent of the teachers participated. The CGTP, including its teachers' federation, opposed the walkout.

A number of leaders of this strike were dismissed, and some were jailed. Although the FDTA and the CGTP protested these measures, they refused to call a general strike in Arequipa over the issue. As a consequence, a group of non-CGTP unions formed the Frente de Defensa del Fuero Sindical. This group called a general strike in November 15. The transport workers, railroaders, and students supported it, although the CGTP claimed later that the city's factory workers had not done so.

This strike generated a good deal of violence. The National Council of the CGTP reported later, "On Tuesday the 20th the violence reached a climax as a result of which two people were killed and various wounded." There were attacks by the mob on SINAMOS headquarters and various other buildings.

In the face of this situation, the FDTA, trying to get control of a situation that it had not created, decided to call its own general strike. The Arequipa federation worked closely with a delegation from the CGTP headquarters headed by Secretary-General Gustavo Espinoza. Meanwhile, the government suspended constitutional guarantees in the city, and the army occupied the city, establishing a curfew.

On November 21, Espinoza returned to Lima "to deal with the Minister of Labor to solve more quickly the trade union petitions raised by the FDTA." He also held a press conference, in which he said, "The Arequipa working class had very little if anything to do with the seditious maneuver begun and directed principally by the repudiated officials of the so-called Sutep, the leaders of transport and the railroads, the large entrepreneurs, the captains of industry and large commerce."

After conferring with the minister of labor, Espinoza returned to Arequipa, "to participate in discussions of the problem with the military authorities in the White city." According to the National Council, "in these conversations a globally correct accord was reached, and an agreement signed of which the contents had been disclosed to the Assembly of the FDTA. Minutes before, the so-called Frente de Defensa del Fuero Sindical suspended also 'its strike' in a most clear and concrete defeat."[91]

Then, in July 1975, about a month before the end of the Velasco regime, another serious situation developed in Arequipa. The FDTA again declared a general strike—for 48 hours—at the same time that the Railroad Federation declared a walkout of unspecified duration on the lines between Arequipa and Cuzco and Puno. The FDTA was protesting the inadequacy of a decree establishing a 400-sol monthly family allowance, but also was demanding expropriation of the local newspaper *Correo*, a general wage increase of 100 soles, and modification of Decree Law No. 21302, which had limited the amount of wage increases that could be gained through collective bargaining.[92]

This strike brought a serious breakdown of law and order. In a public statement by President Isidoro Gamarra and Secretary-General Gustavo Espinoza, the CGTP explained what happened: "Groups of agitators ... this morning organized street actions and confrontations with the police, which gave rise to aggressive repression of the workers. At noon today, guarantees were suspended in the city of Arequipa, which aggravated a situation already very tense."[93]

The government decree establishing a state of emergency in Arequipa said that "some organizations have made demands on the government impossible to satisfy totally, because to do so would have precipitated the country into an insurmountable economic crisis."[94]

The last crisis that imperiled relations between the CGTP and the Velasco government involved the union of workers in Sider Peru, the government steel plant in Chimbote. The conflict there began in May 1973 when a fight broke out in the local fishermen's union, between its secretary-general, Franco Baca Bazán, labeled by the CGTP as a "well-known trade union gangster," and his opponents, who set up a Transitory Junta to administer the union. A general strike of one day, May 24, was called in Chimbote in support of the Transitory Junta. However, there was rioting in the streets that day, and the Republican Guard was called out. Among other things, the Republican Guard attacked the headquarters of the Sider Peru union, in the process mortally wounding Cristóbal Espinola, a leader of that union and member of the National Council of the CGTP.

As a result of all this, the Federación Departamental Sindical de Ancash, which had belonged to the CTP, declared a one-day general strike for May 25, which was supported by the Sider Peru Union. However, that organization decided to extend the strike indefinitely, later voting to continue it "until the ultimate consequences."

The leadership of the CGTP intervened extensively in this situation. It arranged meetings of the union with the Chimbote port captain and the ministers of labor and interior to discuss various grievances the steelworkers had. The Assembly of Delegates finally urged the steelworkers to call of their walkout, but the Sider Peru union refused.

The strike was finally broken. As a consequence, a number of its leaders were arrested and many workers were dismissed. Although the CGTP was able to get freedom for the union leaders, it was unable to get them restored to their jobs.[95]

DEFECTION OF THE MINERS' FEDERATION

From its inception, one of the strongholds of the CGTP had been among the miners in the southern part of the country, grouped in the Miners' and Metalworkers' Federation. Miners' union leaders Manuel Orego and Faustino Baquerizo were vice presidents of the CGTP in 1971, and Victor Cuadros was named to its National Council.[96]

We have already noted the problems that the CGTP and the Miners' Federation had in 1971 with the unions in the Cerro de Pasco complex. Perhaps as a result of these difficulties, CGTP vice president Faustino Baquerizo Camargo, a Communist Party member, was expelled from the La Oroya Union of Metallurgical Workers, one of the 15 Cerro de Pasco unions, in April 1972.[97]

Early in 1973, the Miners' Federation itself withdrew from the Confederación General Trabajadores del Perú. It did so as a result of internal problems within the Communist Party, rather than because of any direct conflict between the Miners' Federation and the CGTP.

The principal legal adviser of the CGTP until 1973 was Dr. Ricardo Díaz Chávez, who also was the lawyer of the Miners' Federation. In reporting on the problem with the miners, the National Council of the CGTP noted, "During the time that lawyer Díaz Chávez advised the Central there were not major difficulties or basic contradictions with the CGTP. On some occasions, he had different criteria with regard to some things, but never were these criteria cause of serious friction."

A meeting of the National Assembly of Delegates of the CGTP in February 1973 issued a statement explaining what had happened with regard to Díaz Chávez:

The attacks against the leaders of the CGTP have been accentuated as a result of a political sanction which, as is publicly known, has been received by Doctor Ricardo Díaz Chávez. It must be made clear that that sanction does not involve the trade union organizations, since it involves a measure that has absolutely no effect on the unions and federations. It concerns rather a disciplinary sanction approved by the Central Committee of the Communist Party against Dr. Díaz Chávez, who was, until recently, a member of the Central Committee of that Party.

The CGTP statement went on,

The CGTP considers that the problems, which have arisen between the Communist Party and lawyer Díaz Chávez, provide no reason to involve the interest and attention of the Unions. For this reason, the CGTP rejects anyone who attempts to introduce in the unions, as part of the discussion of the workers, the internal problems of whatever, which have no reason to be submitted to the consideration of the unions.[98]

However, alluding to the impact of Díaz Chávez's problems with the Communist Party, the CGTP statement said, "The Assembly, at the same time, condemns the fact that some people have used the matter of the aforementioned lawyer to take positions against the Central and against its leadership, assuming, without absolutely any consultation the representation and name of their unions."

However, the fact was that not only was Díaz Chávez expelled from the Communist Party, but so were three of the top leaders of the Miners' Federation. As a consequence, the Miners' Federation withdrew from the CGTP, though some of the individual mining unions stayed with the confederation.[99] A new Miners' Federation was organized by the CGTP with those unions the Communists still controlled. It was headed by Manuel Orrego, who at first had sided with Díaz Chávez and his colleagues, but subsequently changed his position.[100]

THE CGTP AND THE PEASANTS

Throughout the period of military rule, the CGTP sought to bring the peasantry into its ranks. Thus, the Second Congress in December 1971 passed a resolution "to support and give impulse to the organization of the workers of the countryside and their more active participation in the process of Agrarian Reform, particularly through the Departmental and Provincial Federations."[101]

In May 1974, the CGTP convened what it called the First National Peasants Convention. Baltazar Carpio, national secretary of Peasant Affairs of the CGTP, gave the principal report to that meeting. He noted various regional peasant congresses that had been held since enactment of the agrarian reform, although it was not clear how many of these had been under the auspices of the CGTP.

Carpio denounced the two existing national peasant groups, the FENCAP and the Confederación de Campesinos del Perú. He claimed that "the principal peasant organizations of the country have affiliated with the CGTP."

A resolution of this convention endorsed Law No. 19400 of the military regime, which had dissolved the landlords' Sociedad Nacional de Agricultura, and provided for formation of "agrarian leagues" by the peasants. However, it urged that the government "permit the integration of unions and provincial and departmental federations of peasants into the agrarian leagues ... and in the department agrarian federations, as one of the forms of making peasant participation effective."[102]

When the government-sponsored Confederación Nacional de Agricultores (CNA) was established in October 1974, the peasant organizations of the CGTP participated in it. As a consequence, as Daniel Premo noted, the Communists and CGTP "exert[ed] some influence in the peasant sector."[103]

THE CENTRAL DE TRABAJADORES DE LA REVOLUCIÓN PERUANA

From the beginning there were certainly elements in the military regime that were opposed to the collaboration of the government with the Confederación General de Trabajadores del Perú. During the Velasco period, this opposition had various expressions.

The first form such opposition took was the Movimiento Laborista Revolucionario (Revolutionary Labor Movement—MLR), which was established in 1971 with the support of the minister of fisheries, General Javier Tantaleán. It succeeded in getting control of some of the fishermen's unions and soon spread beyond that group.[104]

The crisis faced by the CGTP in May 1973, involving the steel workers' union in Chimbote, began as a struggle between the MLR and those opposed to it and continued within the fishermen's union in Chimbote. More than two years later, the executive committee of that union placed an advertisement in the *Ultima Hora* of Lima, protesting a story that had appeared in *Expresso* alleging that the MLR ex-leader of the union, Franco Baca Bazán, had been barred from attending meetings of the union.[105]

At one time or another, the MLR gained control of the union in the Marcona iron mine, the Sider Peru union, and the Callao dockworkers. In at least some of these cases, opponents were able to dislodge the MLR forces. According to the CGTP, the MLR frequently used force and intimidation to get control of different unions.[106]

A more serious effort to organize a labor movement under control of the military government was undertaken by the Servicio Nacional de Apoyo a la Mobilización Social (SINAMOS). In August 1972, General Leónidas Rodríguez, the head of SINAMOS, announced its intention to "promote the formation of labor unions where needed."

This announcement by General Rodríguez presented a quandary for the Communist Party and the CGTP because SINAMOS was an important institution of the revolutionary military government, which they were pledged to support. But its entry into the trade union field presented a potentially major challenge to the CGTP.

The Communist Party newspaper *Unidad* quickly indicated its reservations about SINAMOS's entry into the trade union field, publishing the following commentary:

The basic question is to define the essence of the participation of SINAMOS. In our opinion, the greater part of it must be aimed at cooperating with labor union leaders to carry out the functions that pertain to them. In absence of an official union, because the labor union is not organized, support should be given to the union organizing committee…. Then it is not precisely that SINAMOS must set up the labor union organizations. This can and must be done under better conditions by the workers themselves with the help of the existing classist labor union organizations.[107]

The CGTP quickly called its Second National Organization Conference to try to deal with the problem of SINAMOS entering the trade union field. That meeting adopted a long resolution that, among other things, proclaimed, "The Conference, reflecting genuinely the positions of the classist labor movement, therefore rejects that through SINAMOS it is attempted to replace the social organizations, disfigure them, manipulate them or destroy trade union democracy, destroying its legitimate independence."[108]

In spite of the protests of the CGTP, there was established in November 1972 the Central de Trabajadores de la Revolución Peruana (Confederation of Workers of the Peruvian Revolution—CTRP), with the patronage of SINAMOS. William Bollinger noted,

While the government's own … CTRP failed to displace either CGTP or the independent left-led federations, it did organize dozens of smaller factories, expanding the reach or organized labor. Workers who had tried in vain to get weak unions recognized by the Ministry of Labor suddenly discovered that government approval was theirs within days if they would affiliate with CTRP. Yet many of these firms were undercapitalized, inefficient competitors, and some of their own were notoriously anti-union. Thus, by the mid-1970s the military regime found itself allied with unions which became embroiled in nasty labor disputes that received heavy play in pro-government newspapers.[109]

The CTRP also organized some of its own federations. For instance, there appeared the Metalworkers' Federation of the Peruvian Revolution.[110]

The government's effort to establish "its own" central labor organization may explain the fact that in 1972 some 410 unions were legally recognized, an all-time record.[111] Over the total period of the Velasco regime, the number of legally recognized unions rose from 2,343 in 1968 to 4,335 in 1975.[112]

The CTRP succeeded in some cases in using government pressure to get unions of the CTP or the CGTP to shift their allegiance to the CTRP. We have already noted such pressure in the CTP-affiliated dockworkers' union of Callao. In 1975 the Ministry of Interior supported the shift of the union of the Marcona mine from the CGTP to the CTRP.[113] Nancy Johnson noted that such change under government pressure "leads to the assumption that many of the members claimed by the CTRP remain ideologically tied to other confederations."[114]

In spite of support from some elements of the military government, the CTRP failed to achieve its obvious objective of uniting all of the labor movement under an organization subordinate to the regime. It never became more than the third-largest of the country's four central labor organizations. According to Nancy Johnson, its principal unions were to be found among fishermen, transport workers, brewery employees, workers in some aspects of the petroleum industry, telecommunications workers, port workers, and "mid-south mining" workers.[115]

As time went on, the CTRP developed an increasingly friendly attitude toward the CGTP. For their part, the Communists of the CGTP sought to avoid any open confrontations with the government-sponsored labor group.

THE CONFEDERACIÓN NACIONAL DE TRABAJADORES

The Confederación Nacional de Trabajadores, the smallest of the four central labor bodies of the 1970s, had its origins in the Movimiento Sindical Cristiano del Perú (Christian Union Movement of Peru—MOSICP), which had been established in 1955 under the aegis of the Christian Democratic Party, which also had been founded in that same year. According to William Bollinger, by 1960 the MOSICP had only seven affiliated unions with 200 members, and by 1968 "comprised only twenty-five minor unions and was plagued by leadership problems."

When the Christian Democrats decided to support the Velasco government in 1969, their labor group received backing from some elements in the regime, particularly from SINAMOS. The MOSICP was converted into the Confederación Nacional de Trabajadores, which was legalized by the government in 1971, when it claimed to have 12 small federations in its ranks. However, according to Bollinger, "Despite financial backing from the Konrad Adenauer Foundation, the CNT made no headway."[116]

During the period in which elements in the government were trying to convert the CNT into a major labor confederation, some officials of the regime sought to get unions that were affiliated with the CTP or the CGTP to withdraw from those organizations and join the CNT. However, these efforts failed completely.[117]

THE FAR-LEFTIST UNIONS

During the period of the Velasco regime, unions and federations that did not belong to any of the central labor organizations played a significant role in the labor movement. Most of these were politically to the left of the pro-Soviet Communist Party and the CGTP. Although there were some efforts made to bring these groups together in a fifth labor confederation, these attempts were not successful.

We have noted that the Federation of Mining and Metallurgical Workers withdrew from the CGTP in 1973, and thereafter it was one of the most important of the far-leftist union groups. Others of major significance were the SUTEP (the Unified Teachers Union of Peru) and the Peasants Confederation of Peru (CCP).

Almost immediately after the October 1968 coup, the Apristas and CTP began to lose control of most of the mine workers' unions. William Bollinger has described this process:

In September 1969 some 5,000 striking La Oroya workers marched on Lima, won their demands, and then disaffiliated from CTP. In December CGTP convened a national mine workers congress, reconstituting Mine and Metallurgical Workers National Federation of Peru (Federación Nacional de Trabajadores Mineros y Metalúrgicos del Perú——FNTMMP). Unions participating included the La Oroya smelter workers, the Cobriza and Tequepala copper miners, and the Marcona iron mine workers. The Southern miners federation was organized by CGTP in 1970, leaving APRA and CTP with almost no influence among mine workers beyond one small northern federation.[118]

The militancy of the mine workers in the period before their break with the CGTP has been discussed previously in this text, and in 1971, 69 percent of "hours lost in strikes were in the mining industry, although mine workers represented only 2 percent of the labor force."[119] The Miners and Metallurgical Workers Federation lost none of its militancy after separating from the CGTP. It was to be particularly active in the struggle against the economic program of the Morales Bermúdez government.

Various far-left political factions were active within the FNTMP. For example, the outstanding figure in the union of the Cuajone mine of the Southern Peru Copper Company was Hernán Cuentas, a leader of the Partido Obrero Marxista Revolucionario, one of several Trotskyist groups then active. Cuentas was arrested on various occasions by the government.[120]

Even more militant than the Miners' Federation was the teachers' organization, the Sindicato Único del Perú—SUTEP. After the failure of the teachers' strike of 1971, this organization emerged as the principal organization of the country's primary and secondary school teachers. It was largely under the influence of the several Maoist-oriented Communist parties of that period, although it also had an Aprista faction within it, which may have controlled some of the SUTEP locals.[121]

Throughout the period of military rule, the SUTEP engaged in numerous strikes. One of these was held in October 1973 and, according to Communist sources, was a failure. The CGTP and the Communists did not support that walkout.[122]

The third major far left–controlled organization within the labor movement during the Velasco period was the Confederación Campesina del Perú (Peasants Confederation of Peru—CCP). This had originally been established by the Communists in 1947, but remained a small group until after the October 1968 military coup.

William Bollinger noted, "When the agrarian reform of the Velasco military regime … bogged down in 1973, groups to the left of the PCP

... reorganized CCP and built it into Peru's most active peasant and farm worker organization. Several of its bases ... initiated a land seizure movement in 1974."[123]

It was largely to confront the CCP that the government sponsored the organization of the National Agrarian Confederation (CAN) in 1974. The pro-Moscow Communists, as previously noted, also supported the CAN.

Understandably, the leaders of the CCP, who were mainly Maoist Communists, were exceedingly hostile to the CAN. They denounced those forming it as "traitors and divisionists" and said that the founding congress of the CAN was "alien to peasant interests."[124]

During the military period, several ad hoc groupings of far left–controlled unions—sometimes with some participation of the CGTP—appeared. One of these, the Comité de Coordinación y Unificación Sindical Clasista (Class Conscious Union Coordination and Unification Committee—CCUSC), was established during the Velasco period, in November 1974. According to William Bollinger, it was established when "*Clasista*-led unions within CGTP joined with independent federations." At one point, it included as many as 100 unions in its ranks.[125]

Opinion was split within the CCUSC concerning what its orientation should be. One U.S. Trotskyist noted, "The CCUSC failed to become a viable alternative leadership, owning to incorrect policies and sectarian bickering among the various Maoist groups that came to dominate it. The Maoists tried to turn the CCUSC itself into a 'revolutionary' federation, dismissing the CGTP as 'bourgeois' and thus isolating themselves from the federation's militant ranks."[126]

NOTES

1. Interview with Ismael Frías, former Trotskyist leader, supporter of Velasco regime, journalist of *La Crónica* of Lima, in Lima, July 13, 1971.

2. Interview with Carlos Delgado, subchief of Sistema Nacional de Apoyo de la Mobilización Social (SINAMOS), ex-Aprista, in Lima, July 13, 1971.

3. Nancy R. Johnson, *The Political , Economic and Labor Climate in Peru*, Industrial Research Unit, The Wharton School, University of Pennsylvania, Philadelphia, 1979, p. 44.

4. Ibid., p. 39.

5. Ibid., pp. 30–31.

6. Ibid., p. 24.

7. *La Prensa*, July 18, 1975; see also *Expreso*, Lima, February 1, 1974, p. 18.

8. Interview with Mary Castillo, member of Executive Committee of Partido Socialista del Perú, in Lima, July 18, 1975.

9. Johnson, op. cit., p. 13.

10. Ibid., p. 19; see also Luis Pasara and Jorge Santistevan in *Movimiento Obrero Sindicatos y Poder en América Latina*, Editorial El Coloquio, Buenos Aires, 1975.

11. *Comunidad Laboral: de la Ficción a la Realidad*, Junaj, Lima, July 8, 1975, p. 26.

12. Johnson, op. cit., pp. 100–101.

13. Interview with Luciano Castillo, leader of Partido Socialista del Perú, in Lima, July 18, 1975.

14. Interview with Arthur Purcell, labor attaché of U.S. Embassy, in Lima, July 9, 1971.

15. Pasara and Santistevan, op. cit., pp. 387–392.

16. Interview with Carlos Delgado, op. cit., July 13, 1971.

17. *Prensa Sindical*, Lima, June 1971, p. 7.

18. *Unidad*, newspaper of pro-Soviet Partido Comunista del Perú, Lima, August 2, 1972, p. 5.

19. Denis Sulmont, *El Movimiento Obrero Peruano (1890–1980), Reseña Histórico*, Tarea, Lima, 1981, p. 104.

20. Johnson, op. cit., pp. 53 and 62.

21. Interviews with Mary Castillo, op. cit., July 18, 1975; and Luis Alberto Sánchez, a major leader of Partido Aprista Peruano, in Lima, July 9, 1971.

22. Interviews with Arthur Purcell, op. cit., July 10, 1972; and Andrés Townsend Ezcurra, a leader of Partido Aprista Peruano, in New York City, November 15, 1975.

23. Johnson, op. cit., p. 126.

24. Interview with Arthur Purcell, op. cit., July 10, 1971.

25. Interview with Julio Cruzado, secretary-general of Confederación de Trabajadores del Perú, in Lima, July 18, 1975; see also William Bollinger, in Gerald Michael Greenfield and Sheldon L. Maram (editors), *Latin American Labor Organizations*, Greenwood Press, Westport, CT, 1987, p. 617.

26. Johnson, op. cit., p. 104.

27. Interview with Wilfredo Chau Villanueva, secretary-general, Federación de Trabajadores de Hospitales, in Lima, July 10, 1972.

28. Interview with Ricardo Temoche, international secretary of Partido Aprista Peruano, former member of Executive of Confederación de Trabajadores del Perú, in Lima, July 7, 1972.

29. Interview with Manuel Ramírez Salas, secretary-general of Federación Chóferes y Anexos del Perú, in Lima, July 10, 1972.

30. Interview with Gustavo Espinoza, secretary-general of Confederación General de Trabajadores del Perú, in Lima, July 12, 1972.

31. Johnson, op. cit., p. 112.

32. See "Consejo Directivo Nacional de la CTP (Periodo de 1973 a 1976)" (typewritten).

33. Interviews with Charles Wheeler, AIFLD country program director of Bolivia and Peru, in Lima, July 17, 1975; and James Creagan, labor reporting officer of U.S. Embassy, in Lima, July 17, 1975.

34. "C.C.I.I. Recien Empieza el Debate," in *Marka*, Lima, July 12, 1975, p. 15.

35. *Times of the Americas*, Miami, February 18, 1976.

36. *Expreso*, Lima, March 9, 1972, p. 16.

37. Joseph Novitski, "Workers in Peru Become Bosses," *New York Times*, May 1, 1972.

38. Interviews with Víctor Torres, secretary-general, Federación de Trabajadores Azucareros del Perú, in Lima, July 8, 1971; and Leónidas Cruzado, president of Federación de Trabajadores Azucareros del Perú, in Lima, July 7, 1971.

39. Federación de Trabajadores Azucareros del Perú, "Modificación del Decreto-Ley No. 17, 716," p. 5.

40. Ibid., p. 6.

41. *El Comercio*, Lima, March 9, 1972, p. 2.

42. Interview with Leónidas Cruzado, op. cit., July 7, 1971.

43. *La Prensa*, Lima, July 10, 1971.

44. *Expreso*, Lima, April 24, 1972, p. 4.

45. *La Prensa*, Sunday supplement, Lima, April 23, 1972, pp. 6–8.

46. *Latin America*, weekly newsmagazine on Latin America, London, April 26, 1974, p. 127.

47. Interview with Rafael Avalos, president of Federación Nacional de Campesinos del Perú, in Lima, July 13, 1971.

48. Interview with Manuel Carranza, secretario de la Selva of Federación Nacional de Campesinos del Perú, in Lima, July 8, 1971.

49. Interview with Marcial Benítez, president of Federación Campesina del Norte of FENCAP and CTP, in Lima, July 13, 1971.

50. Interviews with Manuel Carranza, op. cit., July 8, 1971; and Raúl Carrasco, secretary of organization, Federación Campesina del Perú, in Lima, July 10, 1972.

51. *Latin America*, April 26, 1974, p. 121.

52. Johnson, op. cit., pp. 141–142.

53. *2do Congreso Nacional de Trabajadores del Perú: Conclusiones y Resoluciones CGTP 1–5 de Diciembre 1971*, Lima, p. 3.

54. *CGTP III Congreso Nacional 6–10 Marzo 1974, Lima, Perú*, Lima, 1974, p. 3.

55. Ibid., pp. 122–123.

56. Ibid., p. 28.

57. Ibid., p. 16.

58. Ibid., p. 24.

59. Interview with Isidoro Gamarra Ramírez, president of Confederación General de Trabajadores del Perú, in Lima, July 17, 1975.

60. *2do Congreso Nacional de Trabajadores del Perú, etc.*, op. cit., p. 30.

61. *CGTP III Congreso Nacional etc.*, op. cit., p. 60.

62. Interview with Isidoro Gamarra Ramírez, op. cit., July 17, 1975.

63. *CGTP III Nacional etc.*, op. cit., pp. 60–61.

64. Interview with Gustavo Espinoza, op. cit., July 12, 1972.

65. Interview with Jaime Figueroa, editor of *Unidad*, weekly newspaper of pro-Soviet Partido Comunista del Perú, in Lima, July 12, 1971.

66. *2do Congreso Nacional de Trabajadores del Perú etc.*, p. 62.

67. *CGTP III Congreso Nacional etc.*, p. 117.

68. Interview with Isidoro Gamarra Ramírez, op. cit., July 17, 1975.

69. *CGTP III Congreso Nacional etc.*, p. 8.

70. Interview with Alfredo Abarca, editor of *Unidad*, in Lima, July 17, 1975.

71. Interview with Jaime Figueroa, op. cit., July 12, 1972.

72. Gustavo Espinoza, *1° de Mayo: Intervención de Gustavo Espinoza, S.G. de la C.G.T.P. en el Mitin del 1° de Mayo de 1972*, Lima, 1972, p. 13.

73. Ibid., p. 15.

74. *CGTP III Congreso Nacional etc.*, op. cit., p. 28.

75. *2do Congreso Nacional de Trabajadores del Perú etc.*, op. cit., pp. 28–29.

76. *CGTP III Congreso Nacional etc.*, op. cit., pp. 18–19.

77. Ibid., pp. 19–20.

78. Interview with Mario Guimare, secretary of discipline, Confederación de Trabajadores, del Perú, in Lima, July 10, 1972.

79. *2do Congreso Nacional de Trabajadores del Perú etc.*, op. cit., p. 13.

80. Interview with Major General García Calderón, former subsecretary of labor in government of President Velasco Alvarado, in Washington, DC, January 18, 1977.

81. *CGTP III Congreso Nacional etc.*, op. cit., p. 59.

82. Ibid., p. 64.

83. Ibid., pp. 73–74.

84. *Unidad*, Lima, June 28, 1972.

85. Interview with Arthur Purcell, op. cit., July 10, 1972.

86. *2do Congreso Nacional de Trabajadores del Perú etc.*, op. cit., pp. 18–19 and 23.

87. *Intercontinental Press*, New York, December 13, 1971.

88. *2do Congreso Nacional de Trabajadores del Perú etc.*, op. cit., p. 21.

89. Ibid., p. 22.

90. *CGTP III Congreso Nacional etc.*, op. cit., pp. 30–34.

91. Ibid., pp. 40–45.

92. *La Prensa*, Lima, July, 18, 1975.

93. *Expreso*, Lima, July 18, 1975.

94. *Hoy*, La Paz, July 19, 1975.

95. *CGTP III Congreso Nacional etc.*, op. cit., pp. 34–40.

96. *2do Congreso Nacional de Trabajadores del Perú etc.*, op. cit., p. 89.

97. *Combate*, Lima, April 6, 1972; and *Unidad*, Lima, April 6, 1972.

98. *CGTP III Congreso Nacional etc.*, op. cit., pp. 50–51.

99. Interview with Isidoro Gamarra Ramírez, op. cit., July 17, 1975.

100. *Unidad*, Lima, April 5, 1973; see also *CGTP III Congreso Nacional etc.*, op. cit., p. 51.

101. *2do Congreso Nacional de Trabajadores del Perú etc.*, op. cit., p. 40.

102. *Unidad*, Lima, May 23, 1974.

103. *1978 Yearbook on International Communist Affairs*, Hoover Institution Press, Stanford, Calif., 1978, p. 406.

104. Interview with Isidoro Gamarra Ramírez, op. cit., July 17, 1975; see also Fred Murphy, "The Fight for Class-Struggle Policies in Peru's Unions," *Intercontinental Press*, November 27, 1978, p. 1326.

105. *Ultima Hora*, Lima July 18, 1975.

106. *Unidad*, Lima, June 23, 1975.

107. *Unidad*, Lima, August 24, 1972, p. 5.

108. *Unidad*, Lima, September 14, 1972.

109. Bollinger, op. cit., p. 617.

110. *La Nueva Crónica*, Lima, April 30, 1973.

111. Sulmont, op. cit., p. 103.

112. Ibid., p. 109.

113. Johnson, op. cit., p. 117.

114. Ibid., p. 104.

115. Ibid., p. 117.

116. Bollinger, op. cit., pp. 630–631.

117. Interview with Arthur Purcell, op. cit., July 9, 1971.

118. Bollinger, op. cit., p. 654.

119.   Ibid., p. 655.

120.   "International Campaign to Free Hernán Cuentas," *Intercontinental Press*, March 15, 1976, p. 407; and Miguel Fuentes, "New General Strike on the Agenda in Peru," *Intercontinental Press*, January 15, 1979. pp. 12–13.

121.   Interview with Julio Rosales, Peruvian representative of International Federation of Free Teachers Unions, in Lima, July 18, 1975; see also Bollinger, op. cit., p. 662.

122.   Foreign Broadcast Information Service, October 28, 1973.

123.   Bollinger, op. cit., p. 658.

124.   Daniel Premo in *1980 Yearbook on International Communist Affairs*, Hoover Institution Press, Stanford, Calif., 1980, p. 387.

125.   Bollinger, op. cit., p. 631.

126.   Fred Murphy, "The Fight for Class-Struggle Policies in Peru's Unions," *Intercontinental Press*, November 27, 1978, p. 1326.

CHAPTER 4

Peruvian Organized Labor from 1975 to 1990

General Juan Velasco Alvarado was removed from the presidency of Peru on August 29, 1975. He was succeeded by General Francisco Morales Bermúdez, who until then had been prime minister.

There were at least three reasons for the fall of President Velasco. One was the serious economic crisis that had developed by the mid-1970s. Another was undoubtedly the drastic decline in Velasco's health; he died a few months after his ouster from the presidency. Finally, much of the leadership of the armed forces had become disillusioned with some of the aspects of the "revolution from above," which the military regime had been carrying out since 1968.

The Morales Bermúdez government reversed many of the policies of its predecessor. It converted the industrial community into little more than a profit-sharing scheme; it denationalized the fishing industry and some other enterprises that had been taken over by the government under Velasco, including the newspapers. Morales Bermúdez also returned the government to constitutional civilian control, first calling elections for a constitutional assembly and, when the new constitution had been written, presiding over elections for a new president and Congress.

The victor in the 1980 presidential election was ex-president Fernando Belaúnde Terry. Although he served out his constitutional term of office this time, his second administration was faced with the continuing economic crisis that had helped bring him to power. He also had to confront a new kind of political challenge, in the form of the so-called Sendero Luminoso (Shining Path) Communist Party, which undertook a guerilla war, the beginning of which coincided with Belaúnde's second inauguration.

It presented grave problems not only for the Belaúnde regime, but for the organized labor movement as well.

In the next election, in 1985, the Partido Aprista Peruano for the first time clearly won the contest and was allowed to take power. The Aprista president, Alan García, undertook a different method than his two predecessors had used to try to deal with the continuing economic crisis, which at first seemed to be successful, but subsequently saw a renewal of that crisis. This administration too faced the continuation and extension of the guerrilla war launched by Sendero Luminoso.

The political and economic changes between 1975 and 1990 inevitably had a major impact on the country's labor movement, which had to find ways of confronting the "neoliberal" economic policies adopted by the Morales Bermúdez and second Belaúnde administrations and the collapse of the Alan García government's attempt to find an alternative to those polices.

The "neoliberal" approach began with the Morales Bermúdez regime's adoption of a stringent "economic stabilization" policy, under pressure from the International Monetary Fund. That policy attempted to curb wage increases and free foreign-exchange controls and involved other measures that were unpopular with organized labor.

The upshot of this was that under the Morales Bermúdez regime there began significant changes within the organized labor movement. Although far-left elements within it were particularly militant in their opposition to the government's policies and brought strong pressure on the Confederación General de Trabajadores del Perú, controlled by the pro-Moscow Communists, by the advent of the constitutional regime, there had been a substantial shift against both the far-leftists and the CGTP, an almost complete disappearance of the Velasco government–fostered labor confederation, and some recovery by the traditional Aprista-controlled Confederación de Trabajadores del Perú.

PARTIAL RECOVERY OF THE CTP UNDER MORALES BERMÚDEZ

With the displacement of General Juan Velasco Alvarado by General Francisco Morales Bermúdez in the presidency in August 1975, the political atmosphere changed in Peru. President Morales Bermúdez did not share his predecessor's aversion to the Aprista Party and the CTP, so the government adopted a more friendly attitude toward the Confederación de Trabajadores del Perú than had been characteristic since 1968.

Although the Morales Bermúdez period was marked by a high degree of labor militancy, in protest against the "economic stabilization" program adopted by the president on the insistence of the International Monetary Fund, the CTP generally adhered to a more cautious policy than did the segments of the labor movement dominated by the pro-Soviet Communists and the extreme left parties and groups. However, in 1976 the CTP did call a 48-hour general strike to protest a government decree limiting the level of wage increases that could be negotiated in collective bargaining. The walkout was generally observed in the textile industry, but seems to have been less successful elsewhere.[1]

The CTP usually did not officially back the general strikes called by the CGTP and far left–controlled unions during the Morales Bermúdez period. However, it did support the walkout of May 22–23, 1978, which was the most widely observed strike of the period.[2]

A number of unions that had withdrawn from the CTP during the Velasco period, although remaining under Aprista leadership, returned to the confederación after 1975. Also, the Textile Workers Federation was able to put an end to penetration by far-leftists elements in some of its affiliated unions. In the case of the petroleum workers, the competing two unions that had for long existed were finally merged in 1977 under Aprista leadership.[3]

Writing in 1979, Cecilia Valente said, "In the past year, judging from concessions won and political influence, the CTP has held an edge over the Communist current within organized labor. It is relatively united in its *aprista* orientation, and has cautiously supported the Bermúdez government; while the CGTP, controlled by the orthodox Communist Party suffers from divisions among this and parties and unions to the far Left."

Valente added, "Labor actions, although more numerous than ever, had had milder effects than would have been expected over the past year and have involved political rather than purely economic issues. This is doubtless partly attributable to the weak bargaining position of unions when there is higher unemployment, but it also reflects the restraining influence of the leadership of the CTP and of the Moscow-line Communist party within the CGTP."[4]

Denis Sulmont, a sympathizer with the far-left element of Peruvian Labor, also conceded the partial recovery of the forces of the CTP during the Morales Bermúdez period. Writing soon after the event, he said,

The electoral process that permitted the parties of the right to recompose their political forces, established the bases for an approach between the Military Government and Apra and served as a political counterweight to the popular demonstrations pushed by the Left. The electoral victory, together with support of the authorities and dismissal of "classist" leaders, permitted Apra to recover a certain initiative on the trade union front. In fact, the CTP begins to control some unions in which the clasista left had a presence.[5]

The international organizations with which the CTP and its affiliates were associated were allowed by Morales Bermúdez to resume activities in Peru, which had been restricted in the last years of the Velasco regime. Thus, the International Federation of Plantation, Agricultural and Allied Workers, with which the Sugar Workers Federation and National Peasant

Federation were affiliated, helped to organize a new Confederación Agropecuaria del Perú, which sought to unite those groups "representing democratic Campesinos of the nation." Also, the American Institute for Free Labor Development was allowed to resume operations in Peru in 1978, to extend leadership-training activities. One of the seminars it organized on the subject of the transfer of technology had Víctor Raúl Haya de la Torre as a guest speaker. In November 1978, the Organización Regional Interamericana de Trabajadores (ORIT), with which the CTP was affiliated, held a meeting of its executive in Lima.[6]

THE CGTP DURING THE MORALES BERMÚDEZ PERIOD

With the advent to power of President Morales Bermúdez, both the CGTP and the Communist Party at first declared the change to be a "deepening of the revolution." However, Daniel Premo noted, "As the Morales government became more openly conservative, the PCP followed a vacillating policy, on some occasions giving support to workers' and peasants' struggles ... and at other times seeking a 'dialogue' with the military to create a more orthodox political role for the party."[7] This observation equally describes the policies of the leadership of the CGTP during this same period.

The vacillating policy of both the Communist Party and the CGTP brought the labor confederation under growing pressure from far-left elements inside and outside of the labor movement. This culminated in serious splits within both the party and the CGTP.

The economic policies of the Morales Bermúdez regime, designed among other things to curb the country's galloping inflation and to encourage the return of foreign investment to Peru, caused widespread unhappiness among the working class. The policies resulted in marked declines in real wages, which the labor movement sought to counteract by obtaining wage increases.

During 1975 and the first half of 1976, there were many strikes, particularly in the "industrial sector." Nancy Johnson noted, "Fifty-three percent (421) of the 784 strikes held in 1975 occurred in this sector, especially mining, which is a major source of Peru's export revenue. During the first of 1976, heavy strike activity persisted; 147 strikes took place in the industrial sector."[8]

The government reacted strongly to this situation. In mid-1976 it declared a "state of emergency which prohibited strikes, slowdowns and work stoppages, *inter alia* for the duration."[9] This measure was in effect for a year, but it by no means brought an end to strike activity.

On July 19, 1977, a 24-hour general strike was called with the support of the Confederación General de Trabajadores del Perú to protest the government's decision to raise prices of basic items such as food, gasoline, and transit fares as much as 50 percent. The walkout was marked by rioting, described by the *Christian Science Monitor* as "the most serious in 50 years."

The government cracked down very hard on this strike. The headquarters of the CGTP was raided by the police, and over 300 union leaders were arrested, many of whom were from the CGTP.[10] Nancy Johnson noted, "Allegedly, the CTP intervened and, after a meeting with President Morales Bermúdez in mid-August, obtained the release of the general secretaries of the CGTP, CTRP and the CNT."[11] However, for many months the release of the other arrested labor leaders was a major issue in the labor movement.

Meanwhile, President Morales Bermúdez met with a CGTP delegation early in August. In that meeting he said that he hoped that it would be possible for "antagonism to be overcome and quarrels forgotten." Subsequently, the CGTP denounced efforts of far-left elements to organize demonstrations against the government, labeling them "subversive" and saying that the purpose of such demonstrations was "to undermine the unit of the working class in defense of its rights and interests and the prestige of labor union leaders."[12]

In December 1977 a National Delegates Assembly of the CGTP called another general strike, for 48 hours, on January 23–24, 1978. A Comando Unitario de Lucha (United Struggle Command—CUL), including the CGTP and a number of independent unions, was formed to organize the walkout. A further meeting of the National Delegates Assembly on January 15 renewed the call for the walkout.

However, on January 19, what had become virtually an annual event took place when there was a border clash between Peruvian and Ecuadorian troops. Thereupon, President Morales sent a letter to the CGTP leadership, stating the "hope that we might all collaborate to the best of our abilities in these crucial moments for the fatherland." Thereafter, on the same day, after a meeting with the minister of labor, CGTP secretary-general Eduardo Castillo unilaterally called of the general strike. The CUL reluctantly went along with this decision, although denouncing Castillo and other CGTP leaders.[13]

Pressures from both inside and outside the CGTP forced it to reschedule the general strike, which had been called off. This was done by a National Delegates Assembly on February 10, which set the date for a two-day walkout for February 27–28, 1978. The strike demands included "an across-the-board wage increase, a price freeze on basic necessities, and observance of collective-bargaining agreements," as well as "rehiring of the 5,000 union militants the government ordered fired after the July 19 strike, the release of trade union and political prisoners, and the return of union and political leaders now in forced exile."

Strike leaders claimed that the February general strike was 90 percent effective in Lima, 100 percent effective in some southern cities, and 60 percent effective in northern urban centers. The government said that 185 people were arrested during the walkout, although strike leaders put the number at "at least 2,500."[14]

Meanwhile, a split had developed in both the Communist Party and the CGTP. Daniel Premo reported, "At the beginning of the year a Coordinating Committee of the Regions and the Youth (CCRJ) publicly challenged the PCP's Political Committee for control of the party." It claimed "particularly strong support in the CGTP" and "charged the party's leadership with adopting a 'reformist, bourgeois-liquidationist policy.'"

Premo noted, "One of the reasons for the split in the PCP and the CGTP can be attributed to the latter's reluctance to struggle more vigorously for the reinstatement of the workers fired after the general strike in July 1977…. Gradually the oppositionists broke from the PCP and have been expelled from both the party and the CGTP." The dissidents formed what came to be known as the Partido Comunista del Perú (Mayoría), as opposed to the loyalists' Partido Comunista del Perú (Unidad), each group being identified by its periodical.

Insofar as the CGTP was concerned, Fred Murphy noted, "A cold split thus developed in the CGTP, with the dissidents in control of important unions such as the steel, metal, paper, garment and leather workers, and key provincial federations…. The dissidents constituted themselves as the 'Coordinating Commission of the Ranks of the CGTP.' "[15]

The Morales Bermúdez government's decision on May 14, 1978, to end subsidies of many foods and other articles of prime necessity sparked still another general strike call by the CGTP on May 22–23. It was supported by most of the union groups under far-left control. Again, the government met the strike by arresting union leaders, particularly those affiliated with the left wing of the CGTP, including José Chávez, former assistant secretary-general of the CGTP.[16]

Although the May general strike brought few concrete concessions from the government at that time, on July 16 the government announced that all exiled trade union and political leaders would be allowed to return and, three days later, that all who were being held in prison would be released. However, evidencing the pressure that it was under, the CGTP organized a large rally demanding that all those who had been dismissed after the July 1977 general strike be restored to their jobs. Breaking with tradition, the CGTP leaders even allowed a representative of the far-left SUTEP, as well as Victor Cuadros, the leader of the Mine and Metallurgical Workers Federation, which had split from the CGTP in 1973, to address this meeting.[17]

However, the conflict between the CGTP leadership and the unions controlled by the far left continued. This was demonstrated by the CGTP's refusal to call a general strike in support of a miners' walkout that began on August 4, 1978, arguing that such a general walkout "could have caused the overthrow of the government and its replacement by a Chile-type fascist regime." The Miners and Metallurgical Workers Federation finally called off its strike on September 4.[18]

The struggle for control of the CGTP also continued. Dissident CGTP leaders participated in a "National Trade Union Assembly," attended also by leaders of the Miners and Metallurgical Federation, SUTEP, and other far left–controlled unions, on September 24. That assembly decided that the far-left unions would all try to join the CGTP, obviously in a move to try to take control of it.

However, the Unidad Communists controlling the CGTP took drastic steps to prevent this. In preparation for the Fifth Congress of the CGTP late in September 1978, according to one U.S. Trotskyist source, "Rump provincial federations were set up ion Junín, La Libertad, Pisco, Tarma, and Piura. Parallel unions of metal, garment, and paper workers were put together. The bureaucrats demanded at the last moment that all unions be paid up in dues to be allowed delegates at the congress."

As a consequence of these measures, the Unidad Communists maintained firm control of the Fifth Congress of the CGTP. Requests of far-left unions to join the CGTP were rejected as "opportunist." Elections for the new National Council resulted in all 45 members being from the Unidad slate, although the opposition's candidate got one-third of the votes.[19]

The leadership of the CGTP was in a highly equivocal position. On the hand, the CGTP president, Isidoro Gamarra, joined Communist Party secretary-general Jorge del Prado in attending the Annual Conference of Executives in mid-November 1978, where "before the 300 top businessmen and 100 generals and government officials, del Prado praised the effort to 'restructure' the foreign debt, explicitly rejecting proposals for renouncing or declaring a moratorium … and welcomed foreign investment in Peru."

On the other hand, the CGTP leadership was under renewed pressure from the far left to launch another general strike in protest against the government's economic policies. Such a walkout had been endorsed by the Fifth Congress, although no date for it had been set. Increasingly, elements of the far left both inside and outside the CGTP demanded the setting of a date for the walkout.

Finally, the CGTP called the strike for January 9–11, 1979. The Trotskyite writer Miguel Fuentes noted at the time, "The Stalinists have sought to reassure the regime that the work stoppage will last only three days. CGTP officials have explained in a series of newspaper interviews that 'conditions' are not right for an extended general strike and that this one should not be seen as a prelude for such a struggle. They are in effect telling the regime that if it will sit tight for three days it can weather the storm."[20]

However, the government took stern measures against the January 1979 general strike. Another Trotskyist writer noted that "there was severe repression, both general and selective, during and after the walkout."

Still another 24-hour general walkout was called by the National Delegates Assembly of the CGTP on July 19, 1979, this time in protest against what was seen as an inadequate 35 percent increase in the minimum wage in the face of a 60 percent rate of inflation. This walkout met with less drastic measures by the government than the one six months before.[21]

Considerable labor unrest continued until the end of the Morales Bermúdez government, and the CGTP continued to be no more militant than it had to be. Shortly before Morales Bermúdez gave away to Fernando Belaúnde, who had been reelected in the 1980 election, a strike of government employees, including medical doctors, broke out. The CGTP confined itself to organizing a march in support of a "petition," which it was submitting to the Belaúnde administration "in the light of the new policy it was promised."[22]

THE CTRP AND CNT IN THE MORALES BERMÚDEZ PERIOD

With the intensification of labor unrest during the Morales Bermúdez regime, a split developed within the Central de Trabajadores de la Revolución Peruana, the central labor group that had been organized by elements of the Velasco government. The fishermen's unions finally ousted the Movimiento Laborista Revolucionario (MLR) elements that had largely dominated them, and a new Fishermen's Federation was formed. At the same time, the CTRP in Lima broke with the national organization, using the name CTRP-Lima. These groups aligned themselves with the far-left elements that were defying the Morales Bermúdez government. According to Fred Murphy, "the national CTRP apparatus was left a hollow shell."[23]

The Confederación Nacional de Trabajadores, the central labor group more or less aligned with the Christian Democratic Party, also suffered two splits, as a result of which two organizations emerged using that name, while a third sought to revive the Movimiento Sindical Cristiano del Perú (MOSICP), which had originally given rise to the CNT. These schisms weakened even more the Christian Democratic segment of the labor movement. The CNT unions frequently supported strikes and other activities of the CGTP and of the far-left union groups.[24]

THE FAR-LEFTIST UNIONS IN THE MORALES BERMÚDEZ PERIOD

The far-leftist unions, which did not belong to any of the central labor organizations, were particularly militant during the Morales Bermúdez period. Particularly important were the unions of miners and teachers, and some new independent groups appeared during this period. There were some moves toward grouping these unions into a fifth central labor group, but these were not successful.

The National Federation of Miners and Metallurgical Workers of Peru (FNTMMP) was particularly active in the struggle against the economic program of the Morales Bermúdez administration. On August 4, 1978, it launched a general miners strike over several issues. These include demands for reinstatement of miners dismissed after the July 1977 general strike; abrogation of an emergency mining decree, "which denied miners the right to strike and greatly restricted union activity in the mines"; and protest against a "labor stability decree," which had permitted the mines "to carry out mass layoffs and extended the probation period for newly hired workers from three months to three years." The mines also demanded wage increases and settlement of a number of local grievances.[25]

The miners carried the message of their strike to the nation's capital. Denis Sulmont commented, "In the process of this strike, some 10,000 miners of the Central Sierra carried out 'a march of sacrifice' to the center of Lima, where they camped during various weeks and carried out spectacular street demonstrations."[26]

The government acted strongly against this strike. Although making some concessions that were not accepted by the federación, it relied largely on force to break the walkout. Martial law was declared in five departments, and troops were moved into the ex-Cerro de Pasco area as well as in the Marcona iron mining region and the Southern Peru Copper Company's holdings.

As noted already, the CGTP refused to call a general strike in support of the miners. So, after some of the strikers began to straggle back to work, the Miners Federation called off the walkout on September 8, 1978.[27]

Various far-left political factions were active within the FNTMMP. For example, the outstanding figure in the union of the Cuajone mine of the Southern Peru Copper Company was Hernán Cuentas, a leader of the Partido Obrero Marxista Revolucionario, one of several Trotskyist groups then active. Cuentas was arrested on various occasions by the government.[28] There were also Maoist and other dissident Communist elements active in various parts of the federation.

Another very militant far left–oriented union during the Morales Bermúdez period was the teachers' union, the Sindicato Único de la Educación del Perú—SUTEP. Its most spectacular work stoppage during those years occurred in 1978 and lasted more than two months. The union was demanding legal recognition as well as salary increases, the reemployment of union members who had been dismissed, and various other things. The government for long refused even to negotiate with the SUTEP leadership, many of whom were arrested, while others went into hiding. The government denounced the strike as being political and organized by "ultra Leftists" to undermine the regime.[29]

However, on July 28, 1978, after 81 days, this walkout was settled. The government "granted most of the teachers' demands for union recognition, a wage increase and better working conditions."[30]

An even longer walkout by SUTEP in the following year was less successful. It featured a "hunger strike" in sympathy with the teachers, participated in by, among others, Jorge del Prado, secretary-general of the pro-Soviet Communist Party; a leader of the Revolutionary Socialist Party (organized by some of the military men who had been active in the Velasco administration), the miners' leader Victor Cuadros, and the Trotskyist Hugo Blanco. However, "SUTEP called off its strike on 2 October with the government still refusing to negotiate with its leaders."[31]

A new independent union of more or less far-left orientation appeared during this period. This was the Confederación Intersectorial de Trabajadores Estatales, formed by government employees in 1978. In September of that year, it launched a protest strike against the Morales Bermúdez government's decision to limit job tenure. This walkout was marked by numerous street demonstrations.[32]

In spite of their opposition to the policies of the established central labor organizations, the far-left union groups did not organize a unified national organization to confront them. Although ad hoc groups including many of the far-left unions did function from time to time, none of them emerged as a permanent national confederation.

The first of these ad hoc groups was the Comité de Coordinación y Unificación Sindical Clasista, which, as previously noted, had been established in 1974, near the end of the Velasco administration. It continued to exist for some time during the Morales Bermúdez presidency, and after the July 1977 general strike, when the government declared a "state of emergency" and banned all strikes, the CUSC attempted to organize a defiance of this measure. However, their call for a further general strike "went unheeded by the workers."[33] The comité seems to have disappeared soon thereafter.

A second ad hoc group was the Comando Unitario de Lucha (United Struggle Command—CUL). It included at first the CGTP, as well as a faction of the CNT, the CTRP dissident group CTRP-Lima, the miners, and various other unions. It was under its auspices that the July 19, 1977, general strike was organized. However, after that walkout, the CGTP and CNT groups withdrew from CUL. The groups that remained in it then sought to organize a new general strike on September 20, particularly to protest the dismissal of large numbers of workers in the wake of the July 19 walkout. But that strike was a "total failure," and the CUL soon disappeared.

However, the CUL was revived in preparation for the general strike of January 23–24, 1979, which had been called by the CGTP. Again, the far-leftist unions and the CGTP participated in the CUL. When the CGTP leaders unilaterally called off that walkout, the CUB grudgingly agreed, although denouncing the CGTP leaders as "traitors to the working class and the people of Peru."

Then, when the CGTP renewed its general strike call for February 27–28, 1979, the CUL endorsed that walkout. However, there was little coordination between the CUL and the CGTP in organizing the strike, the effectiveness of which was relatively limited. The CUL also endorsed the CGTP's call for still another two-day general strike on May 22–23, 1979, which was a s futile as the others in obtaining its avowed objective—changing the economic policies of the Morales Bermúdez government.

In September 1978, the CUL joined with CGTP dissidents in issuing a call for "all the forces of the trade union movement … to hold a united national assembly in order to plan strategy and tactics for trade union unity … to strengthen the CGTP, and to advance toward a single federation of the Peruvian proletariat." The resulting National Trade Union Assembly on September 24 was the group that called for the entry into the CGTP of all of the far left–controlled union groups, a move that was thwarted by the Fifth Congress of the CGTP early in October.[34] The far-leftist union groups apparently made no effort to form a central labor organization of their own after being rebuffed by the CGTP.

Another new group, limited to the Lima area, was the Federación Departamental de los Trabajadores de Lima (Lima Departmental Workers Federation—FEDETRAL). According to William Bollinger, this group, "founded in 1979 by union forces to the left of the Peruvian Communist Party … was an effort to consolidate a network of combative unions in the nation's capital…. FEDETRAL affiliates were disenchanted with PCP leadership of the General Confederation of Peruvian Workers. The founding congress (with 255 delegates representing 106 locals) was marred by intra-left polemics."[35] It survived until after the end of the military regime but did not become a national confederation.

Thus, all efforts by the unions under far-leftist leadership to organize their own central labor organization during the military regime failed. Undoubtedly, the major cause of this failure was the political rivalries among the various Maoist and Trotskyist groups, which shared the leadership of these workers' organization.

A SUMMARY OF THE ROLE OF ORGANIZED LABOR IN THE 1968–1980 MILITARY REGIMES

There is no doubt that the 12 years of military rule, 1968–1980, were marked by one of the greatest outbursts of militancy in the history of Peruvian organized labor. Much of this militancy was led by elements of the political far left and the largely independent unions under their control. The Confederación General de Trabajadores del Perú, under leadership of the pro-Moscow Communist Party, was generally more cautious than the far left–led independents, seeking to follow a policy of general support for the military regime without losing backing of its own members. The government-fomented Central de Trabajadores de la Revolución Peruana began with a policy of discouraging "excessive" militancy, although elements within it became increasingly aggressive and finally broke away from the CTRP. The Aprista-led Confederación de Trabajadores del Perú was the most cautious group of all, always fearful that with their ingrained hostility toward APRA, the military regime (particularly under President Velasco) would use any marked militancy on the CTP's part as an excuse to try to stamp it out altogether—although in the one significant situation in which the CTP did stand up to the government (in the case of the sugar workers), it won out.

So long as the economic situation was favorable, as it was in the first years of Velasco government, labor militancy seemed to pay off. The "revolutionary" government was not anxious to have a showdown with organized labor and in fact welcomed the rise of the CGTP (which came about particularly because of its relative militancy) as a challenge to the CTP. However, when the economic situation turned difficult, and particularly after General Velasco was succeeded by General Morales Bermúdez, organized labor paid a heavy price for its increasingly active challenge.

Michael L. Smith has sketched the cost paid by the labor movement, particularly after 1977. He wrote, "The high water mark of labor militancy came with the July 1977 general strike. It forced the military government (1968–1980) to begin handing back power to civilians. However, the strike action resulted in the sacking of five thousand seasoned labor leaders nationwide, decapitating the union movement and wiping out a large share of fifteen years' political work."

Smith went on:

Recession and the liberal shift in economic policy took an additional toll of union leadership and rank and file. Management removed troublesome union leaders through administrative procedure or blackballing and cut back on their stable work force. Between 1976 and 1981, Lima's manufacturing plants shrank from an average of thirty-four workers to twenty-three workers. Although some leaders remained active, thanks to support from their parties, community organizations, or sheer perseverance, others drifted back into private life.[36]

Undoubtedly another factor that was working to undermine organized labor by the end of the military regime was the rapid growth of the "informal," "second," or "underground" economy, particularly in the Lima-Callao region, but also to a lesser degree in other larger cities. This was expanding as a result of the massive movement of people from the Peruvian countryside in search of better living and working conditions. The influx into Lima-Callao and other cities far outran the ability of pre-existing industries, commerce, and other traditional economic activities to provide work for the migrants.

As a consequence of this situation, the migrants were forced to generate their own employment. They became artisans and petty merchants and carried out other activities. These kinds of work were largely outside the range of governmental control or regulation. They were also virtually immune from trade union penetration, as a result of the smallness of most enterprises in the secondary economy and the lack of governmental control that might have been used to enforce labor laws, including those legalizing unions and supporting collective bargaining.

END OF THE MILITARY REGIME

A year after assuming the presidency, General Morales Bermúdez announced his intention of returning to an elected civilian government. The first step in that direction was the election in mid-1978 of a constitutional convention, in which the Aprista had a plurality and Víctor Raúl Haya de la Torre served as chairman.

With adoption of a new constitution, general elections were finally held on May 18, 1980. These were won by ex-president Fernando Belaúnde Terry and his party, Acción Popular, which had refused to participate in the constitutional assembly election two years before. Belaúnde received about 40 percent of the total vote.

Belaúnde's victory was undoubtedly due to several causes. On the one hand, the death of Haya de la Torre in mid-1979 had provoked a struggle between various factions within the Aprista ranks, which undoubtedly reduced their vote in the 1980 election. On the other hand, the far-left forces, which had been more or less united in the 1978 election and had done relatively well, also split into several competing factions in the 1980 poll.

As the Franco-Peruvian sociologist Denis Sulmont noted, Belaúnde received a considerable portion of the vote that in 1978 had gone to the far left. He wrote,

The results confirmed the impact of the division of the left on the popular masses. Belaúnde with a very diffuse program, an able and richly financed demagogic campaign (promise of a million jobs ...) understood how to capitalize on the democratic, anti-dictatorial militarist, and anti-Aprista movement. Some of those who supported the left in 1978 voted this time for Belaúnde as president, although some of them supported the left for senators and deputies. Belaúnde was considered "the lesser evil" in the face of Apra and a symbol of the rejection of military rule.... His victory did not arouse any popular enthusiasm.[37]

THE SECOND BELAÚNDE GOVERNMENT AND ORGANIZED LABOR

The second administration of President Fernando Belaúnde quickly came into conflict with organized labor. In part, this was due to the extravagant promises that he had made to the workers during the election campaign. In part, also, it was due to the very difficult economic situation that the country still faced and to the Belaúnde government's policies for dealing with it. Finally, the relations between the Belaúnde government and organized labor were complicated by the outbreak, virtually at the same time that Belaúnde took office, of a serious guerrilla war, led by the so-called Sendero Luminoso (Shining Path) faction of the Maoist Communists.

Among the things that Belaúnde had promised while running for president were the generating of a million new jobs and an amnesty for workers who had been dismissed during the military regime for violating anti-strike decrees. These and other proposals had generated "a climate of great expectations among long-suffering workers."[38]

However, the economy was faced with a situation that Sandra Woy-Hazleton categorized as "the worst in a century." This was provoked both by a series of natural disasters that "destroyed 60 percent of the nation's agricultural production" and by a very large foreign debt acquired during the military regime, as well as by mounting inflation and an unfavorable balance of payments.

Belaúnde very quickly resorted to very orthodox economic measures ("neoliberalism") to try to deal with this crisis. As Sandra Woy-Hazleton noted, "The administration's economic policy consisted of monetarist stabilization policies dictated by the International Monetary Fund, reprivatization of the economy, and liberalization of trade. But the promised economic growth and increased employment were not forthcoming. During most of 1983, inflation was over 100 percent, unemployment and underemployment topped 59 percent, exports declined in value and growth was –6 percent."[39] In the same year, the gross domestic product fell by 12 percent, and manufacturing output fell by 17.2 percent. However, inflation not only continued, but increased, with prices going up 125 percent in 1983, 111.5 percent in 1984, and 158.3 percent in 1985.[40]

By the end of 1984, according to Woy-Hazleton, "Peru was more than $345 million in arrears on a $13.5 billion debt, the servicing of which accounted for one-third of the year's budget.... Almost every statistic for the year was gloomy. Growth in 1984 was just over 2 percent in real terms, domestic savings were at 1950s levels, new investment loans were only 16 percent of the 1983 level, and inflation raged at 125 percent."[41]

The outbreak of the Sendero Luminoso guerrilla campaign, beginning in the Ayacucho region and spreading extensively through central and southern Peru, as well as (to some degree) in the Lima region, tended to harden the Belaúnde government's attitude toward any evidences of social unrest. It also made the president unwilling to divert resources from the military (which accounted for 25 percent of the 1984 budget) to social services (which took up only 15 percent of the budget) that might have helped alleviate that unrest.[42]

During its first years, the new Belaúnde administration sought to reach some kind of accommodation with the labor movement and the political left in general. In February 1981, Belaúnde established a National Tripartite Commission, with representatives of the four labor confederations, employers' organizations, and government agencies. When the CGTP objected that that body was not dealing with the economic policy issues to which the labor movement objected, Belaúnde established a National Labor Council, "to achieve consensus among government, employers and workers." The four labor groups withdrew from that council in November 1981.

The result of the Belaúnde government's economic policy was the collapse of the president's efforts to reach some kind of accord with organized labor. He, according to William Bollinger, then "embarked upon a neo-liberal labor policy, withdrawing the Ministry of Labor from much of its mediator role and extending anti-union devices introduced by the military regime. The 1978 law deferring job stability rights for three years, which Belaúnde had promised to repeal, kept in place, as was the 1976 decree placing mine workers under a state of emergency which suspended their right to strike."

Belaúnde went even further in his antilabor measures. He proposed to Congress a law extending workers' "provisional" status on the job to 20 years in some parts of the country, as well as a bill to, on a permanent basis, seriously restrict the right to strike. He sought to put a definite end to the industrial communities that had been set up under Velasco and that still existed, although in a very attenuated form.[43]

Belaúnde also resorted to a general crackdown on elements of the labor movement and the opposition in general. As Sandra Woy-Hazleton noted, by 1983,

a major concern of the Left was harassment of political, labor and peasant leaders. Examples included a campaign against schools run by unions, popular groups, or municipalities ... and the detention of persons who organized or participated in strikes or meetings critical of the regime or even possessed 'subversive material' such as books by Marx, Mariátegui, or Lenin.... In June, more than 15,000 police were mobilized in Lima, and 500 people were arrested; although most were freed when no evidence of terrorism could be found, for many this meant months of detention.

Among those jailed (for a week) was Isidoro Gamarra, the 78-year-old president of the Confederación General de Trabajadores del Perú.[44]

All of these governmental actions undermined the labor movement. William Bollinger observed,

While some of Belaúnde's anti-labor measures were blocked by concerted union and leftist parliamentary opposition, by 1984 some 50 percent of all workers employed in industry were without job stability protection.... Such neo-liberal polices weakened the labor movement ... fewer qualifies union members were willing to devote time to union affairs or stand for election to union office. Union solidarity was undermined as stronger unions concentrated primarily on their own economic goals. The number and duration of strikes declined as they proved ineffective, and demoralization spread. Some unions in the hardest-hit industries concentrated instead on collection of severance pay to enable members to gain a foothold in the burgeoning underground economy.[45]

THE CGTP AND FAR-LEFTIST UNIONS IN THE SECOND BELAÚNDE PERIOD

The Confederación General de Trabajadores del Perú continued throughout the second Belaúnde administration to be the largest of the country's central labor organizations. The CGTP continued to be under the control of the pro-Soviet Communist Party, although there was a tendency for union groups controlled by elements to the left of that party to join or rejoin the CGTP and for members of some far-left parties to be admitted to the National Council of the CGTP.

The Confederación held two congresses, its sixth and seventh, during the Belaúnde period. In the first of these meetings, held in January 1982, the far-left SUTEP teachers' union was admitted to the CGTP, and the confederation's own teachers' federation was declared defunct. Subsequently, the old miners' federation, augmented by the membership of the SIDERPERU steel workers' union, as well as the far left–controlled Confederación Campesina del Perú, also joined the CGTP. At the Sixth Congress, five leaders of "other Left currents" were elected to the CGTP National Council.[46]

At the Seventh Congress, in 1983, PCP Central Committee member Isidoro Gamarra was once again reelected as president of the CGTP. Eduardo Castillo was succeeded as secretary-general by another member of the pro-Soviet Communist Party, Valentín Pacho. However, the new National Council was said to include "independents, pro-Soviet PCP members, Trotskyists, and members of the Maoist-led UNIR."[47]

At first, the CGTP tried to establish a modus vivendi with President Belaúnde. Thus, even before he took office, the CGTP organized a march "to submit a petition to Belaúnde."[48] In January 1982, the CGTP invited minister of labor Alfonso Grados Bertorini to address its congress—the first time that a minister of labor had ever received such an invitation.[49] Also, the CGTP participated—for a while—in both the National Tripartite Commission and the National Labor Council established by Belaúnde during his first year, although it finally withdrew from both of these.[50]

Subsequently, the CGTP took the lead in organizing general strikes against the economic policies of the Belaúnde administration. These walkouts were of varying effectiveness.

The first general strike called by the CGTP in January 1981, before the Communist Party and CGTP had largely broken with the Belaúnde government, won comparatively wide backing. Although the strike was organized by the CGTP and a group of independent unions, it also had the support of the Aprista-led CTP and the remnants of the CTRP, which had originally been established by the Velasco regime. William Bollinger reported that the walkout "was especially successful in provincial capitals where the IU [Izquierda Unida] had won control of city halls, providing further evidence of the importance of the political arena in bolstering the trade union movement's fading power." "Such action," he wrote, "helped workers gain a slight increase in real wages by early 1982, although salary rates still stood at only 75 percent and 66 percent of 1973 levels for blue-collar and white-collar employees, respectively."[51]

However, the CGTP's efforts to launch general strikes in 1982 were less efficacious. David Scott Palmer recorded that in 1982,

the CGTP was less successful in gaining worker adherence to repeated calls or threats to call general strikes. A 15 January initiative to protest government price increases was only 30 percent effective … a 22 September effort against the anti-strike law, even less so. Threats of stoppages in April and August were "postponed" in the face of worker reluctance…. The problem for CGTP was that its calls for general strikes were perceived as intended to accomplish political goals during a period in which most workers were concerned about economic ones.[52]

In 1983 the CGTP refused to participate in a new National Labor Council and Social Pact organized by the government, although the other labor confederations did join the organization for a short while. Inflation took off during the year, reaching the level of 70 percent, as a result of which strikes increased. The two principal peasant groups, the Confederación Campesina del Perú and the Confederación Nacional Agraria, led walkouts, as did the Sugar Workers Federation in the North.[53]

Strike activity continued in the first months of 1984, and in March the CGTP called another general walkout, which Sandra Woy-Hazleton categorized as "its most successful stoppage since Belaúnde took office." It was backed by the three other labor confederations and took place in spite of the government's declaration of a state of emergency, banning all public assemblies. CGTP general secretary Eduardo Castillo claimed that in Lima 34 percent of the workers answered the strike call and that it was a "total success" in a number of provincial cities.

Still another general walkout of 24 hours was called by the CGTP on September 27, 1984, demanding establishment of price controls on food and gasoline. CGTP secretary-general Valentín Pacho claimed that "100 percent of the CGTP bases adhered to the strike," but its principal success seems to have been in Arequipa.[54]

Two more general strikes took place in 1985, on March 22 and November 23, being jointly called by all four labor confederations. In each case, the government suspended constitutional guarantees, but the walkouts were widely observed. The March 1985 stoppage was "second only to the 1977 strike that brought the military's move toward democracy. In the provinces, the strike was almost total.... The secretary-general of the CGTP, Valentín Pacho, said that 90 percent of all unionized workers observed the 29 November strike despite government intimidation."[55]

It was notable that as the number of general strike walkouts increased during the Belaúnde administration, the number of purely economic strikes by individual unions fell dramatically. The research periodical *Análisis Laboral* indicated that, whereas in 1980 something near 600,000 workers had participated in these local walkouts, in 1984 the number had fallen to about 350,000. The number of such strikes was estimated at about 850 in 1981, but had fallen to less than 500 in 1984, whereas the number of man-hours lost as result of them had declined by 50 percent between 1982 and 1984.[56]

The independent unions led by elements to the left of the pro-Soviet Communist Party formed a National Union Coordinating Committee (CNS) early in the Belaúnde administration. That committee tended to work relatively closely with the CGTP, and as we have noted, a number of the independent unions actually joined the Confederación General de Trabajadores.[57] In 1983 the independent unions of the CNS and the CGTP established the National Unitary Struggle Command (Comando Nacional Unitario de Lucha), which was in charge of organizing the general strikes of March and September of that year.[58]

THE CTP AND OTHER LABOR CENTRALS DURING THE SECOND BELAÚNDE ADMINISTRATION

The Aprista-controlled Confederación de Trabajadores del Perú continued to be the second-largest central labor organization throughout the second Belaúnde administration. It was marginally more willing than the CGTP to reach an accommodation with the government, but in most cases supported the general walkouts that characterized the Belaúnde years. The CTP also suffered considerable internal dissension during this period.

After Belaúnde took office, Julio Cruzado, the secretary-general of the CTP, indicated a preliminary willingness to work with the president to bring together organized labor, employers, and the government. He also had the CTP join with factions of the CTRP and the CNT to establish the Democratic Union Front (Frente Sindical Democrático—FSD).[59] However, given the economic policies of the Belaúnde regime, the cooperation of both the CTP and the FSD with it was short-lived.

The CTP supported the January 1981 general strike.[60] It also participated in the March 1984 walkout. However, although first taking part in planning the September 1984 strike, it withdrew its backing "because of internal problems."[61] The internal problems of the CTP were in part a reflection of struggles within the Aprista Party. Haya de la Torre had died in 1979, and there followed dispute within the party. It was reflected within the CTP.

An opposition to CTP secretary-general Julio Cruzado developed under the leadership of Luis Negreiros Criado, son of the Aprista labor leader murdered during the Odría regime. It succeeded in getting Cruzado expelled (temporarily) from the Aprista Party, but in the CTP's 1983 congress, Cruzado was reelected secretary-general. In spite of these internal difficulties, the Aprista Party (and the CTP) began to make modest gains in union influence.[62]

The other two central labor organizations, the Central de Trabajadores de la Revolución Peruana and the Confederación Nacional de Trabajadores, remained very minor factions within the Peruvian labor movement. They generally reflected the militant mood of organized labor during the second Belaúnde regime.

SENDERO LUMINOSO AND ORGANIZED LABOR

A new and disturbing element in the Peruvian labor picture in the 1980s was the activity of the Partido Comunista del Perú Sendero Luminoso (Communist Party of Peru Shining Path), led by Abimael Guzmán. This party was a splinter of the pro-Chinese elements who had split from the traditional Communist Party in the early 1960s. It preached (and practiced) the doctrine that the only road to power and to an egalitarian society was terrorism and guerrilla war.

During the 1970s, Sendero Luminoso had established a base in the region of Ayacucho, where it recruited students, as well as some following among the slum dwellers in the city and among peasants in the vicinity. It spent several years in preparing for the armed uprising, the beginning of which coincided with the taking of power by President Belaúnde.

Sendero Luminoso preached the destruction of the existing society. Exactly what it proposed to put in place of the status quo remained vague. Some of the opponents felt that the nearest thing to a model that it had was the regime established by the Pol Pot–led Communists of Cambodia.[63]

In the beginning, the Luminoso was not so much concerned with taking control of already-existing unions as with establishing organizations of its own. Carlos Iván Degregori noted, "A fundamental characteristic of Sendero's activity is disregard for grass-roots organizations: peasant communities, labor unions, neighborhood associations. These are all replaced by generated organisms—that is, by the party that decides everything."[64]

The "generated organism" among the urban workers was the Workers and Laborers Movement (MOTC). Martin L. Smith said that the MOTC was "an ideologically pure 'generated organization' similar to those the party had forged in Ayacucho. Although MOTC did not control unions, it was tenacious in supporting strikes. It applied a ten-man team to aid strike committees, setting up a soup kitchen, supplying, supplying food and material, and mobilizing people.... It used the occasions to preach its message of the people's war just over the horizon."[65]

Sendero Luminoso played almost no role in the general strikes of the early 1980s. Carlos Iván Degregori noted that its attitude toward these general strikes "varied between absolute indifference and frontal opposition."

However, Sendero Luminoso decided to support the ninth general strike, that of January 1988. But Degregori noted that "Sendero's participation was limited to very minor actions. They burned tires on the Central Highway and disrupted the rally of the General Workers Confederation in the Plaza de Mayo, shooting slogans and setting off dynamite caps."

Regardless of the marginal importance of Sendero Luminoso's role in the January 1988 strike, they pictured it as of "historical" significance. Degregori said that "on the next day, the headline in *El Diario*, the semiofficial party mouthpiece, read 'historic Day for the Peruvian Proletariat.' Obviously it was not a historic day because of the magnitude of the strike, but because the party decided to back it, producing a kind of proletarian Pentecost that marked 'A new direction for the working class, nourished for the first time by a more elevated experience of struggle!' "[66]

ORGANIZED LABOR DURING THE APRISTA REGIME

More than 50 years after it was established, the Partido Aprista Peruano finally was allowed in 1985 to win an election and take office. Its successful candidate for president was Alan García, a relatively young man still in his forties, and the party also won a majority in both houses of Congress.

The 1985 election campaign was notable, according to William Bollinger, because "for the first time in Peruvian history, all major presidential candidates formally courted organize labor." This was facilitated by a National Workers Conference organized by the Confederación General de Trabajadores del Perú and independent unions at which all three candidates—the relatively conservative ex-mayor of Lima and dissident Christian Democrat Luis Bedoya Reyes; Alan García; and Alfonso Barrantes, nominee of the Izquierda Unida (United Left)—presented their positions.[67]

Upon taking office, President Alan García launched a socioeconomic program that was effective for a couple of years and that generated relative calm on the labor front. However, during the last years of his administration, the García program began to fail, and labor militancy resumed.

President García "declared a 'war on misery and crisis' and promised a government of 'social and economic democracy of participation' to attack the 'deep crisis of poverty, unproductiveness and dependence, and the negative criminal expression in response to that crisis as demonstrated by Sendero Luminoso.' " To that end, he established an "economic reactivization program." This provided wage increases, devaluation of the Peruvian currency, price and exchange controls, and reduction of interest rates. As a consequence, inflation fell from an average monthly rate of 10.9 percent, during January to August 1985, to 3.5 percent in September.

García's program also rescinded contracts with three foreign oil companies, banned remittance of profits to foreign firms, and adopted measures to protect national industry and agriculture. The president also announced that payments on the foreign debt would be limited to 10 percent of the country's foreign-exchange earnings.[68]

To try to combat the influence of Sendero Luminoso in rural areas, the García government also launched a program of large grants to the Indian communities, which the communities spent largely on local public works projects. President García also made extensive visits to rural communities, where he talked with local people in Quechua, being the first Peruvian president who was able to do this.[69]

During the first year of the Aprista government, the economic effects of its policies appeared to be positive. Sandra Woy-Hazleton commented, "The economic situation in Peru improved in 1986. Slowly but steadily, the inflation was cut to 44 percent from 158 percent, the growth was increased to 6.5 percent, and salaries rose 150 percent from August 1985 to October 1986, thus outpacing inflation.... García was able to increase public sector wages, which in turn stimulated demand for food and simple goods and helped to revive the domestic market."[70]

Immediately upon taking office, President Alan García was faced with a labor crisis involving government employees. The Intersectional Confederation of State Workers (CITE), an organization that had no legal recognition but had wide support among government employees, had launched a strike in March 1985, which involved workers in several ministries as well as in some state-owned enterprises. Then, in June it began a "50-day action," which also paralyzed the functioning of key government departments. The government announced a substantial wage increase for government employees, which ended the strike.[71]

One of the first steps of the Alan García government was to seek a "social pact" among the four central labor groups, employers' organizations, and the government. Although this idea was rejected by the CGTP, it was accepted by the other three central labor organizations.[72]

The Aprista government also met one of the major demands of all parts of the labor movement. This was the enactment of a "job stability law," providing that after only three months' employment, workers would receive "stability," which meant that they could only be dismissed for justifiable causes set forth in that law; this replaced a law passed under Belaúnde's second administration that had granted such stability only after three years of employment.

However, the union leaders, particularly those of the CGTP, claimed that the job-stability law was undermined by other moves taken by the García government. As part of its efforts to reduce unemployment and underemployment, the government allowed employers to hire workers

on a "temporary" basis, and the union leaders claimed that many of the
employers used this proviso to substitute these "temporary" workers for
those whose job stability was supposedly assured.[73]

Nevertheless, during the first months of the García regime, there was
clearly a new attitude on the part of the government toward organized
labor, and the period was marked by relative labor peace. Carmen Rosa
Balbi noted,

During the period from August to December 1985 there were few conflicts and
there was evident a capacity to deal with them, a different way of handling labor
conflicts, as was shown in the conflicts in middle-sized mining, generated in
the previous government, and in the later banking conflict, which received the
attention of all labor sectors. The strike was declared legal with the fulfillment of
the formal requirements, thus breaking the tradition of illegality with which the
Ministry labeled all work stoppages.[74]

As late as early 1987, Sandra Woy-Hazleton noted, "Labor unrest under
García has been less than it was under Belaúnde. The organized sectors
have held off national strikes in favor of negotiations on a union-by-union
basis." In February and May 1986, strikes by miners, doctors, teachers
and state employees were settled by negotiation. Also, Alan García met at
length with the president of SUTEP, the militant teachers' union, the first
time a president had done so.[75]

One of the declared objectives of the Aprista government was that
the workers' real income be increased. According to Carmen Rosa Balbi,
real wages in 1996 were only about half of what they had been 10 years
earlier.[76]

The objective of raising real wages was facilitated in the first part of the
García administration by a substantial economic recovery. This affected all
sectors of the economy except fishing and mining. Output in manufacturing rose by 12.2 percent and in construction by 17.1 percent. The general
gross domestic product increased by 8.5 percent from 1985 to 1986. At the
same time, unemployment decreased, falling by 10 percent in 1985 and by
5.4 percent in 1986.[77]

Real wages rose substantially from 1985 to 1986. In sectors covered by
collective bargaining, wages increased 36.6 percent for manual workers
and 23.5 percent for white-collar employees, whereas among workers
not subject to collective bargaining, real wages rose 6 percent for manual workers and 19.5 percent for white-collar workers. For government
employees, real wages increased by 10 percent, and for workers receiving the minimum wage (estimated at between 20 and 25 percent of the
workforce), the rise was 3 percent.[78]

However, by 1987 the economy had taken a turn for the worse. The
old problems of intensified inflation, balance of payments difficulties, and
limited growth in the economy reappeared. These developments tended
to undermine the popular support for the Aprista regime, which suffered

also from widespread rumors of corruption in the Alan García administration, the continuation and even intensification of the Sendero Luminoso guerrilla campaign, and growing factionalism within the Aprista Party.

All of these factors had an impact on the labor movement, particularly that part of it not under the leadership of the Apristas. This became evident when, on May 19, 1987, the CGTP called a one-day general strike, to support a long list of demands on the government, including demands that the government break relations with the International Monetary Fund, enact 15 changes in labor policy, and end all efforts to privatize segments of the state-owned parts of the economy.[79]

In a statement issued after the May 19 walkout, the CGTP listed a number of other complaints against the Aprista government. These included the violent and bloody repression of a riot of Sendero Luminoso prisoners in the La Frontón penitentiary and the government's handling of a police strike several days before the general walkout.[80]

Versions differed concerning the effectiveness of the May 19, 1987, strike. The Ministry of Labor claimed that only 35 percent of the workers in the Lima area participated.[81] However, the CGTP statement already referred to claimed that those who obeyed the strike call included not only virtually all industrial workers, but also government employees, fishermen, social security system doctors, peasants, and workers throughout the interior.[82]

In spite of this general strike, President Alan García did not break off relations with the CGTP. Subsequently, he had a meeting with the leaders of the organization.[83] Also, when in October 1987 Prime Minister Guillermo Larco Cox called for labor cooperation in trying to "reactivate" the economy, a vice president of the CGTP said that it was ready for such cooperation, "always and when this is real, when [the government] takes seriously the requests of the working class represented in the trade unions." He added, "I am sure that the government, the industrialists and workers in general will have no problem in having dialogue and reaching honest accords in clear defense of the interests of the country."[84]

In July 1987, the CGTP organized what it called the Second National Conference of Workers, the purpose of which was to draw up a National and Popular Project. The call to this meeting proclaimed, "We are the Alternative of Government and Power."[85]

In January 1988, the CGTP organized a second general strike against the Aprista government. It served to underscore the intensifying social and economic crisis facing the country. It was followed by an exchange of letters between the CGTP leadership and President García. However, these did not bring about any fundamental change in government policy or in the critical attitude of the CGTP leadership toward the García administration.[86]

Throughout the Aprista period in power, the Confederación General de Trabajadores del Perú remained the country's largest central labor organization. Estimates of its size varied considerably. Leaders of the CGTP claimed its membership at 1.2 million, whereas Sandra Woy-Hazleton credited it with only about 300,000 members.[87]

The CGTP continued to be controlled by the pro-Soviet Communist Party. However, there were also some members of its National Council who belonged to the Partido Comunista Patria Roja faction of the Maoists. There were also some Trotskyists among leaders of the CGTP affiliates, although no Trotskyist was a member of the National Council.[88]

The Confederación de Trabajadores del Perú (CTP) continued to be the second largest central labor group and continued to be controlled by the Apristas. It was credited by CTP leaders with having between 400,000 and 500,000 members, although Sandra Woy-Hazleton placed the number at 90,000.[89]

According to William Bollinger, "APRA continued to make modest gains in union influence, especially in the public sector." The internal quarrels in the organization, which had plagued it during the second Belaúnde period, were somewhat ameliorated, and CTP secretary-general Julio Cruzado was restored to membership in the Aprista Party.[90]

The other two central labor groups, the Central de Trabajadores de la Revolución Peruana (CTRP) and the Confederación Nacional de Trabajadores (CNT), continued to trail far behind the two major central labor bodies in membership and influence. The CNT suffered certain internal tensions between elements belonging to the Christian Democratic Party and those whose association was principally with the Latin American Confederation of Workers (CLAT). Sandra Woy-Hazleton credited each of these groups with about 15,000 members, and a leader of the CGTP said that by 1987 the CTRP was the smallest of all of the central labor groups.[91]

Throughout the period of the Aprista regime, Sendero Luminoso continued its violent attacks on the existing labor organizations. Between January and May 1989, it was reported to have assassinated more than 51 union leaders throughout the country, and in October it murdered Enrique Castillo, an important textile-union leader. It also gunned down the labor relations director of a factory on the Central Highway. It gained influence in three unions in that area.

Martin L. Smith noted,

Sendero's union strategy in the late 1980s relied on drawing out the work stoppage, sometimes up to one hundred days. It did not negotiate at the peek leverage point for the best settlement. It pushed strikes for the sake of the conflict. Although Sendero almost always had a minority position in the union leadership, it had an effective veto in strike assemblies because it could accuse more flexible leaders of selling out the union and the working class to management.

Smith added, "The reaction of the rank and file was fear and a feeling of being overrun by Sendero. Other parties' work had slackened in unions, radical groups supported the armed struggle rhetorically, which played into the hands of Sendero and confused the rank and file.... Sendero also used intimidation, with outsiders brought in to reinforce the SL line."[92]

However, Sendero Luminoso did not become a major factor within the Peruvian organized labor movement. In the Lima-Callao region, its influence seems to have been limited to one portion of the Central Highway area. At least for a time, it may have had a more serious impact on the labor movement in Ayacucho and some other areas where its terrorist and guerrilla activities were more widespread—most of the union leaders killed by Sendero were from the mine workers' union in the Ayacucho region.[93]

CONCLUSION

By the end of the 1980s, the Peruvian labor movement was undoubtedly considerably weaker than it had been a couple of decades earlier. Only about 11 percent of the "economically active" population belonged to the trade unions, and not all of these had collective agreements.[94] The continuing economic crisis, which Peru had suffered for nearly two decades, as well as the political uncertainties that had had plagued the country had both undermined the labor movement. Undoubtedly, the great growth of the "informal economy," stimulated by the economic crisis and by the mass migration of rural folk to Lima and other large cities, had also been detrimental to organized labor, which had little membership or influence in that secondary economy.

The labor movement also continued to be split politically, as it had been virtually since its inception. As had been true since at least the 1930s, the two principal political forces in organized labor were the Aprista Party and the pro-Soviet Communist Party, although starting in the 1970s, various Maoist and Trotskyist groups had also acquired considerable significance. The part of the labor movement fomented by the Velasco regime had all but disappeared 15 years later.

In the election of 1990, at the end of the Alan García administration, the victor was Alberto Fujimori, a Japanese-Peruvian, who until the election campaign was a little-known political figure. His victory was widely interpreted as a rebuke to all the country's principal parties, although his followers did not receive a majority in parliament. Fujimori ruled—with the support of the military and secret police—in an authoritarian manner. In economic terms, his policies followed extreme neoliberal policies.

The advent of Fujimori to power meant that the future of organized labor in Peru was very problematic. But that story goes beyond the confines of the present volume.

NOTES

1. *Times of the Americas*, Miami, February 18, 1976.

2. Denis Sulmont, *El movimiento obrero Peruano, 1890–1980, reseña histórica,* Tarrea, Lima, 1981, p. 117.

3. Interview with Juan Miranda Donayre, secretary-general of Sindicato Mixto Central de Generación y Similares de Electrolina, in New York City, February 24, 1979.

4. Nancy R. Johnson, *The Political, Economic and Labor Climate in Peru,* Industrial Research Unit, The Wharton School, University of Pennsylvania, Philadelphia, 1979, pp. 210–211.

5. Sulmont, op. cit., p. 121.

6. Johnson, op. cit., pp. 214–215.

7. *1979 Yearbook on International Communist Affairs,* Hoover Institution Press, Stanford, CA, 1979, p. 375.

8. Johnson, op. cit., p. 125.

9. Ibid., p. 124.

10. Judy White, "Peruvian Workers Say 'No' to Price Increases," *Intercontinental Press,* New York, August 1, 1977.

11. Johnson, op. cit., p. 125.

12. *1978 Yearbook on International Communist Affairs,* Hoover Institution Press, Stanford, CA, 1978, p. 406.

13. Fred Murphy, "Peruvian Union Militants Go On Hunger Strike," *International Press,* New York, February 27, 1978, pp. 330–331.

14. Fred Murphy, "Peru—2,500 Arrested During General Strike," *International Press,* New York, March 20, 1978, p. 337.

15. *1979 Yearbook on International Communist Affairs,* op. cit., pp. 378–379.

16. Fred Murphy, "Starvation Decrees Touch Off Workers Upsurge," *Intercontinental Press,* New York, June 5, 1978, pp. 660–661.

17. "30,000 in Lima Demand Amnesty for Fired Union Militants," *Intercontinental Press,* New York, July 31, 1978.

18. Fred Murphy, "Peru: Repression Forces Miners to Suspend Strike," *Intercontinental Press,* New York, October 2, 1978, p. 1081.

19. Fred Murphy, "The Fight for Class Struggle Policies in Peru's Unions," *Intercontinental Press,* New York, November 27, 1978, p. 1327; see also Sulmont, op. cit., pp. 123 and 149.

20. Miguel Fuentes, "New General Strike on Agenda in Peru," *Intercontinental Press,* New York, January 15, 1979, pp. 12–13.

21. Aníbal Vargas, "General Strike Shuts Down Peru," *Intercontinental Press,* New York, August 6, 1979, p. 776.

22. Foreign Broadcast Information Service, July 3, 1980.

23. Fred Murphy, op. cit., November 27, 1978, p. 1326.

24. Johnson, op. cit., p. 114.

25. Fred Murphy, op. cit., October 2, 1978, p. 1081.

26. Sulmont, op. cit., p. 119.

27. Fred Murphy, op. cit., October 3, 1978, p. 1081.

28. "International Campaign to Free Hernán Cuentas," *Intercontinental Press,* New York, March 15, 1976; and Miguel Fuentes, op. cit., pp. 12–13.

29. *El Nacional,* Caracas, July 9, 1978.

30. Daniel Premo in *Yearbook on International Communist Affairs*, Hoover Institution Press, Stanford, CA, 1979, p. 378; see also Sulmont, op. cit., p. 116.

31. Daniel Premo, op. cit., 1980, p. 387; see also Sulmont, op. cit., pp. 126 and 133.

32. Sulmont, op. cit., p. 118.

33. Fred Murphy, op. cit., November 27, 1978, p. 1327.

34. Ibid., pp. 1327–1328; see also William Bollinger in Gerald Michael Greenfield and Sheldon L. Maram (editors), *Latin American Labor Organizations*, Greenwood Press, Westport, CT, 1987, p. 661.

35. Bollinger, op. cit., p. 651.

36. Michael L. Smith in David Scott Palmer (editor), *Shining Path of Peru*, St. Martin's Press, New York, 1992, p. 130.

37. Sulmont, op. cit., p. 176.

38. Bollinger, op. cit., pp. 662–663.

39. Sandra Woy-Hazleton in *1984 Yearbook on International Communist Affairs*, Hoover Institution Press, Stanford, CA, 1984, p. 165.

40. Carmen Rosa Balbi, *Las Relaciones Estado-Sindicalismo en el Peru 1985–1987*, Fundación Friedrich Ebert, Lima, November 1988, pp. 12–13.

41. Woy-Hazleton, op. cit., 1985, p. 122.

42. Ibid., p. 122.

43. Bollinger, op. cit., p. 624.

44. Woy-Hazleton, op. cit., 1984, p. 168.

45. Bollinger, p. 624.

46. Ibid., p. 623.

47. Woy-Hazleton, op. cit., 1984, p. 165.

48. Foreign Broadcast Service, July 3, 1980.

49. David Scott Palmer in *1982 Yearbook on International Communist Affairs*, Hoover Institution Press, Stanford, CA, 1982, p. 137.

50. Bollinger, op. cit., p. 624.

51. Ibid., p. 623.

52. Palmer, op. cit., 1982, p. 137.

53. Palmer, op. cit., 1983, p. 123.

54. Woy-Hazleton, op. cit., 1984, pp. 165–166.

55. Woy-Hazleton, op. cit., 1985, p. 123.

56. *Análisis Laboral*, scholarly monthly dealing with "Socio-Economic and Legal Aspects," Lima, April 1985, p. 1.

57. Bollinger, op. cit., p. 623.

58. Ibid., p. 625.

59. Ibid., p. 640.

60. Ibid., p. 623.

61. Woy-Hazleton, op. cit., 1985, p. 123.

62. Bollinger, op. cit., p. 638.

63. Interview with Eugenio Valdivia Fulchi, leader of Aprista students at University of San Marcos, in Lima, October 6, 1987.

64. Carlos Iván Degregori, in David Scott Palmer (editor), *Shining Path of Peru*, St. Martin's Press, New York, 1922, p. 39.

65. Martin L. Smith in David Scott Palmer (editor), *Shining Path of Peru*, St. Martin's Press, New York, 1992, p. 131.

66. Degregori, op. cit., p. 40.

67. Bollinger, op. cit., p. 626.

68. Woy-Hazleton, op. cit., 1986, p. 134.

69. Interview with Aprista leader Nicanor Mujica, minister of the presidency of Peru, in New York City, June 10, 1986.

70. Woy-Hazleton, op. cit., 1987, p. 133.

71. Woy-Hazleton, op. cit., 1986, p. 134.

72. Ibid., pp. 134–135; and Bollinger, op. cit., p. 626.

73. Balbi, op. cit., p. 42.

74. Ibid., p. 16.

75. Woy-Hazleton, op. cit., 1987, p. 133.

76. Balbi, op. cit., p. 14.

77. Ibid., p. 20.

78. Ibid., p. 23.

79. Woy-Hazleton, op. cit., 1988, p. 114.

80. "Informe Sobre el Balance del Paro Nacional Unitario y Popular del 19 de Mayo de 1987, Aprobado por el Consejo Nacional de la CGTP" (mimeographed), pp. 4–5.

81. Woy-Hazleton, op. cit., 1988, p. 114.

82. "Informe Sobre el Balance," op. cit., p. 7.

83. Ibid., p. 1.

84. Hoy, Lima, October 7, 1987.

85. Confederación General de Trabajadores de Peru, CONADET 87: Somos Alternativa de Gobierno y de Poder, Lima, 1987, pp. 1 and 2.

86. Balbi, op. cit., pp. 61–63.

87. Woy-Hazleton, op. cit., 1986, p. 134; and interview with Hernán Espinoza Segovia, secretary of culture of Confederación General de Trabajadores del Perú, in Lima, October 6, 1987.

88. Interview with Hernán Espinoza Segovia, op. cit., October 6, 1987.

89. Woy-Hazleton, op. cit., 1986, p. 135.

90. Bollinger, op. cit., p. 626.

91. Woy-Hazleton, op. cit., 1986, p. 135; and interview with Hernán Espinoza Segovia, op. cit., October 6, 1987.

92. Martin L. Smith in Palmer, op. cit., pp. 138–140.

93. Ibid., p. 140.

94. Woy-Hazleton, op. cit., 1986, p. 135.

CHAPTER 5

Organized Labor in Ecuador before 1948

Before the coming of the Spaniards, Ecuador constituted the northern part of the Inca Empire, having been conquered by the Incas only about a generation before the Spanish Conquest. As elsewhere in the Spanish domains, the indigenous peoples, or Indians, of Ecuador and the land on which they lived were distributed among the conquistadores. Until well into the second half of the twentieth century, the descendants of the conquerors continued to control most of the land of the highlands of Ecuador and to keep the Indian peasants there in one or another form of servitude.

In some parts of the country, ancient Indian communities continued to function. But in most of the highlands, the land was in the hands of large landowners. Some of these had managers who cultivated their land—people who received only a nominal wage, if any, but were given a little piece of land on which they could cultivate their own crops, have their houses, and keep their own animals and who in return for this worked the landowners' land. Still other landlords did not want to be bothered with having anything to do with managing their holdings and so rented them out at a fixed rental sufficient to bring an income with which they were satisfied.[1]

However, the Republic of Ecuador, which was one of the countries "liberated" from Spanish control under the aegis of Simón Bolivar, was always sharply divided between the largely Indian highlands centering on the national capital, Quito, and the much more heterogeneous coastal area, focused on the port city of Guayaquil. Economic, social, and political rivalry between these two parts of the republic was a major element in the country's history in the nineteenth and twentieth centuries.

Until the middle of the twentieth century, Ecuador remained one of the more "backward" of the Latin American countries. The colonial landholding patterns of the highland regions remained largely intact. The economy of the country remained overwhelmingly agricultural, and the society remained resistant to change, particularly in the mountainous part of the nation.

However, as early as the last decade of the nineteenth century, winds of change began to blow through Ecuador. In 1895 the Liberal Party seized power under the leadership of General Eloy Alfaro. It attacked the entrenched power of the Roman Catholic Church and launched a program of economic liberalism, which encouraged the growth of exports and undertook some development of the infrastructure, most notably the construction of a railroad to link Quito with the port city of Guayaquil, which was opened in 1903.

During the first half of the twentieth century, Ecuador became more closely associated with world markets. Along the coast various more-or-less modern plantations were developed, producing cacao, sugar, and (after World War II) bananas, largely for export. Then, in the 1970s important petroleum reserves in the East began to be exploited, largely by foreign firms, bringing a rather short-lived economic euphoria.

Also, the first half of the twentieth century saw the modest beginning of industrialization, which gained much greater impetus during and after the Great Depression. Factories appeared, producing textiles, shoes, processed foods and beverages, construction materials, and other manufactured products. These tended to be centered particularly in Quito and Guayaquil, although some factories were also built in a few other provincial cities. At the same time, the infrastructure of the economy also expanded, with the building of roads and expansion of electricity, telephones, and other means of communication.

Until the middle of the twentieth century, the backwardness of the economy was reflected in the organized labor movement. As late as the 1940s, Ecuador was the only South American country in which a clear distinction had not appeared between mutual benefit societies and trade unions. Local and national central labor organizations continued until well after World II to have both kinds of workers' groups as affiliates. In some cases, mutual benefit societies evolved into trade unions; in others, new unions took on some aspects of mutual benefit societies.

As in other Latin American countries, the labor movement of Ecuador was thoroughly politicized. In the early years, anarchist influence was notable; subsequently, leadership of organized labor was largely in the hands of the Socialist and Communist parties. There also evolved a Catholic labor movement, at first largely confessional but subsequently evolving into a more purely trade union movement. Finally, starting in the 1960s, there developed a branch of organized labor that rejected the leadership of the Socialists and Communists, as well as all connection with the Roman Catholic Church and Catholic social philosophy.

EARLY BEGINNINGS

A few labor organizations began to appear in the years before the Liberal Revolution of 1895. Perhaps the oldest of these was the Sociedad de Artesanos "Amantes del Progreso" ("Lovers of Progress" Artisans Society), which Richard Lee Milk described as "the dean of Guayaquil's mutual aid societies." It was established by a group of carpenters led by Andrés Miranda as a mutual benefit society, providing "credit, burial and medical care," but also maintaining a library and organizing "an artisan-industrial fair every two years." It was outlawed by the government in 1874, but then was revived in 1879.[2]

At least two workers' groups were established in Quito before the Liberal Revolution. One was the Sociedad de Carpinteros (carpenters), which was likewise a mutual benefit group.[3] There was also a Sociedad de Mastros Sastres "Union y Progreso," established by the tailors of Quito and led by Manuel Chiriboga Alvear in 1886. Subsequently, it took a lead in organizing what amounted to the first central labor group in Quito, the Artistic and Industrial Society of Pichincha.[4]

However, the first important impetus came with the organization of the Ecuadorian artisans by the Liberal Revolution of 1895. General Eloy Alfaro, leader of the revolution and one of the major figures in the country's history, sought to stimulate organization among the craftsmen of both Guayaquil and Quito.

As Richard Lee Milk wrote, Alfaro and his followers

actively supported the establishment of workers' societies as a means to mobilize support for the Liberal regime and implement their social goals. The governmental support not only led to the formation of organizations associated with the Liberal Party, but also spurred the Church to establish worker groupings, the Catholic Workers' Centers and Circles. It was also during this period that the anarchists established their first groups, such as the association of street vendors.[5]

An organization known as the Hijos del Trabajo (Sons of Labor) was founded in Guayaquil late in 1895 under the direct patronage of General Eloy Alfaro. It was originally a tailors' society, although it soon expanded to include workers of other crafts. It was organized by a Cuban who had had some contact with labor organizations in Cuba and in Spain. He had anarchist tendencies, and the organization did too, in its early days. It became a species of central labor federation in Guayaquil. It was aided financially by the government in spite of its anarchist inclinations, and in the early days it had its own small press, a library, and schools for workers.

Most of the other early labor groups in Guayaquil were organized under its wings.[6]

Meanwhile, in Quito the Sociedad Artística e Industrial de Pichincha, originally established in 1892 as a mutual benefit group, also received aid from Eloy Alfaro. The government gave the sociedad a headquarters, which it occupied for half a century. The sociedad served the same purpose in Quito as the Hijos del Trabajo did in the port city, although it was not until 1917 that it formally transformed itself into the central labor body of the capital city.[7]

There was at least one other city, Cotopaxi, where the Revolution of 1895 resulted in the formation of a craft workers' organization of some importance, the Sociedad Artesanos de León, which was established in the year of the revolution.[8]

These mutual benefit societies played an exceedingly important part in the history of the labor movement for half a century or more. The majority of the more important mutual benefit societies of Guayaquil were founded in the early 1900s, such as the Sociedad de Carpinteros, the Sociedad de Zapateros (shoemakers), the Hijos de Volcán (Sons of Vulcan—a blacksmiths' and mechanics' group), and the Federación de Gráficos (printers). All of these were under anarchist influence, and there existed in addition to these mutualist groups some specifically anarchist political centers such as the "Adelante" (Forward) group and the "Luz y Trabajo" (Light and Labor) society, both of which dated from the 1890s.[9] In 1905 the Confederación Obrera del Guayas was established in Guayaquil, made up of most of the city's workers' groups.[10]

The first strike in Ecuador of which we have record was that launched by the Sociedad de Carpinteros of Guayaquil in 1896. Richard Lee Milk noted, "The society is also associated with militant, pro-labor activity up through the 1940s."[11]

The first strike in Quito took place among the tailors in June 1917. The movement was led by Miguel Angel Guzmán, and it occurred without any previous organization. Although the strikers had had no experience in carrying out work stoppages, they established a strike fund, raised from among sympathizers. They set up flying squads to enforce the strike and created a secret information service to keep the strike committee informed of the trend of events. This strike lasted 15 days and was lost because of government intervention. The Sociedad de Operarios Sastres, which was formed during the walkout, did not survive the strike, although it was revived several years later under the same name.

The printing-trades workers of Quito, who had been among the first to organize in the early 1900s, called what was probably the third walkout in the country's history, in 1919.[12] No information is available concerning the outcome of this strike.

Two labor centers were established in the World War I period: the Federación del Trabajo in Guayaquil, which claimed 3,000 members in

1919 and 2,000 in the next year; and the Confederación Obrera Ecuatoriana in Quito. The latter continued in existence throughout the decade of the 1920s and held three "National Labor Conferences," the last of which took place early in 1925.[13]

THE BAPTISM OF FIRE

Most later leaders of the Ecuadorian labor movement and political parties associated with it dated the effective birth of the modern labor movement from November 15, 1922. The situation leading up to the tragedy of that day began with a strike on the Quito-Guayaquil railroad, which was successful, gaining the workers a wage increase and release of all the strikers jailed during the walkout.[14] However, the railroaders' strike had stimulated a number of other labor conflicts that culminated in the first citywide general strike (in Guayaquil) in the country's history. The government, perturbed by the situation, sent in troops to "control" it.[15]

The clash between workers and troops, which resulted in the death of several hundred demonstrators, occurred when a crowd of railroaders went to the police detention barracks to greet their coworkers who were being released from jail after the settlement of their walkout—and were fired upon by the troops.[16]

Several people who were to play an important part in the country's history in later years were involved in the events of November 15, 1922. Dr. Carlos Arroyo del Rio, later president of Ecuador, was at this time secretary to President Tamayo, and workers' organizations placed on him much of the responsibility for the incident. Dr. José Vicente Trujillo, later foreign minister, but at that time a student, was one of the leaders of the strike movement. He is said to have remarked after the massacre, "Until now, we have dressed in sheep's clothing, but today we change to the tiger's skin."[17]

The year 1922 had seen the formation of several important labor organizations. One was the Confederación de Sindicatos Obreros (Confederation of Workers Union). It is not clear whether this was in fact a national organization or whether it was confined to Quito, but it was significant in being established by unions rather than mutual benefit groups. It was credited with having brought some effective pressure on the government to pass labor legislation.[18]

Meanwhile, the anarchists had launched the Federación Obrera Regional Ecuatoriana (FORE), with its base in Guayaquil. The Railroad Workers Federation, which called the 1922 strike on the Quito-Guayaquil Railroad, was affiliated to the FORE, which was the most militant labor group of that time.[19] It was outlawed by the government a few months after the November 15, 1922, incident.[20] Richard Lee Milk noted, "Overshadowed by the Guayas Labor Confederation and the Artistic and Industrial Society of Pichincha, FORE nevertheless was important in setting an example of militancy, commitment to labor goals, and independence from national leaders."[21]

A political development that was to have very wide repercussions on the labor movement began in 1924. A group of young men, including Ricardo Paredes, Jorge Carrera Andrade, and Luis F. Maldonado Estrada, launched a periodical called *La Antorcha* (*The Torch*). Its first issue appeared on December 31, 1924, with a lead editorial entitled "Toward a Socialist Party." The paper attacked the government of the day with great severity, and because of an article entitled "The Disciples of Mephistopheles," which attacked ex-president Leónidas Plaza Gutíerrez, the periodical was closed down for a month.

Early in 1925, the Grupo Socialista "La Antorcha" was formed around the periodical *La Antorcha*. Three months later, another Grupo Socialista "La Reforma" was formed in the provincial city of Tulcán.[22]

La Antorcha carried numerous articles by members of the group, but also reprinted pieces by Marcelino Domingo and Fernando de los Rios, Spanish Socialists, and by Gorki and others more sympathetic to the Bolsheviks. The general tone of the publication indicated the group to be Socialist, although with sympathy for the Soviet regime.

Meanwhile, labor organizations were having frequent difficulties with the government. In May 1925 an alleged Communist plot in Guayaquil was used as an excuse to close most of the labor groups there. However, there were not very many strikes in this period. The principal one of note was a walkout of the bakers of Riobamba.[23]

The principal labor organization from the point of view of militancy was still the Federación Obrera Regional Ecuatoriana, which was revived late in 1924. The Federación Ferroviaria was established at the same time. Among the leaders of the FORE was Luis Maldonado Estrada, its secretary-general.[24] The anarchist elements had strictly political groups also, such as Solidaridad, which from time to time published the periodical *La Protesta*.[25]

The Confederación Obrera Ecuatoriana continued to be active in Quito. It was affiliated with the Pan American Federation of Labor[26] and was "reformist." At one time, it claimed to have 35 groups affiliated with it, and it published the periodical *El Faro* (*The Beacon*).[27]

THE REVOLUTION OF 1925

The Revolution of July 19, 1925, was a Liberal revolt with Socialist overtones. The president of its first Revolutionary Government Committee was Luis Napoleón Dillon, a member of the La Antorcha group who later was one of the founding members of the Partido Socialista, although he never was very active in that party. Other members of the La Antorcha group were also active in the 1925 Revolution.[28]

At the time of the 1925 uprising, Ricardo Paredes wrote that it was "directed mainly against the financial plutocracy, which had dominated the country for thirty years, against the corrupt State officials, the army chiefs and the big landlords." He claimed that the revolutionary regime had "a certain Soviet structure," being based on military councils and delegates from labor groups, with the latter having only a consultative status, however. The manifestos of the military councils stressed the "proletarian demands" of the revolution, according to Paredes. The new government expropriated several privately owned monopolies and passed a law for the expropriation of certain rural estates. The "petty bourgeois" press was suppressed, the clergy were treated roughly, and for some time strikes were encouraged by the army.[29]

Alexander Lozovsky, then head of the Red International of Labor Unions, poked fun at the enthusiasm of Paredes and other Ecuadorians for the Revolution of 1925. He noted, "There is a certain confusion in Latin America between social revolution and socialist revolution."[30] Dr. Paredes and his friends undoubtedly strained somewhat to find parallels between this revolution and the Russian experience.

ESTABLISHMENT OF THE COMMUNIST PARTY

The periodical *La Antorcha* had died a couple months before the 1925 Revolution. However, members of the group that had gathered around the paper formed the country's first Socialist Party on May 16, 1926. Like the group out of which it grew, the Partido Socialista was Socialist in orientation, but was distinctly friendly to the Russian Revolution.[31]

The new Socialist Party was reported to have "been formed on the model of the Belgian Labor Party. It is based on individual membership and collective affiliation of trade union organizations under the leadership of the Communist Party."[32] The so-called "Communist Party" was actually a group known as "Amigos de Lenin." It was avowedly Bolshevik in inspiration and was headed by Enrique Terán, a musician. It published a periodical known as *La Fragua* (*The Forge*). Ricardo Paredes represented both the Amigos de Lenin and the Partido Socialista Ecuatoriano at the 1928 Congress of the Communist International.[33]

Ricardo Paredes went to Moscow early in 1927 and stayed there during most of that year and 1928, attending the tenth anniversary celebration of the Russian Bolshevik Revolution in November 1927 and the Sixth Congress of the Communist International in August 1928.[34] He also had credentials from the Railwaymen's Federation of Ecuador and the Labor Federation of Chimborazo, and in that capacity he signed a proclamation that led to the 1929 Montevideo Congress of Latin America and pro-Communist trade union groups and the formation of the Confederación Sindical Latino Americana (CSLA).[35]

The Socialist Party's first periodical was *La Vanguardia*, which appeared during the later months of 1927. It had a pro-Communist bias, and it published official proclamations of the Comintern, such as the report of

Lozovsky on the meeting of the Pan Pacific Labor Congress. In the January 1, 1928, issue there was a critical article about the life and theories of the anarchist leader Bakunin and a note on a visit to Ecuador by Pedro Albizu Campos, the Puerto Rican Nationalist leader,

A further step in the evolution of the Partido Socialista came with the return of Ricardo Paredes from Moscow and his assumption of the general secretaryship of the party. The November 15, 1928, issue of *La Vanguardia* carried the first notice of the adhesion of the Partido Socialista Ecuatoriano to the Communist International, noting that the request for admission to the International had been accepted by the 1928 Congress of the Comintern.[36] While accepting the PSE's affiliation as a "sympathetic" party, the Comintern instructed its executive committee to give the party the "necessary direction, advice and help" to make it a real Communist party, to have it change its name and form of organization and "make it more ideologically communist."[37]

Those members of the PSE who objected to its increasingly Communist orientation broke with the party in the late 1920s and early 1930s. Most left in 1928–1929, although some, such as Luis Maldonado Estrada, remained in the party until 1932.[38] The dissidents formed two groups: Transformación Social, centered in Quito, which in 1932 took the name Partido Socialista Ecuatoriano; and another called Renovación Social, with its principal force in Guayaquil, which in 1930 took the name Partido Social Cooperativista and ran a candidate in the 1932 presidential election. In 1933 these two parties joined forces under the name Partido Socialista Ecuatoriano, a name it continued to hold for several decades.[39]

César Endara was secretary-general of the first Partido Socialista at the end of 1927, and he continued in the party long after it became Communist. However, with his exception, all of the members of the 1927 Directing Committee of the Partido Socialista were either members of the Socialist Party or were independent 20 years later.[40]

POLITICAL CURRENTS IN THE LABOR MOVEMENT

After 1930 the labor movement was almost completely in the hands of the Communists and Socialists, with the exception of the small Catholic labor group that grew up in the latter half of the 1930s. There still remained some small anarcho-syndicalist influence in spite of the fact that the Communists in 1929 claimed that they had "completely collapsed."[41] In October 1933, the anarchists launched the Federación Obrera Regional Local in Guayaquil, which was their principal center of strength. This FORL was based principally on the Sindicato de Transporte Rodante Manual, made up of pushcart peddlers. However, the organization did not last long and thereafter the anarcho-syndicalists did not have any noticeable influence.[42]

The Socialist-Communist group from its foundation played a leading part in the labor movement. The founding of the Grupo Socialista "La Antorcha" was commented on favorably by the labor periodical *La Voz del Proletariado* (*The Voice of the Proletariat*) in Guayaquil.[43] The La Antorcha group worked within the Sociedad Artística e Industrial of Quito as early as 1925, and they continued to work within the unions and mutual benefit societies that made up the labor movement of the time. In 1929 the Communists were instrumental in organizing the Federación Obrera Agricola of Naranjito, near Guayaquil,[44] and the Asociación General of Maestros del Ecuador (General Association of Teachers of Ecuador).[45]

ORGANIZED LABOR IN THE 1930S

During the early 1930s there were several important strikes. In January 1930 there was a series of walkouts in the provincial city of Ambato, as well as a students' strike in the Juan Montalvo School in Quito. A few months later, there was a walkout of municipal workers in Guayaquil.[46]

The year 1931 was marked by "sporadic strikes, demonstrations and peasant revolts," which of course, the government blamed entirely on the Communists.[47] May Day 1934 provided a tug of war between the government of the day and the unions. The latter decreed a general strike for that day, whereupon the government declared the day a national holiday. The unions then countered by calling out workers from the railroads, telephones, and other services that normally never closed down even for a national holiday. There were some skirmishes between workers and police during the demonstrations in Guayaquil.[48]

A series of partial strikes in Guayaquil in 1935 was followed by a one-day general strike in the city, one of the first such moves that had occurred in Ecuador.[49]

Trade unions began to appear by the mid-1930s among the slowly growing class of industrial workers in Quito and a few other urban centers. The first walkout among this class of workers was in the Quito textile plant "La Internacional" in 1934. The Sociedad Artística e Industrial and other groups aided this strike with money and advice, but the walkout was lost because of government opposition. However, as a result, the Sindicato de Trabajadores de "La Internacional" was formed and continued in existence, and the movement for organization of the textile workers received a considerable impulse. Most of the important textile plants in the country were soon organized, and in 1936 a Federación Textil was formed, uniting the various textile workers' unions. However, this federation soon lapsed into inactivity and was only revived again after the revolution of 1944.[50]

Organizations were appearing among other groups of workers. Some time in the early 1930s, a union was organized among the trolley-car workers of Guayaquil. In 1936 the chauffeurs formed a Federación de Chóferes, which, like the Federación Textil, soon became inactive.[51]

An attempt was made in 1935 to launch a national labor federation, when the Union of Customs House Employees of Guayaquil invited all of the country's unions to a convention in the port city. Representatives attended from organizations of municipal workers, commercial employees, railroaders, shoemakers, barbers, carpenters, miners, agricultural workers, and small merchants. However, no central labor group actually emerged from these deliberations. The meeting's political complexion can be judged by the fact that honorary membership in the congress was conferred upon Ambrosio Lazo, a Communist leader then in jail for leading an uprising among the Indians.[52]

An attempt to form a united front among the various political elements active in the labor movement was made in Guayaquil in 1934. A Unity Committee against Speculation, including Socialists, Communists, and anarchists, was established on the initiative of the Communists. It tried with only limited success to force the municipal council to act against speculation. Soon, the anarchists withdrew from the committee, and a little while later, the Socialists also pulled out of it.[53]

Central labor groups were established both in Guayaquil and in Quito during 1937, the former being called the Confederación de Trabajadores de Guayas, the latter the Unión Sindical de Trabajadores de Pichincha. Socialists and Communists shared the leadership in both of these.[54]

In 1939 another attempt was made to launch a national labor confederation, with the establishment of the Confederación General de Trabajadores, with its headquarters in Guayaquil. However, it proved to be stillborn, as did the Centro Obrero Nacional, which was organized in 1940.[55]

Meanwhile, several new national craft and industrial federations were established. The petroleum workers organized a Federación de Petroleros in 1938. Most of the unions in this federation were along the coast, although the single most powerful unit of the organization, the union of the workers of the Shell Oil Company, was in the forest region of eastern Ecuador. Other federations formed during this period were the Federación de Peluqueros (barbers), established in 1937, and the Federación Ferroviaria, which was revived in 1938.[56]

THE CATHOLIC LABOR MOVEMENT

An important labor development of the late 1930s was the founding of a successful Catholic labor movement. As early as the first decades of the 1900s, Workers Circles were established under the aegis of the Church. Thereafter, there were sporadic attempts to organize an effective Catholic labor movement. Such an effort was the attempt of the Centro Católico de Obreros to bring together a number of isolated Catholic labor groups in 1926. This centro published a periodical, *La Defensa*, with vigorous propaganda against the riding Marxist influence among the Ecuadorian urban workers.[57]

Intensive efforts were begun in 1938 to establish specifically Catholic labor unions and mutual benefit societies. At that time the regime in power in Ecuador, headed by General Henríquez, was quite sympathetic to the Socialists and had seen to it that they received one-third of the members of the then-current constitutional assembly. The Socialists had held a national labor congress in the provincial city of Ambato, which had received a good deal of publicity and aroused considerable interest among the workers.[58]

This upsurge of Socialist influence and the Ambato conference, in particular, provoked the calling of the First Congress of Catholic Workers, presided over by Pedro Velasco Ibarra, a lawyer, brother of a former and future president of the republic, José María Velasco Ibarra, and a prominent Catholic layman. It adopted resolutions in favor of the formation of "pure trade unions, which will be made up wholly of workers of the same trade." These unions, said the resolutions, were not to conduct "systematic warfare with the employers," but rather were meant to be "instruments employed by the workers for the defense of their rights and interests against anyone who ignores or interferes with them"; the resolutions urged "free discussion with the employers' unions, which are necessary as workers' organizations."

The congress suggested that those Catholic trade unions bear the title "sindicato Católico" and that each of them have an ecclesiastical adviser "to safeguard the Dogma and interpret correctly Catholic social doctrine." Although one resolution stated that "Catholic unions are not political organisms," it noted, "As a complement to trade union action we recognize the necessity of political action to defend the general interests of the working-class families."[59]

The congress went on record as basing its doctrine on the encyclical "Rerum Novarum" of Pope Leo XIII.[60] Some confusion is indicated in statements such as that of the congress president Pedro Francisco Velasco Ibarra, who referred to the French Socialist Leon Blum as "the leader of French Communism."[61] The congress drew up various resolutions in favor of agrarian reform and changes in the country's social security and labor legislation.

SIZE OF LABOR MOVEMENT IN THE EARLY 1940s

Both the Catholic and secular labor movements consisted largely of government-recognized organizations. In 1942 the Ministry of Social Welfare and Labor published a list of the labor organizations that had been recognized by the government. There were 451 groups listed, with a total of 22,779 members. The province of Guayas, in which Guayaquil is located, had 122 organizations, and the province of Pichincha, which includes Quito, had 97 groups in the list. However, Pichincha had 6,163 organized workers, against only 2,951 in Guayas. No other province had more than 37 organizations, or 2,111 workers in recognized groups.

These figures were not complete. Many of the organizations listed did not report any membership figures. Many of the groups listed no doubt had passed out of existence before the report was issued, but were not removed from the list of the Dirección General del Trabajo.

There were nine labor groups that reported more than 400 members, five of which were in Pichincha, two in Guayas, and one each in Inbabura and Asuay. The biggest reporting member of all was the Sindicato Único de Chóferes de Pinchincha, which had a reported membership of 981. The largest industrial union was the Sindicato Textil "La Industrial" of Quito with 737 members. The Sindicato Textil "La Internacional," also in Quito, reported 650. Only eight-tenths of 1 percent of the Ecuadorian population was then reported as belonging to any recognized labor group.[62]

THE LABOR MOVEMENT AND WORLD WAR II

During World War II, the urban laboring population of Ecuador was subjected to considerable propaganda from both groups of belligerents. Naturally, Allied efforts were channeled through the existing labor groups, which, at least after June 22, 1941, were pro-Allied. The Germans, on the other hand, were forced to start their own publications and organizations.

The principal pro-Nazi periodical, which was intended to circulate among the workers, was *Voz Obrera* (*Labor Voice*). This magazine regularly carried a page of "Overseas News" from the official Nazi Transocean News Agency, which was described as "the most truthful agency in the World." Typical of the propaganda of *Voz Obrera* was an article on "'Nazi Penetration' in Ecuador," which first ridiculed the idea that there was such penetration and then went on to say,

Be that as it may, it is certain that world masonry, having been defeated in Europe, thanks to the power of the valorous and united German people, has taken refuge in the New Continent, where it has talked of its love for "democracy," "liberty," "the people." In fact, though Masonic Judaism has drunk the blood of the people, has enslaved the nation and has degraded the name of democracy by imposing in its name tyranny and despotism, always using gold to fatten its victims.[63]

By July 1941, *Voz Obrera* was carrying proudly on its front page the statement, "This review is listed on the Black List of the Masonic-capitalist English Government."[64]

Aside from straight pro-German propaganda and attacks on Britain and the United States, the magazine carried news on labor. In one issue it carried a complimentary article on the Centro Católico Obrero of Quito and had a front-page appreciation of a priest, Manuel Humberto Mejía Ayala, who had been active in the Catholic workers' movement and had just died.[65] Emphasis was always on Catholic labor and on Catholicism in general. The publication's choicest attacks were reserved for the Masons, and one article told how masonry had been "swept from Europe" by Salazar, Franco, Hitler, and Mussolini.[66] The periodical had a page of "social news" on the comings and going of workers.

During the first part of the war, the Nazi propagandists were joined by Communist ones. In 1940 there appeared a newspaper called *El Trabajador*, which, although it gave no indication as to who published it, followed the international Communist line of the time. It proclaimed itself to be "in the service of the exploited, the workers, peasants, soldiers." It had a feature on "The Workers of Ecuador and the European Imperialist War," which urged that the Ecuadorian workers endorse a policy of the strictest neutrality and referred to "the 'democracies'—among which is the United States of North America, the barbarians of the North."[67]

The third issue of this newspaper carried a long story on "The Experience of France," justifying the antiwar position of the French Communist Party and denouncing the Socialists for their support of the war, saying that "once more History confirms the fact that the Socialist International is a police agent of the bourgeoisie in the working class." The last article on the first page of this same issue was headlined "All the workers of the world applaud the socialist peace policy of the Soviet Union."[68]

With the entry of Russia into the war, the tone of the Communists and their friends immediately changed. In the later part of 1942, Vincent Lombardo Toledano, president of the Confederación de Trabajadores de América Latina, visited Ecuador and was welcomed by the government, the press, and the unions, including those controlled by the Communists. He addressed a public meeting in company with President Arroyo del Rio, and 20,000 people heard him urge all-out support of the Allied war effort.[69]

TOWARD A NATIONAL LABOR CONFEDERATION

The visit of Lombardo Toledano to Ecuador gave a considerable impulse to the formation of a national central labor organization. While he was there, a conference was held in Guayaquil, at which it was decided to call a congress to launch a national labor confederation.[70] This congress was scheduled for March 1943, and all labor groups in the country were invited to send delegates. However, Quito Archbishop Carlos María de la Torre urged that the Catholics not attend the meetings, saying that it was a "Communist attack on Christian civilization" and that the workers were being "tricked into backing atheism and communism. As a result of this denunciation, the Confederación Ecuatoriana de Obreros Católicos decided not to send delegates to the meeting and asked that the government prevent its taking place.[71]

On the other hand, the Sociedad Artística e Industrial de Pichincha, the Federación de Trabajadores de Guayas, and the Longshoremen's

Association of Guayaquil (which was of anarcho-syndicalist orientation) all supported the call to the congress. They urged that the new central labor body be nonpolitical and without international affiliation. Other commentators suggested that teachers, government employees, and farm workers be excluded from the congress.

The meeting finally convened in Quito, with 200 delegates present. One hundred sixty of these voted to affiliate with the CTAL; to have teachers, government employees, and farm workers as members of the new confederation; to condemn the Nazis; and to send fraternal greetings to workers' organizations in Mexico, the United States, Great Britain, and the USSR. A minority of 20 delegates appealed to the government to intervene against the meeting.[72]

The government did intervene and arrested most of the left-wing leaders of the congress. However, this occurred after the election of a Comité Nacional de Trabajadores del Ecuador, made up mainly of Socialists and Communists.[73] After the breaking up of the congress by police and soldiers, the pro-government delegates organized a Confederación de Trabajadores del Ecuador, with the blessings of the Arroyo del Rio government.[74]

With the exit of most of the left-wing leaders from jail in August 1943, the first meeting of the Comité Nacional de Trabajadores was held. It considered two questions. First, it began to lay plans for the overthrow of President Carlos Arroyo del Rio.[75] In the second place, it discussed its principal task of bringing together the workers' organizations in a national confederation. That it had some prospects of success in this endeavor was indicated by the fact that by October 1944 it was reporting some 5,000 members in 150 affiliates and the fact that it was undertaking organizing campaigns among urban transport, maritime, railway, and mine workers.[76] Early in 1944 it was reported that there was a "truce" in effect between the trade unions and President Arroyo del Rio's government.[77]

However, during the second meeting of the Comité Nacional de Trabajadores, the final touches were put on plans for overthrow of the president. There was one serious stumbling block in the way of these plans: the position that U.S. troops, who were in the country under wartime accords, would take in case there was an uprising against the government. One member of the Revolutionary Committee was commissioned to contact the U.S. authorities, and after a few days, the committee received word that the U.S. troops would stay in their barracks and take no part on one side or the other. It was only after this word had been received that the coup against Arroyo del Rio was carried out.[78]

THE MAY 1944 REVOLUTION

The overthrow of President Arroyo del Rio occurred on May 29, 1944, and was engineered by the Alianza Democrática, which consisted of the Liberal Independent, Conservative, Communist, Socialist, and Socialist

Revolutionary Vanguard parties. A temporary Revolutionary Committee was established, which included General Luis Larrea Alba of the Socialist Revolutionary Vanguard, Julio Teodoro Salme of the Liberal Independent Party, Mariano Suárez Veintinilla of the Conservatives, Gustavo Becerra of the Communist Party, and Manuel Agustín Aguirre, a Socialist.[79] The actual uprising began in Guayaquil when the military began to distribute arms to the workers. At the same time, the Comité Nacional de Trabajadores called a general strike in all cities held by Arroyo.[80]

With the victory of the insurrection, the insurgents invited R. José María Velasco Ibarra, the ex-president who had been deposed about a decade before, to return from exile and be chief executive once again. In his earlier term of office, he had governed as a Conservative, but during his exile he had come into close contact with the Socialists and Communists in Argentina and Chile and had developed a reputation as a "Man of the Left." At the same time, because of his past, he was satisfactory to the Conservatives.

Soon after coming back to office, President Velasco Ibarra called elections for a constitutional assembly. The election was won by a Democratic Alliance, consisting principally of the leftist parties, which won 60 seats against 25 for the right-wing Electoral Front. The Comité Nacional de Trabajadores supported the Democratic Alliance.[81]

ESTABLISHMENT OF THE CONFEDERACIÓN DE TRABAJADORES DEL ECUADOR

The Comité de Trabajadores del Ecuador returned to the task for which it had originally been established—to organize a national central labor organization—after the overthrow of Arroyo del Rio. It called a National Congress of Workers, which convened on July 4, 1944. Out of this meeting came the Confederación de Trabajadores del Ecuador (CTE). The original group with this name, which had been patronized by the Arroyo del Rio government, was not heard from after the fall of that regime.

The founding congress of the CTE was held in Quito, and there were 1,030 delegates present.[82] The new confederation's officers were chiefly Socialists and Communists, with Communist Pedro Saad, who had been president of the Comité Nacional de Trabajadores, as president, and Dr. Juan Isaac Lovato, one of the principal Socialist leaders, as vice president.[83]

The Confederación de Trabajadores del Ecuador immediately set about establishing new labor organizations in various parts of the country. This work was done on two levels. In the first place, it attempted to organize a provincial labor federation in each province. During the quarter of a century before establishment of the CTE, at least one attempt had been made to set up provincial labor federations in Guayaquil, Pichincha, Imbabura, and Carchi (a bi-provincial organization established in 1940),

El Oro (1926), Manabi (1920, 1929, and 1933), Azuay (1939), Chimborazo (1917), and Tungurahua (1929).[84] In the three years following establishment of the CTE, provincial groups were set up in Carchi, Imbabura, Pinchincha, Cotopaxi, Tungurahua, Chimborazo, Bolivar, Azuay, Loja, El Oro, Esmeraldas, Manabí, Guayas, and Los Rios.[85]

Without doubt the most important regional federations were those in Guayas and Pichincha (Guayaquil and Quito). The Guayaquil organization included both mutual benefit societies and trade unions. Among the former were organizations of shoemakers, carpenters, hat makers, cocoa handlers, and stevedores. Some other mutual benefit groups such as the Hijos de Volcán, the meat sellers, and the Hijos del Trabajo did not affiliate to the Federación del Trabajo de Guayas because of the strong Communist influence in that organization.

In addition to those mutual benefit groups, there were *sindicatos*, that is, trade unions, in a variety of trade and industries. These included railroaders, trolley-car men, maritime workers, shipbuilders, chauffeurs, street cleaners, municipal public-works laborers, stevedores, and a half-dozen agricultural workers' unions from the environs of Guayaquil. In all, there were about forty *sindicatos* affiliated to the Federación Provincial de Trabajadores de Guayas by the middle of 1947.[86]

The Federación de Trabajadores de Pichincha (FTP) was organized on October 9, 1944. It was also composed of both mutual benefit societies and trade unions.[87] It was organized with some 80 affiliated groups, with about 10,000 members. However, 15 to 20 of these organizations were Indian groups, and when an Indian Federation was established early in 1947, these withdrew from the Pichincha federation.

A coup by President Velasco Ibarra against his left-wing allies on March 30, 1946, undermined the FTP, and immediately after that coup there were only 35 organizations affiliated with it. However, by the middle of 1947, the FTP had 65 active affiliates. There were 15 other nominal affiliates that did not function. Eight member groups were mutual benefit societies, 35 were *sindicatos,* and the rest were *comités de empresas*—special types of labor organizations established under the Ecuador Labor Code for the purpose of profit sharing, which were not supposed to function as trade unions. In fact, however, many did so function. In some instances there were both a *comité de empresa* and a *sindicato* in the same plant.

The Federación de Trabajadores de Pichincha tried to emphasize the trade unions rather than mutual benefit societies and looked forward to the day when the two groups would be organized in different central bodies.[88] It was very busy in the mid-1940s organizing trade unions, and by 1947 most of the industrial plants in Quito were unionized. These included the textile plants La Industrial, La Victoria, and La Compana and the sparkling water plants La Orangini and La Guitig. Also among the organized plants were spaghetti products factories, candy kitchens, and soap factories, as well as the chemical plant La Life.[89]

Aside from its organizing activities, the Federación de Trabajadores de Pichincha had a considerable cultural program. In 1945 it first organized a popular university, the expenses of which were originally covered by a 7,000 sucre appropriation by the government and 7,000 sucres appropriated by the National University. This financial aid was withdrawn after March 30, 1946, when President Velasco Ibarra broke with the left-wing and labor groups. The popular university started with a single course in constitutional law and expanded to include history, geography, and labor law (the three most popular courses) and hygiene, mathematics, and elementary physics and chemistry. It was established with an administrative committee of nine, seven of whom were university students—who served as the university's faculty—and two of whom were appointed by the FTP. The classes of the popular university were taught in the headquarters of the various unions. It was estimated in the middle of 1947 that there were between two and three thousand workers in the Popular University.[90]

NATIONAL INDUSTRIAL AND CRAFT FEDERATIONS

In addition to organizations on a regional basis, the Confederación de Trabajadores del Ecuador established labor federations on an industrial and craft basis. Soon after establishment of the CTE, several federations that had been formed earlier but had lapsed into inactivity were established, including the Federación de Chóferes, the Federación de Petroleros, the Federación Textil, and the Federación Ferroviaria.[91] New ones were also established, including the Printing Trades Workers Federation, the Educators, the Accountants, the Shoemakers, and the White-Collar Workers Federation.[92]

All of these were affiliated with the Confederación de Trabajadores del Ecuador, although by the end of the second Velasco Ibarra administration in 1947, the Railroad Workers Federation's membership in the CTE appeared to be largely nominal, and it was reported that the federación was closely allied with the government and was working with Velasco Ibarra against the CTE.[93]

The establishment of a White-Collar Workers Federation was a new development. The unionization of this type of worker was slow in getting started, although during World War II, a number of such unions appeared. In 1940 and 1941 there was such a group formed among the clerks in the La Industrial textile factory, and there was a pharmacy employees' union, a movie employees' union, and a union of employees of the Social Insurance Fund. All of these Quito organizations were brought together in January 1941 into a Sociedad de Empleados de Comercio, which soon changed its name to Unión General de Empleados de Comercio and began to publish a periodical, *La Justicia*.[94] This publication continued to appear with fair regularity, presenting the white-collar workers' case against inflation and favoring union organization.[95]

An Ecuadorian Miners' Congress was held in Guayaquil in May 1945, with representatives present from 17 branches of mining labor. The congress adopted resolutions in favor of minimum wages and family allowances and a number of other demands.[96] Apparently no federation was actually formed at this time.

PARTY POLITICS WITHIN THE CTE

During its first two years, the Confederación de Trabajadores del Ecuador was controlled by the Communists, and Pedro Saad was its secretary-general. What use the Communists made of their control of the labor movement is demonstrated by an article in the organ of the Federación de Trabajadores de Pichincha, backing the Russian position at the London Foreign Ministers' Conference in the latter part of 1945. The article said that the United States' attitude in favor of participation in the proposed Peace Conference of all those countries that had declared war on the Axis was only a guise to get a lot of votes for positions favored by the United States and against those favored by the Soviet Union. The votes were to come, said the article, "from virtually colonial nations subordinated to the influence of the northern country." It said that if the United States were to win this point, it would mean "the defeat of the true interests of world democracy."[97]

There was rivalry within the confederación between the Communists and the Socialists. This reached a high point in the Second Congress of the CTE, which met in November 1946. At that time, the Socialists took control of the confederación away from the Communists, putting seven Socialists on the CTE Executive Committee, against four Communists.[98]

However, the change in party control did not mean any change in the fundamental policies of the CTE, given that the Socialist Party of Ecuador was ideologically not in great conflict with the Communists, which was due in part to the joint origin of the two groups and personal friendships between their leaders. It was due in part, also, to the lack of clarity in the ideological position of the Ecuadorian Socialists. Like some other Socialist groups, the Ecuadorian party became very discontented with the supposed ineffectiveness of democratic process and was prone to use Marxist-Leninist phraseology.

During the early 1940s, there grew up a very strong anti-Communist group within the Socialist Party, which for a short time in 1947 controlled the party under the leadership of Luis Maldonado Tamayo as secretarygeneral.[99] However, when Maldonado Tamayo resigned as secretary-general during the revolution of August 1947, the group that was most friendly to the Communists came back into power within the party.[100]

LABOR AND THE SECOND VELASCO IBARRA PERIOD

The Confederación de Trabajadores del Ecuador of course benefited considerably from the friendly attitude that the government of Velasco

Ibarra took toward it right after the revolution of 1944. However, in less than two years, the president had fallen out with the leftists and the CTE. In March 1946, President Velasco Ibarra carried out a coup d'état against the left, ousting the Socialist and Liberal members of his government and arresting many leftist political and trade union leaders. From March 30, 1946, until the meeting of the next Constituent Assembly in August, there was a reign of terror in Ecuador, and many of the imprisoned leaders were ill-treated. After the opening of the new Constituent Assembly, which was completely controlled by the Conservative Party because all other parties refused to participate in the elections, the Velasco Ibarra regime again was modified. Exiles returned and opposition leaders were released from jail.[101]

Velasco Ibarra was finally ousted in August 1947 after a quarrel with his minister of war. The coup—made by the General Staff under Colonel Mancheno and a civilian group led by Luis Maldonado Tamayo—was intended to launch a thorough-going social revolution. However, a counterrevolution led by the Conservatives, and presumably backed by the Catholic Church, ousted Mancheno within two weeks.[102] In subsequent elections in 1948, independent Liberal Galo Plaza was elected president.

During the second Velasco Ibarra regime, the Catholic labor movement made some headway. The Second National Congress of Ecuadorian Catholic Workers was held in July 1944. Pedro Velasco Ibarra was again president of the congress, and his brother, José María Velasco Ibarra, president of the Republic, addressed the opening session.[103] The congress sent greetings and good wishes to the British, French, and U.S. embassies, which were duly acknowledged. Correspondence was also exchanged with the Comité Nacional de Trabajadores Ecuatorianos, which was making final preparations for the congress that launched the Confederación de Trabajadores del Ecuador, and each group wished the other well in its endeavors.[104]

The Second Catholic Workers Congress adopted resolutions concerning education—with emphasis on the necessity and desirability of Catholic education, as well as stress on the necessity for education of the blacks—and urged passage of a trade union law that the Catholic workers' groups had backed but the secular trade unionists had opposed. It also urged establishment of a family allowance system, called for reform of the Labor Code to ban all night work for women of whatever age, and proposed a number of other reforms. It asked that appropriations that Congress regularly made for organizations with legal personality, which included the unions, be divided equally between the Catholic and secular unions. There were numerous other resolutions.[105]

A Third Catholic Workers Congress was held in 1946, and at that session the Confederación Nacional de Trabajadores Católicos was established, as an organization superior to the existing Confederación Ecuatoriana de Obreros Católicos (CEDOC). The CEDOC was to include only factory workers and craftsmen, whereas other groups were to be organized for white-collar workers and agricultural workers. All three would be part of the Confederación Nacional de Trabajadores Católicos.

A year later, the confederations of white-collar employees and agrarian workers had not been established. In fact, there were few if any agricultural workers in the Catholic labor movement, although there were three white-collar employees' groups—in Quito, Cuenca, and Guayaquil. The Confederación Nacional de Trabajadores Católicos was stillborn, and CEDOC continued to be the country's Catholic labor group.

The best-organized Catholic labor movement in the country was in Cuenca, where there were 18 Catholic unions under energetic leadership. In Quito there were 20 to 25 Catholic labor groups in July 1947, but they were not as united or as well run as the Cuenca movement.

According to Pedro Velasco Ibarra, there were 18,000 to 20,000 workers in the Catholic labor movement in mid-1947. This was about half the number in the secular labor movement, according to Velasco Ibarra.[106]

THE SECULAR LABOR MOVEMENT IN THE LATE 1940s

As in most other Latin American countries, it was difficult to estimate how strong the labor movement was numerically in Ecuador. The World Federation of Trade Unions credited the Confederación de Trabajadores del Ecuador with 100,000 members in 1947. However, Pedro Saad, ex-secretary-general of the CTE, reported in July 1947 that there were only 80,000 in the organization. At the same time, he estimated that there were only about 10,000 workers in the Catholic trade unions.[107]

Miguel Angel Guzmán, vice president of the CTE, estimated at about the same time that there were about 110,000 workers listed as members of the CTE, but only about 50,000–60,000 were "effective" members.[108] It can be presumed that the union leaders did not understate the strength of their own organization.

Whatever the exact size of the labor movement in Ecuador, by the late 1940s, most urban workers who were eligible for membership in the labor movement were in some kind of organization. However, the Ecuadorian labor movement remained backward, in the sense that it lacked a clear separation between trade unions and other types of labor groups, although there was a growing tendency, particularly in the secular unions, to differentiate between mutual benefit societies and trade unions.

The Confederación de Trabajadores del Ecuador continued to be affiliated with the Communist-controlled Confederación de Trabajadores de América Latina (CTAL), in spite of the fact that some Socialist leaders of the CTE had expressed sympathy for the aims and organizations of the anti-Communist International Confederation of Free Trade Unions, which was established in 1949.[109] The CTE showed its loyalty to the CTAL and its national affiliates when it protested to President González Videla against his campaign against the Communist faction of the Confederation of Workers of Chile.[110]

The Inter-American Confederation of Workers (CIT) and its successor, the Organización Regional Interamericana de Trabajadores (ORIT), which were organized in competition with the CTAL, had as their Ecuadorian affiliate the Confederación Obrera de Guayas, the oldest central labor group in Guayaquil. The Confederación Obrera de Guayas was composed mainly of mutual benefit groups, although a few industrial trade unions were also part of it.[111]

There were several strikes of importance in the late 1940s, notably petroleum and textile workers' walkouts in 1948, which won wide support throughout the country's labor movement. The oil workers' strike won international support, and the Oil Workers International Union of the United States sent $1,000 to aid the walkout,[112] with the Mexican petroleum workers' union also sending several hundred dollars.[113]

LEGAL STRUCTURE OF ECUADORIAN UNIONISM

Although by the late 1940s most Ecuadorian labor organizations were still mutual benefit societies, the legal framework within which trade unions were supposed to function was in place. It provided that in order to acquire legal recognition, a union had to submit to the Ministry of Labor a copy of its statutes, although the law did not specify what exactly should be in those documents. Once the statutes were approved by the ministry, the union was given legal recognition, *personaria jurídica*.

The law provided that the principal functions of a union were to defend its members vis-à-vis the employer and to organize special projects such as cooperatives. However, the law also provided for another kind of organization, the "enterprise committee" (*comité de empresa*) to negotiate and sign collective agreements with the employer. Where an enterprise committee did not exist, a *sindicato* (trade union) could serve that function.

The unions were forbidden by law to engage in politics. Of course, this was a provision honored more in the breach than in the execution, although political participation was one of the few reasons for which a union could be deprived of legal recognition.

When a union or *comité de empresa* presented a series of demands to an employer, the law provided that there should first be direct negotiations between the two parties, and only if these failed did an inspector of labor enter the situation, to try to bring about conciliation. Failing such mediation, a Special Tribunal, consisting of representatives of both sides and presided over by a labor inspector, made further efforts to reach an agreement. If that failed, a union was legally free to strike, and an employer to declare a lockout. Meanwhile, the Special Tribunal was to continue its efforts to reach a conclusion as to how the matter should be settled. Either party could then appeal to the general director of labor, who would give a decision intended to be final. Within three days of that decision, a continuing strike or lockout was to be declared illegal.

In the case of individual workers' grievances, direct negotiation was the first recourse under the law. If it failed, the matter passed to the Comisario del Trabajo, a kind of labor court. That body's decision could be appealed to a regular Court of Appeals, and if necessary to the Supreme Court.

Unlike the labor codes of several Latin American countries, the Ecuadorian legislation did not provide for interference by the Labor Ministry in either the finances or the elections of unions.[114]

NOTES

1. Interview with J. Osvaldo Espinosa, secretary of Cámara de Agricultura de la Primera Zona, in Quito, September 7, 1956.

2. Richard Lee Milk in Gerald Michael Greenfield and Sheldon L. Maram (editors), *Latin American Labor Organizations*, Greenwood Press, Westport, CT, 1987, p. 301.

3. Interview with Miguel Angel Guzmán, vice president of Confederación de Trabajadores del Ecuador, in Quito, July 4, 1947.

4. Milk, op. cit., p. 304.

5. Ibid., p. 291; see also interview with Pedro Velasco Ibarra, president of Confederación Ecuatoriana de Obreros Católicos, in Quito, July 7, 1947.

6. Interview with Humberto Gaybort Rada, member of Executive Committee of Federación Provincial de Trabajadores del Guayas, secretary-general of Partido Socialista of Guayaquil, in Guayaquil, July 1, 1947; see also Milk, op. cit., p. 304.

7. Interview with Miguel Angel Guzmán, op. cit., July 4, 1947; see also Milk, op. cit., p. 296.

8. Interview with Miguel Angel Guzmán, op. cit., July 4, 1947.

9. Interview with Humberto Gaybort Rada, op. cit., July 1, 1947.

10. Ibid.

11. Milk, op. cit., p. 304.

12. All of the foregoing from interview with Miguel Angel Guzmán, op. cit., July 4, 1947.

13. *American Labor Year Book 1923–24*, Rand School Press, New York, 1924, p. 360; and *La Antorcha*, Quito, February 21, 1925.

14. *American Labor Year Book, 1923–24*, op. cit., p. 360.

15. Milk, op. cit., pp. 291–292.

16. *American Labor Year Book 1923–24*, op. cit., p. 360.

17. Interview with Humberto Gaybort Rada, op. cit., p. 360.

18. Moisés Poblete Troncoso, *El Movimiento Obrero Latinoamericano*, Fondo de Cultura Económica, México, D.F., 1946, p. 204.

19. Interview with Ricardo Paredes, founder and secretary-general of Partido Comunista del Ecuador, in Quito, July 5, 1947.

20. Stephen Naft, "Labor Organizations in Latin America," unpublished manuscript.

21. Milk, op. cit., p. 299.

22. Interview with Ricardo Paredes, op. cit., July 6, 1947.

23. *La Antorcha*, Quito, May 9, 1923.

24. *La Antorcha*, Quito, December 20, 1924.

25. *La Correspondencia Sudamericana*, publication of South American Secretariat of Communist International, Buenos, Aires, April 20, 1926.

26. *La Antorcha*, op. cit., December 20, 1924.

27. *La Correspondencia Sudamericana*, op. cit., April 30, 1926.

28. Interview with Ricardo Paredes, op. cit., July 6, 1947.

29. *La Correspondencia Sudamericana*, op. cit., September 25, 1928 (article by Ricardo Paredes).

30. Alexander Lozovsky, *El Movimiento Sindical Latino Americano—Sus Virtudes y Sus Defectos*, Ediciones del Comité Pro Confederación Sindical Latino Americana, Montevideo, p. 14.

31. Interview with Ricardo Paredes, op. cit., July 5, 1947.

32. *International Press Correspondence*, periodical of Communist International, October 17, 1928.

33. Interview with Ricardo Paredes, op. cit., July 5, 1947.

34. Ibid.

35. *International Press Correspondence*, op. cit., October 17, 1928.

36. *La Vanguardia*, Quito, official publication of Partido Socialista Ecuatoriano, November 15, 1928.

37. *International Press Correspondence*, op. cit., November 23, 1928.

38. Ibid.

39. Interview with Dr. Carlos Palacios Sáenz, leader of Socialist Party of Guayaquil, in Guayaquil, July 2, 1947.

40. Interview with Ricardo Paredes, op. cit., July 5, 1947.

41. *El Movimiento Revolucionario Latino Americano*, Report of First Conference of Latin American Communist Parties, Buenos Aires, 1929, p. 140.

42. Interview with Ricardo Paredes, op. cit., July 5, 1947.

43. Ibid.

44. *La Vanguardia*, Quito, February 3, 1929.

45. Interview with Ricardo Paredes, op. cit., July 5, 1947.

46. Ibid.

47. *American Labor Year Book 1932*, Rand School Press, New York, 1932, p. 228.

48. *International Press Correspondence*, op. cit., September 14, 1934 (article by Ricardo Paredes).

49. Interview with Pedro Saad, first secretary-general of Confederación de Trabajadores del Ecuador, Communist leader, in Guayaquil, July 8, 1947.

50. Ibid.

51. Interviews with Ricardo Paredes, op. cit., July 5, 1947, and Pedro Saad, op. cit., July 8, 1947.

52. *International Press Correspondence*, op. cit., September 1, 1934.

53. Ibid.

54. Poblete Troncoso, op. cit., p. 204.

55. Ibid., p. 205; see also *El Telégrafo*, Quito, June 1940.

56. Interview with Pedro Saad, op. cit., July 8, 1947; see Milk, op. cit., p. 302.

57. See *La Defensa*, weekly publication of Centro Católico de Obreros, Quito.

58. Interview with Luis Maldonado Tamayo, secretary-general of Partido Socialista Ecuatoriano, in Quito, July 6, 1947.

59. *Primero Congreso Católico Nacional,* Quito, 1935, pp. 30–31.
60. Ibid., p. 83.
61. Ibid., p. 5.
62. *Asociaciones de Trabajadores del Ecuador, 1942,* Quito, 1942.
63. *Voz Obrera,* September 29, 1940.
64. *Voz Obrera,* July 20, 1941.
65. *Voz Obrera,* September 29, 1940.
66. Ibid., September 15, 1940.
67. *El Trabajador,* #1, June 22, 1940.
68. *El Trabajador,* #3, July 30, 1940.
69. *Allied Labor News,* pro-Communist newssheet, New York, October 28, 1942.
70. Interview with Pedro Saad, op. cit., July 8, 1947.
71. *National Catholic Welfare Conference News Service,* Washington, DC, March 8, 1943.
72. *Daily Worker,* Communist daily newspaper, New York, May 27, 1943.
73. Interview with Pedro Saad, op. cit., July 8, 1947.
74. *International Labor Review,* monthly of International Labor Office, Montreal, June 1943.
75. Interview with Pedro Saad, op. cit., July 8, 1947.
76. *Allied Labor News,* op. cit., May 19, 1944.
77. Daily Worker, op. cit., February 7, 1944.
78. Interview with Carlos Palacios Sáenz, op. cit., July 2, 1947.
79. Associated Press, May 29, 1944.
80. *Allied Labor News,* op cit., May 31, 1944.
81. *Allied Labor News,* op. cit., July 25, 1944.
82. *La Tierra,* daily newspaper of Partido Socialista del Ecuador, Quito, July 9, 1947.
83. Interview with Pedro Saad, op. cit., July 8, 1947.
84. Asociaciones de Trabajadores del Ecuador, op. cit.
85. *La Tierra,* op. cit., July 9, 1947.
86. Interviews with Humberto Gaybort Rada, op. cit., July 1, 1947.
87. Interview with Miguel Angel Guzmán, op. cit., July 4, 1947.
88. Interview with Miguel Angel Cevallos Hidrobo, president of Federación de Trabajadores de Pichincha, in Quito, July 8, 1947.
89. Interview with Miguel Angel Guzmán, op. cit., July 4, 1947.
90. Interview with Miguel Angel Cevallos Hidrobo, op. cit., July 8, 1947.
91. Interview with Pedro Saad, op. cit., July 8, 1947.
92. Interview with Miguel Angel Guzmán, op. cit., July 4, 1947.
93. Ibid.
94. *La Justicia,* organ of Unión General de Empleados de Comercio.
95. *La Justicia,* op. cit., September 22, 1942.
96. *International Labor Review,* op. cit., October 1945.
97. *Trabajadores,* periodical of Federación de Trabajadores de Pichincha, Quito, October 9, 1945.
98. Interview with Miguel Angel Guzmán, op. cit., July 4, 1947.
99. Interview with Luis Maldonado Tamayo, op. cit., July 6, 1947.
100. Letter from Luis Maldonado Tamayo, secretary-general of Partido Socialista Ecuatoriano, to Robert J. Alexander, December 5, 1947.

101. Interview with Ricardo Paredes, op. cit., July 5, 1947.

102. Letter from Luis Maldonado Tamayo, op. cit., December 5, 1947.

103. *Segundo Congreso Nacional de Obreros Católicos Ecuatorianos, Quito, 30 de Junio al 2 de Julio de 1944*, Quito, 1944, p. 16.

104. Ibid., pp. 5–6.

105. Ibid., pp. 90–108.

106. Interview with Pedro Velasco Ibarra, president of Confederación Ecuatoriana de Obreros Católicos, in Quito, July 7, 1947.

107. Interview with Pedro Saad, op. cit., July 8, 1947.

108. Interview with Miguel Angel Guzmán, op. cit., July 4, 1947.

109. Arturo Jáuregui, "Democratic Tendencies in the Labor Movements of Panama, Colombia and Ecuador," in *Inter-American Labor News*, periodical of Interamerican Confederation of Workers (CIT), Washington, DC, April 1950.

110. *Noticiero de la C.T.A.L.*, Mexico, D.F., January 10, 1949.

111. Jáuregui, op. cit.

112. *Noticiero de la C.T.A.L.*, op. cit., August 9, 1948.

113. *Noticiero de la C.T.A.L.*, op. cit., September 6, 1948.

114. Interview with Luis Alfonso Zhannafría T., assistant to labor inspector of Quito, in Quito, September 7, 1956.

CHAPTER 6

Organized Labor in Ecuador from 1948 to 1990

The selection of Galo Plaza to the presidency in 1948 marked the beginning of an unusual period of constitutional government. Galo Plaza served out his four-year term and was followed by an elected successor, ex-president José María Velasco Ibarra, who also completed his constitutional period in office—the only time during his office periods as president that he was able to do so. He was also succeeded by a man who was duly elected, Camilo Ponce Enríquez, the first Conservative to be president since the Revolution of 1895.

In his turn, President Ponce Enríquez gave way in 1960 to his elected successor, the ever-present José María Velasco Ibarra. However, this time, Velasco Ibarra was forced out of office by the military on November 8, 1961, and the presidency was assumed by his vice president, Carlos Arosemena. But Arosemena, who suffered from alcoholism, was finally forced out of office by the military as well on July 11, 1963, and for the three following years the country was governed by a military junta regime.

The military regime of 1963–1966 was mildly reformist, enacting the beginning of an agrarian reform. However, it was not particularly friendly to organized labor, and in fact, the Confederación de Trabajadores del Ecuador played a key role in the civilian "uprising," which brought down that government early in 1966 by calling a general strike.[1]

ORGANIZED LABOR IN THE 1950s AND EARLY 1960s

Throughout the 1948–1966 period, the Confederación de Trabajadores del Ecuador continued to be the country's largest central labor organization. It was under the ostensible control of the Socialist Party, which in 1952 claimed to control all of the regional federations of the CTE except that of Guayas, which the Communists dominated. The Socialists also had 7 of the 11 members of the National Executive of the CTE. However, the CTE continued to belong to the Communist-controlled world and Latin American regional organizations, the World Federation of Trade Unions (WFTU) and the Confederación de Trabajadores de América Latina (CTAL), respectively. An effort by some of the Socialist leaders of the CTE to have it withdraw from these groups was finally abandoned because of fear that pressing that issue might split the Confederación de Trabajadores del Ecuador.[2]

During the administration of Galo Plaza (1948–1952), the Socialists for two years had members in his cabinet. This fact assured certain stability in labor relations during that period. However, according to at least one important Socialist leader of the CTE, his party lost certain support within the labor movement because of the Socialists' desire not to create political difficulties for the government of which they were part.[3]

Sometimes there were expressions of resentment by unionists at the supposed lack of concern for the workers' problems by the Plaza government. For instance, at the beginning of 1951, the CTE affiliate in the Quito region, the Federación de Trabajadores de Pichincha, claimed that the only gains made by labor had been "the great organizing impulse of the workers themselves." It demanded that measures be taken to curb inflation, that land grants be made to unemployed workers, and that workers be given control over the Social Security Institute.[4]

Fear of disunity in the CTE was particularly strong during the administration of President José María Velasco Ibarra (1952–1956) and Camilo Ponce Enríquez (1956–1960). This was due to the political background and policies of these two chief executives.

Velasco Ibarra had spent much of the time between his ouster from power in 1947 and his return to office in 1952 in Perón's Argentina. There was considerable fear in the labor movement that he might seek to exert the kind of control over organized labor that Perón had established in Argentina.

At the inception of the third Velasco Ibarra presidency in 1952, there seemed to be some evidence to sustain this idea. For one thing, the Peronistas had been active in the period before Velasco Ibarra's return to office in trying to recruit backing in the Ecuadorian labor movement. They had not had much success, except among the railroad workers, where the Asociación Ferroviaria, a mutual benefit society with about 450 members and an affiliate of the Railroad Workers Federation, sent a delegation to Argentina, where it was feted by the Peronista labor leaders. However, the overall Federación Ferroviaria refused to have anything to do with the Peronistas.[5]

Another factor that worried the leaders of the CTE, insofar as the election of Velasco Ibarra as president was concerned, was the support that he had

had in his campaign from the Agrupación Revolucionaria Nacionalista del Ecuador (ARNE). This was a party with affinities for the Falange Party of Franco Spain. A number of its leaders had spent time in Spain being indoctrinated by the Franco regime. There was fear among the CTE labor leaders that elements of the ARNE might get Velasco Ibarra to adopt the Spanish fascist model of labor relations in Ecuador.[6]

Another development that worried the leaders of the CTE at the beginning of the Velasco Ibarra administration was the appearance of the new National Labor Front (Frente Nacional del Trabajo) a few days before Velasco Ibarra took office. It announced that it would "undertake the establishment of different trade union organisms associated with this central labor organization." It also proclaimed itself "essentially anti-Marxist as a response to the systematic and anti-national exploitation of the cause of the worker made by the leaders of the left, servants of the imperialism of Moscow."[7]

Most of those founding the Frente Nacional de Trabajo were people unknown as labor leaders or politicians. The only exception was César Gangotena, a Socialist lawyer who had sought election as his party's secretary-general and who, upon failing to achieve that, resigned from the party, charging that it was dominated by the Communists.[8]

This Frente, which at first had the active encouragement of Velasco Ibarra, drew what following it achieved from the ranks of the Catholic labor group CEDOC. However, by the end of Velasco Ibarra's period in office, the Frente had virtually disappeared.[9]

With the assumption of office by President Camilo Ponce Enríquez, there was again considerable fear in the labor ranks that he would mount an antiunion policy. One reason for this assumption was that he came from the ranks of the Conservative Party, which was seen by the CTE union leaders as the spokesman *par excellence* of the landed aristocracy and the Catholic Church.[10]

Another factor that worried the union leaders about the advent of Ponce Enríquez to the presidency was his behavior during the two years he had been minister of government in the third Velasco Ibarra administration. He not only had shut down temporarily two key opposition newspapers, *El Comercio* and *La Nación,* as well as four radio stations,[11] but also had suspended the legal recognition of part of the Railroad Workers Federation.[12]

However, the administration of President Ponce Enríquez proved to be largely uneventful insofar as labor was concerned. It did not have an attitude any more hostile toward the organized workers than had most other Ecuadorian governments.

One issue that was of considerable concern to the leadership of the Confederación de Trabajadores del Ecuador during both the Velasco Ibarra and Ponce Enríquez governments was the effort made to oust the "functional" senators representing the organized labor movement. The functional senators were an innovation of the 1938 constitution. They represented particular interest groups rather than the general citizenry. There were two functional senators each for agriculture, industry, commerce, and the workers and one each for the armed forces, the universities, and journalism and cultural institutions, for a total of eleven.[13]

In 1952 there was a major effort by the Catholic workers' organization CEDOC to challenge the election of Pedro Saad (a Communist and secretary-general of the CTE from 1944 to 1947) as the labor functional senator for the coastal area and Miguel Angel Guzmán (a Socialist and former president of the CTE) as the labor functional senator for the Sierra.

The CEDOC challenged the credentials of the two labor functional senators (particularly those of Pedro Saad) on the grounds that they were not in fact workers at all. A throwaway the CEDOC published during this campaign asked, "Why does the working class have to have as its representatives in the National Congress intellectuals who know nothing or almost nothing of the needs of the Worker? What has 'comrade' Pedro Saad done for the worker since 1944 when he began to have an income as a Deputy, in addition to what he gets from his property? Has not this foreign 'comrade' who is repudiated by the Ecuadorian working class failed miserably on more than one occasion?"[14]

Pedro Saad himself claimed that the principal backing for this attempt to oust him and Guzmán came from Arne, the Ecuadorian group inspired by the Falange of Franco Spain. In any case, the effort failed.[15]

In 1956 there was a second effort made to oust the CTE leaders as functional senators for the workers. It failed completely insofar as the senator for the highland area (sierra) was concerned, although Pedro Velasco Ibarra of the CEDOC was chosen as alternate functional deputy there. In the case of Pedro Saad's representation of the coastal workers was concerned, two elections were necessary; in the runoff Saad received a unanimous vote.[16]

The Socialist–Communist leadership of the CTE also fought efforts during this period by the Organización Interamericana de Trabajadores (ORIT) and the U.S. foreign aid program to foster establishment of a rival central labor group to the CTE, efforts that in 1962 gave rise to the founding of the Confederación Ecuatoriana de Organizaciones Sindicales Libres (CEOSL). Thus, in 1958, when a leader of the CTE's Federation of Workers of Pichincha accepted a grant from the U.S. Agency for International Development to attend a labor training course at the University of Puerto Rico, he was promptly expelled from his union.[17]

There were relatively few strikes called by the CTE unions during the 1948–1960 period. A labor inspector noted in September 1956 that there had only been one strike in Quito in the previous four years.[18]

One of the most dramatic walkouts was a general strike called by the CTE in October 1951. Its objectives were to obtain passage of a law establishing the autonomy of the railroads from direct government control and a law ending compulsory work by the citizenry—which in fact meant compulsory services by the Indians—as well as to gain a general wage increase. According to Pedro Saad, the two laws for which the strike was called were passed as a result of the walkout, although the general wage increase was not obtained.[19]

Although the unions did not make extensive use of strikes during the administrations of Velasco Ibarra and Ponce Enríquez, they were active in lobbying both with the ministries and with Congress for decrees and legislation favorable to the workers. Among the measures for which they fought were laws providing for dismissal pay for workers laid off by their employers (a measure to discourage dismissal of union leaders), general wage increases, and augmentation of payments to retired workers.[20]

SPLITS IN LEFTIST PARTIES

Both the Communist and the Socialists, the parties that had dominated the CTE, experienced serious splits during the early 1960s. In the case of the former, a group broke away to form a pro-Maoist party, the Partido Comunista Marxista-Leninista. Although the majority of the trade union leaders of the party stayed with the orthodox, pro-Moscow Partido Comunista del Ecuador, still led by ex-trade unionist Pedro Saad, this Communist split nonetheless caused the party considerable problems subsequently, insofar as the labor movement was concerned.

For their part, the Socialists broke into three groups. Following the Cuban Revolution, one faction broke away from the Partido Socialista Revolucionario (PSR), with strong sympathies for the Castro regime. The Partido Socialista del Ecuador, on the other hand, tended to be more or less friendly to the military regime in power between 1963 and 1966. With fall of that regime, a sizable part of the PSE, as well as smaller numbers of members and leaders of the PSR withdrew from those parties to form the Partido Socialista Unificado.[21] This division in the Socialist ranks turned out to be more significant for the labor movement than the split among the Communists, resulting in virtually complete control of the CTE by the Partido Comunista del Ecuador.

The early 1960s were also marked by several attempts to launch a guerrilla war in Ecuador. The first such effort in 1962 was easily thwarted. Elements of both the pro-Maoist Communist Party and the Partido Socialista Revolucionario participated in a much more serious effort in 1963. The CTE was reported to have contributed 50,000 sucres to the war chest for this attempt. The pro-Chinese party had also sent someone to China to raise funds. The whole effort failed when that man returned and was arrested at the airport and was discovered to have $25,000 in his possession.[22]

Although the Confederación de Trabajadores del Ecuador continued through the years 1948 to 1960 as the largest central labor organization, some of the most important events within the organized labor movement took place outside of its ranks. These were the reorganization and orientation of the Catholic union, CEDOC, and the appearance of an entirely new central labor group, the Confederación Ecuatoriana de Organizaciones Sindicales Libres (CEOSL).

REORGANIZATION OF CEDOC

One of the most important developments in the Ecuadorian labor movement during the 1950s and early 1960s was the transformation of the Confederación Ecuatoriana de Obreros Católicos. This began in 1952, with the affiliation of the CEDOC with the International Federation of Christian Trade Unions (IFCTU), the worldwide Catholic trade union group. At that time it was, according to Pedro Velasco Ibarra, the only Latin American labor organization belonging to the IFCTU.[23]

In the early 1950s, an important law sponsored by the Velasco Ibarra government had a significant impact on the CEDOC. This was the Law for the Protection of Artisans, which established apprenticeship procedures and provided for exemption of the artisans from paying social security on their workers, although promising the establishment of a special security law for that group.

As a result of this law, a separate Confederation of Artisans was established, which came to include most organized workers of that class. Because the CEDOC had traditionally had a substantial number of artisans in its ranks, establishment of that new confederation could not help but have an impact on the CEDOC, making its affiliated trade unions and peasant groups the most important elements in the organization, rather than the few remaining artisan groups that stayed in CEDOC.[24]

Then in 1957, the longtime leader of the CEDOC, Pedro Velasco Ibarra, retired as its president. He was an intellectual rather than a laborer (obrero), and his retirement meant that the leadership of the organization thereafter was in the hands of manual workers rather than intellectuals or Church dignitaries, although the Catholic Church continued for some time to have considerable influence in the organization.[25]

The association of CEDOC with the international Catholic trade union movement also stimulated changes in the nature of the Ecuadorian organization. It not only joined the IFCTU, but when a Latin American regional organization of the world group, the Confederación Latino Americana de Sindicalistas Cristianos (CLASC), was established in 1954, the CEDOC also became part of it. At the time of the May 1957 congress of the CEDOC, José Goldsack, the Chilean president of CLASC, brought greetings to the meeting from both the CLASC and the IFCTU.

One consequence of affiliation of the CEDOC with the international Catholic labor organizations was that the CEDOC began to receive modest financial aid from them. As a result, five Ecuadorians were able to participate in a study trip sponsored by UNESCO, after which there was signed "an agreement with CLASC in view of the transformation of the structure of the movement," providing for the CLASC to "provide active collaboration" with the CEDOC.

In the beginning, this "collaboration" consisted to a considerable degree of financing of leadership-training courses for the Ecuadorian Catholic labor movement. The first of these courses was held in Quito, attended by 105 people from 12 provinces, the coast, the sierra, and the eastern parts of the country. In charge of the first training program was Hernán Troncoso, a Chilean Catholic labor leader, and those lecturing at these sessions included some of the most important leaders of the unions affiliated with the CEDOC. The first session of this course was attended by the Cardinal-Archbishop of Quito, the Papal Nuncio, and the minister of labor, as well as representatives from various political parties.[26]

In subsequent years, although CEDOC sought to instill in its members the necessity of paying dues to their unions, as well as the need for the unions to contribute to the federations to which they belonged, and the federations to help finance CEDOC itself, the CEDOC received very significant financial help from the international Catholic labor movement. The Latin American organization, CLASC, was by 1996 paying organizers in Quito, Guayaquil, and several provincial cities.[27]

With the evolution of the CEDOC, the nature of its affiliates changed. The purely confessional groups that engaged in trying to get workers to carry out their religious duties, which had played a significant, if not major role, in the CEDOC, ceased to do so. Also, as noted, artisans' organizations declined drastically in importance in the confederation.

The CEDOC undertook to organize (or capture) unions of industrial workers and other groups of wage earners, both in the coastal region and in the highland one. Among the most important new unions in the CEDOC was the Federation of Fruit Loaders, formed in 1963, which included most of the port workers involved in loading bananas, which in the 1960s were the country's most important export product. By 1966, it had collective agreements with the principal employers and claimed some 20,000 members.[28]

The CEDOC leaders also claimed to have won over to their ranks several textile workers' unions formerly affiliated with the Confederación de Trabajadores del Ecuador.

The CEDOC likewise sought to organize peasants and agricultural workers. It grouped these in a Peasants Federation, which CEDOC leaders claimed in 1966 had 25,000 members. In a few cases, they had succeeded in negotiating collective contracts for rural workers' groups, although most of the organizational work among the peasants centered on formation of cooperatives of various sorts. The CEDOC organizations also helped—with only modest success—to get the government to grant peasants land under the terms of the agrarian reform law passed by the 1963–1966 military regime.[29]

With these changes in CEDOC, it lost much of its purely Catholic emphasis. By the mid-1960s, it was welcoming into its ranks not only Catholic workers, but Protestants and those with no religion as well.[30]

After a visit to Ecuador in 1966, during which I had a chance to observe the labor movement, I wrote,

In the labor field, the most important factor is the growth of CEDOC, the Catholic labor group, which has been converted from a highly sectarian movement of artisans, into a real labor movement. It is probably the second strongest labor movement in Ecuador now, only a little bit, if any, behind the CTE, the traditional Socialist-Communist labor group. It seems to be very well organized and equally well-financed—in part at least, by CLASC.[31]

ESTABLISHMENT OF CEOSL

A third central labor organization appeared in Ecuador in the early 1960s, largely through the help and encouragement of the ORIT (the American regional group of the International Confederation of Free Trade Unions—ICFTU), the American Institute of Free Labor Development (AIFLD), and the United States Agency for International Development. It was aligned with the ORIT and ICFTU.

Soon after the establishment of ORIT, the Confederación Obrera de Guayas (COG) joined it in 1952, and for a decade was the only Ecuadorian affiliate of the ORIT and ICFTU.[32] The COG was one of the country's oldest labor organizations. However, in the 1950s it consisted mainly of mutual benefit societies, only three of its affiliates being trade unions.[33]

In March 1959 the ORIT sent a Paraguayan exiled trade union leader, Julio Echeverry, to Ecuador as its representative.[34] His first public act was to give a speech in Quito, in which he announced plans to organize a labor-education seminar in Guayaquil late in the month. That first five-day seminar, organized with the help of four International Trade Secretariats, was attended by 69 students, from 4 COG organizations, 9 independent unions, and 14 organizations belonging to the Confederación de Trabajadores del Ecuador. This original course was followed by a number of others in the following year.[35]

As a byproduct of these labor training efforts, there was established the Bloque de Instituciones Clasistas Libres del Litoral, which had as its objective the defeat of Pedro Saad as functional senator for the workers of the coastal region in the June 1960 election. Unlike the two previous attempts to unseat Pedro Saad, this one succeeded, and a trade unionist, Alberto Miranda Gifón, was elected to that position.[36]

The victory over the CTE gave rise to a more permanent organization, the Comité Coordinador de Sindicalistas Libres del Ecuador. It undertook a much wider program of training courses, involving sessions on trade union organization, union administration, collective bargaining, structure of the international trade union movement, parliamentary procedure, labor legislation, and social security. Some 17 two-week sessions were held in the later months of 1960, in 1961, and in the first months of 1962. Most of the lecturers were themselves trade union leaders, given a kind of ad hoc tutoring by Julio Echeverry on the techniques of teaching.[37]

The culmination of this process was establishment of the Confederación Ecuatoriana de Organizaciones Sindicales Libres (CEOSL) at a convention held from April 26 to May 1, 1962. A U.S. Department of Labor publication commented, "This history demonstrates how, by coordinating and effective help from the International Free Trade Union Movement, it was possible to broaden the representation of Ecuadorian trade unions from a single province (Guayas) to a regional and finally to a national organization."

The new confederation voted to join the ORIT and the International Confederation of Free Trade Union. It also urged its affiliates to join their appropriate International Trade Secretariats. Soon there were Ecuadorian unions belonging to the International Transport Workers' Federation; the International Federation of Commercial, Clerical and Technical Employees; the Postal, Telegraph and Telephone International; and the Inter-American Federation of Working Newspapermen's Organizations.[38]

The founding convention of the CEOSL also voted to establish the Instituto de Capacitación Sindical, as a leadership training group subject to the confederation's secretary of organization. In the following years, it organized a large number of courses of varying length. These included basic sessions for local leaders, more advanced ones for those who attended the elementary sessions, special courses for those engaged in the labor-education process, and courses designed particularly for leaders of individual affiliates of the CEOSL.

In these leadership training activities, the CEOSL had the collaboration of the American Institute for Free Labor Development (AIFLD). It began to operate in Ecuador under a U.S. unionist, John Wasson, who was soon succeeded by Pablo Jaime Garzón, of the Unión de Trabajadores de Colombia.[39]

The leadership-training activities of the CEOSL and AIFLD paid particular attention to collective bargaining and the signing of collective agreements. Over a considerable period of time, this had an important impact on Ecuadorian labor relations. There were very few collective agreements in effect before 1962—the number was reported to be as few as eight in the whole country. But by 1975 there were said to be as many as 1,000 such contracts in effect. These involved not only unions belonging to the CEOSL, but also unions belonging to the Confederación de Trabajadores del Ecuador and the CEDOC.[40] In 1975 an official of the Chamber of Industry of Guayaquil commented that collective contracts were "very widespread" by then.[41]

The CEOSL grew with considerably rapidity in the years following its establishment. Richard Lee Milk has claimed that this was due in considerable part to the hostile attitude of the military regime that was in power between 1963 and 1966 toward both the Confederación de Trabajadores del Ecuador and the CEDOC.[42]

INDEPENDENT UNION GROUPS

A substantial part of the labor movement stayed out of all of the central labor organizations. Two of the most important of these were the railroaders and the chauffeurs.

Through the 1950s, the principal railroad workers' group was the Federación Ferroviaria, founded in 1945, consisting of unions of the various branches of the state-owned railroad system. It suffered a severe blow during the second Velasco Ibarra administration, when its union on the Guayaquil-Quito line was deprived of its legal recognition. Various reasons were offered for this action of the government. The leaders of the Federación Ferroviaria claimed that the action was taken because leaders of the union had forcefully demanded payment of five weeks' unpaid wages.[43] Government officials insisted that the canceling of legal recognition was due to the fact that the union had engaged in "political activity."[44]

In any case, by the early 1960s, the railroaders had been reorganized in the Sindicato Ferroviario Ecuatoriano, covering the whole rail system. Although the Federación Ferroviaria had been affiliated with the Confederación de Trabajadores del Ecuador, the Sindicato Ferroviario Ecuatoriano withdrew from the CTE and, although maintaining friendly relations with the new CEOSL, did not join that group.[45] One leader of the Sindicato was in 1962 a member of the Chamber of Deputies, an independent with sympathies for the Liberal-Radical Party.[46]

The Federación de Chóferes del Ecuador was established by the country's truck drivers in 1953. Most trucks were driven by their owners, although some of these had a small number of employees, and the Federación had both driver-owners and their workers in its ranks. The federation belonged to the CTE during the 1950s and was of key importance to that confederation because of the strategic role of the union's members in handling most of the country's over-the-road transport.[47]

Within the CTE, the chauffeurs did not submit to control of either the Communist or the Socialist Party. In fact, it constantly warned the CTE of the danger of the confederation being subject to the dictates of any party.[48]

In 1960 the Chauffeurs' Federation withdrew from the CTE. Richard Lee Milk argued that this withdrawal was caused by "the inherent conflict between the self-interest of owner-operators and overall goals for labor, including salaried drivers."[49] However, the Chauffeurs' Federation continued to be regarded both by itself and by the rest of the labor movement to be an integral part of organized labor. Subsequently it came to include taxi and bus drivers.

POLITICAL EVOLUTION OF ECUADOR
FROM 1966 TO 1990

With the overthrow of the three-year-old military junta in early 1966, Ecuador was governed for a bit more than two years by a provisional regime, which called elections in September 1968. At the end of that period, the four-time president José María Velasco Ibarra returned to power once more.

The phenomenon of Velasco Ibarra was unique in Ecuador and in all Latin America. Although he had already been president four times, had been overthrown thrice, and had no real political party supporting him, he emerged once again as the country's most important politician.

Writing a few months after the overthrow of the military junta, I noted, "The most serious thing about Ecuador these days is that José María Velasco Ibarra still is dominating its political life. He is by all odds the single strongest politician. Those politicians who are opposed to him are convinced that in a direct presidential election, he could win a fifth term as president."[50]

These politicians were correct. Velasco Ibarra was elected once again and took office in September 1968. As he had done twice before, Velasco Ibarra, who was faced with an unfriendly Congress, established a dictatorship in June 1970, sending Congress home, and beginning to rule by decree. However, as had happened three times before, Velasco Ibarra was ousted, this time by the military, on February 16, 1972.

The new military regime was headed by General Guillermo Rodríguez Lara. To some degree, this regime seems to have been inspired by the Peruvian government of General Juan Velasco, which had seized power in the neighboring republic in October 1968. It pictured itself as reformist and nationalist. To make the latter point, it recognized the Castro government in Cuba and took other steps to show its "independence" of the United States.

The Rodríguez Lara regime came to power at the beginning of a short-lived oil boom, resulting from the beginning of exploitation of substantial petroleum reserves in the eastern part of the country at a period when oil prices were at record highs. The government suddenly had more money available than any of its predecessors. Some of these financial resources were spent on development projects, but much of the funds went to pay for a very rapid expansion of government employment, largely on the basis of patronage, and perhaps even more was dissipated in corruption.

On January 9, 1976, Rodríguez Lara was overthrown by his fellow military men and was succeeded by a triumvirate, representing the three armed services. With great hesitation, this leadership started the process of returning power to a civilian government. The first step was elaboration of a new constitution—the country's eighteenth. Finally, two versions were submitted to a plebiscite early in 1978, one a modification of the existing constitution, the other essentially a new document. The latter was accepted by the people.

There then followed a first-round presidential election. The victor was Jaime Roldós Aguilera, a candidate of a coalition headed by the Concentration of Popular Forces (CFP), a party that had been dominant in the Guayaquil area for several years. The runner-up was Sixto Durán, a candidate supported by the forces of the economic and social status quo. Because the armed forces were much opposed to the CFP, they waited several months before announcing the result of the election. When they did so, a run-off election was necessary between Roldós and Durán, as a result of which Roldós won, with Osvaldo Hurtado as his vice president. Also elected was a Congress in which the CFP had the largest representation.

However, a deadlock soon developed between Congress and the president, when Assad Bucarama, head of the CFP, who had been voted as his party's presidential candidate by the military but had been elected to Congress, organized a majority in that body against President Roldós. This deadlock persisted until the accidental death of President Roldós on May 24, 1981.

Vice President Osvaldo Hurtado succeeded to the presidency. However, he was faced with an economic crisis, caused in part by the drastic fall in the price of oil, which was by far the country's most important export, and in part by the extravagance and pilfering of the previous military regime. Hurtado had to adopt very unpopular economic policies.

At the end of President Hurtado's term in 1984, he was succeeded in August by León Febres Cordero, who was supported by the large landholders and other conservative forces. He too adopted economic policies that were unpopular, particularly with the organized labor movement.

Finally, President Febres Cordero was succeeded by Rodrigo Borja, head of the Izquierda Democrática (Democratic Left), a relatively new party, established by people originally drawn from the ranks of the Liberals and Socialists, which had relatively close contacts with the Confederación Ecuatoriana de Organizaciones Sindicales Libres (CEOSL).

Starting with the second phase of the 1972–1979 military regime, organized labor experienced a period of militancy, largely in protest against government economic policies, such as it had never had before. All elements of the labor movement participated to a greater or lesser degree in this militancy.

ORGANIZED LABOR DURING THE FIFTH VELASCO IBARRA REGIME

For many years relations between the organized labor movement and José María Velasco Ibarra had been strained. This continued to be the case during his fifth period in the presidency.

In May 1970, the Confederación de Trabajadores del Ecuador spoke for most of the labor movement when it "expressed opposition to economic measures adopted by the government and called on 'workers, peasants, students, and public employees to form a big action front to stop the greed of the oligarchy.'"

When, a month later, President Velasco Ibarra established his dictatorship, he ordered the arrest of many labor and student leaders, including Bolivar Bolaños, the CTE's organization secretary, who was released a month later. Subsequently, the CTE demanded "abrogation of all the decrees that harm the life of the people and the rights of the workers" and also demanded a 40 percent general wage increase, which, of course, the president was unwilling to grant.[51]

Relations between the president and the Confederación Ecuatoriana de Organizaciones Sindicales Libres (CEOSL) were no better than those with the CTE. In July 1971, Velasco Ibarra and his minister of social security met with leaders of the CEOSL's Guayas regional federation FETLIG, in connection with a number of unresolved labor disputes in the Guayaquil area. The union announced after this meeting that nothing had resulted from it, that there had been "conversations and nothing more." As a consequence, the FETLIG declared an eight-hour general strike of the workers of the Guayas area.[52]

However, during both the provisional governments of 1966–1968 and the Velasco Ibarra administration, the labor movement continued to expand. A number of new unions were established both on the local basis and in terms of federations. For instance, in 1966 an Electrical Workers Federation of Guayas was established, as an affiliate of CEOSL. It was almost immediately able to negotiate a collective agreement with the employer.[53] A Hotel Workers Federation, also belonging to the CEOSL, was established in 1971, with affiliates in Guayaquil, Quito, Cuenca, and Manatí. Its local unions were also able to negotiate collective agreements with various hotels.[54]

Not atypical was the case of the union established in 1968 at the Empresa de Cristalerías del Ecuador, one of the largest glass factories and the only one making beer bottles and soft drink bottles. From its first year, this union was able to negotiate annual collective agreements, which won higher wages and life insurance beyond what the workers got through social security, as well as family allowances and vacation pay.[55]

After many years of struggle, the workers in most of the coastal sugar plantations were able to establish effective unions. For instance, at the Ingenio San Carlos, where a union had first been established following the Revolution of 1944, but had been very weak, a five-day strike in 1969, in the process of which one striker was killed by the police, finally was won by the workers. Thereafter, the workers and their employer annually negotiated a collective agreement, through which the workers gained wage increases, improvements in housing, and establishment of schools for the workers' children.[56]

The CEDOC also expanded in the years following the overthrow of the 1963–1966 military regime. It was aided substantially by the Konrad Adenauer Foundation of the West German Christian Democratic Party, which financed both educational and organizational activities of CEDOC and its affiliated unions.[57]

ORGANIZED LABOR DURING THE RODRÍGUEZ LARA REGIME

There was relative labor peace during the government of General Guillermo Rodríguez Lara (February 1972–January 1976). There were undoubtedly several reasons for this. One was the relative prosperity that the country experienced during those years as a consequence of the oil boom. That made it relatively easy for employers to make wage and other concessions in negotiating with their workers' organizations and also made it unnecessary for the government to adopt economic policies designed to limit wage increases or take other measures that might have aroused labor opposition.

Another factor was that the Rodríguez Lara dictatorship was relatively mild. There was not very much persecution of the opposition to the regime—and most of those persecuted were Conservatives for whom the leaders and members of organized labor had little sympathy. Restrictions on the freedom of press and on organization were quite limited, and the political parties—although generally having no role in the regime—were allowed to continue to hold meetings and otherwise function, except, of course, that there were no elections during that period.

Certainly another factor in the situation was the fact that the pro-Moscow Partido Comunista del Ecuador, which still largely controlled the Confederación de Trabajadores del Ecuador, strongly supported the Rodríguez Lara regime. John D. Martz noted, "The PCE promptly praised the regime as 'revolutionary and nationalist.' Legalized in 1973, it was the only party to back the Rodríguez government. It continued its support until Rodríguez was deposed by fellow military officers on 11 January 1976."[58] Indicative of the friendly relationship between the PCE and the Rodríguez Lara government was the fact that the secretary-general of the party, Pedro Saad, was a frequent lecturer at the Military Academy and at the recently established Center of Higher Military Studies during this period.[59]

Soon after the takeover of the government by General Rodríguez Lara, the Confederación de Trabajadores del Ecuador put out a communiqué saying that the new regime's announced program included "some national aspirations which the Ecuadorian labor movement, specially the CTE, had been striving to achieve, such as better wages, the improvement of living conditions, the elimination of unemployment, improvements in the educational system, social security, housing and so forth." It also suggested that there were some important issues that were not dealt with in the new regime's program "related to the democratic and social rights and role of the labor movement in the revolutionary process."[60]

Reflective of the attitude of the CTE leadership toward the Rodríguez Lara government were the comments made to me by the secretary-general of the CTE's Guayas provincial federation in July 1975. He said that the impact of the country's new oil income was misunderstood by many people, who felt that it ought to be divided among the people. He commented that that would be very shortsighted and would not take the future into account at all. He argued that this income should be used to invest in the development of the economy and that this was exactly what the Rodríguez Lara government was doing.

This CTE official added that, although it was true that the bureaucracy of the government was very much increased as a result of the oil boom, this was natural—that when there were more state activities to be undertaken, an additional bureaucracy was necessary to carry them out. Thus, when the state built a new oil refinery, new people were needed to run it. In sum, he said, the increase in the bureaucracy had been the natural result of the fact that the government had greater responsibilities.[61]

The Rodríguez Lara government was happy to have the support of the Communist Party and the CTE. It demonstrated this friendliness toward the CTE on various occasions. For instance, when a convention of the CTE met early in 1975, President Rodríguez Lara received a delegation of CTE leaders and foreign Communist "fraternal delegates," including North Koreans, at that congress.[62]

The reasons for the Ecuadorian Communist Party's (and hence the CTE's) support of the Rodríguez Lara government were undoubtedly similar to those brining the Peruvian pro-Moscow Communists to back the government of General Juan Velasco Alvarado, upon which the Rodríguez Lara regime was to some degree modeled. The Communists hoped that through supporting the "revolution," which Rodríguez Lara proclaimed, they might be able to influence it to move in a direction that might ultimately make it possible for them to become the ultimate beneficiaries of that "revolution." Meanwhile, it helped the Communists develop some influence among the military and other elements supporting the regime. Also, it helped to assure a friendly government attitude toward that faction of the labor movement under Communist control.

In mid-1975 there were rumors within the organized labor movement that the Rodríguez Lara government might seek to establish a new central labor organization under its own control, as the Velasco regime in Peru had done. People who had been expelled from the CEDOC and other groups announced their intention to establish a Central Nacional de Trabajadores. Although the minister of labor claimed that he was opposed to such a move, some leaders of the existing labor confederations feared that he might not be speaking for the government.[63] In any case, if President Rodríguez Lara had such a move in mind, he was not able to carry it out before he was overthrown in January 1976.

Near the end of the Rodríguez Lara regime, one reasonably informed foreign observer estimated that there were 264,340 people in the country's organized labor movement. He credited the CTE with having 53,000, the CEDOC with 11,600, and the CEOSL with 23,400. However, by far the majority of the organized workers were in unions that did not belong to any central labor organization.

The most important groups in independent unions, according to this source, were public service employees, with 75,000 members, and chauffeurs with 85,000. A Federation of Free Campesinos had 4,500 members, the harbor workers' union also had 4,500 members, and the railroad union had 2,500. There were only 40 members of a merchant marine union, 1,000 in postal workers' unions, 1,000 organized telephone and radio employees, and 1,000 in independent electrical workers' organization.[64]

THE BEGINNINGS OF LABOR MILITANCY

Beginning in the last months of the government of General Rodríguez Lara, Ecuadorian organized labor began to show a degree of militancy—particularly in confronting government policies—such as it had seldom had before. This was provoked by a growing economic crisis, which began in large part because of the misguided economic policies of the Rodríguez Lara regime (including the accumulation of a massive foreign debt) and which would be intensified later by the collapse of the worldwide oil boom in the early 1980s and an accumulation of natural disasters. Successive governments were forced by circumstances and the International Monetary Fund to adopt regressive economic programs to face this crisis, against which the organized movement reacted strongly.

Although throughout the period 1975–1990, the three central labor groups—the CTE, CEDOC, and CEOSL—usually worked together in opposing government policies through an umbrella-like organization, the Frente Unido de Trabajadores (FUT), there was some dissension among them, depending on the individual confederation's general attitude toward the government in power at any particular time. The central labor groups also continued to be plagued by a considerable degree of internal dissension, which in the case of the CTE gave rise in 1982 to a fourth group, the Unión General de Trabajadores del Ecuador (UGTE).

The new labor militancy first became evidenced on November 13, 1975, when the three central labor groups jointly called a nationwide 12-hour general strike to protest "against the oligarchies, against imperialism and fascism" and for "a wide array of concessions to labor." According to John Martz, this walkout proved effective.[65]

Less than two months later, the Chauffeurs' Federation declared a general strike on February 5, 1976, to protest a 20 percent increase in bus fares. This event provided the excuse, three days later, for his fellow generals to depose President Rodríguez Lara.[66]

DIVISIONS WITHIN THE LABOR CONFEDERATIONS

During the early 1970s, all three Ecuadorian central labor organizations—the Communist-controlled Confederación de Trabajadores del Ecuador (CTE); the originally Catholic CEDOC; and the ORIT-ICFTU affiliate, the Confederación Ecuatoriana de Organizaciones Sindicales Libres—suffered degrees of internal dissension. In all these confederations, these quarrels brought splits in the organizations.

Dissension within the CTE arose from the division of the Communist Party between pro-Moscow elements (the Partido Comunista del Ecuador) and those loyal to Beijing (Partido Comunista Marxista-Leninista del Ecuador). Although the pro-Moscow group continued to control the Confederación de Trabajadores del Ecuador, the Maoists caused considerable trouble. William Ratliff noted in 1975, "The party has condemned 'desperate attempts by pro-Peking adventurers to sow discord in the ranks of the revolutionary democratic forces of the people' ... particularly in the Trabajadores de Guayas) in Guayaquil."[67]

Richard Lee Milk noted the continuing dissidence within the CTE. He commented that "the split within the party between the traditionalists and the 'Marxist-Leninists,' compounded by the presence of the Revolutionary Socialist Party (Partido Socialista Revolucionario), the strongest and most radical wing of Ecuadorian socialism, kept the CTE from developing a united and continuous program."[68]

As a result of this turmoil, a fourth central labor group was established late in November 1982. This was the Unión General Trabajadores del Ecuador (UGTE), under control of elements to the left of the traditional Communist Party. The head of the new group, Patricio Aldáz, proclaimed that its objective was to put the control of the labor movement in the hands of real workers instead of "a bureaucracy of lawyers," who, he said, had controlled it until then.[69]

The CEDOC had continued its evolution away from being a confessional group, which had begun in the mid-1950s. The change in the organization was reflected in 1972 when it altered its name from Confederación Ecuatoriana de Obreros Católicos to Confederación Ecuatoriana de Organizaciones Clasistas.[70]

This evolution of the CEDOC continued in a congress held early in 1975, which repudiated the longtime association with the Christian Democratic Party and elected a new, more left-wing leadership. As one of the members of the new Directorate of CEDOC said, the new leadership felt that the CEDOC "must work toward Socialism," although without having anything to do with either of the Communist parties.[71]

The CEDOC continued to be active in both the regional organization of the Catholic-oriented labor movement (itself rechristened the Confederación Latino Americana de Trabajadores—CLAT) and the worldwide group (renamed the World Confederation of Labor—WCL). One leader of CEDOC was a member of the executive committee of each of these organizations.[72]

The CEDOC also continued to be heavily subsidized from abroad. The Konrad Adenauer Foundation, the subsidiary of the West German Christian Democratic Party working in the developing countries, began operations in Ecuador in 1966. By the mid-1970s, the foundation was largely financing the CEDOC, although it was trying to convince the Ecuadorians of the need to be self-supporting. At that point, the CEDOC had 56 activists on its payroll, some involved in a leadership-training operation, the Instituto Ecuatoriana de Educación, others doing organizing work, and still others involved in the bureaucratic work of the CEDOC.[73]

In May 1976 there was a split in the CEDOC. This had been preceded by a division in the Federación Sindical de Trabajadores de Guayas (FESITRAG), the CEDOC organization in the Guayaquil area. The national leadership of the CEDOC refused to recognize the credentials of the leadership of FESITRAG and established a different group to run that organization.[74]

Those who split with the main CEDOC organization in 1976 were particularly vituperative in their attack on the Konrad Adenauer Foundation, as well as on the CLAT and the WCL. They also claimed that the leadership of the CEDOC was continuing to work with the Christian Democratic Party. They expressed their intention of supporting the Frente Amplio de Izquierda, the coalition organized by the pro-Soviet Communist Party to participate in the 1978 elections.[75] The split in CEDOC persisted for several years.[76]

The Confederación Ecuatoriana de Organizaciones Sindicales Libres (CEOSL) also suffered a split in the mid-1970s. It centered both on relations of the CEOSL with the American Institute of Free Labor Development and on discontent within the CEOSL with its long-term leader, Luis Villacrés Arandi.

In 1964 the American Institute for Free Labor Development, which had begun operations in Ecuador a couple of years before, reorganized its activities as the Instituto de Educación Sindical Ecuatoriana (IESE). The country program director of AIFLD financed and supervised the IESE.[77]

Until Agustín Torres Lazo's arrival as AIFLD country program director in 1973, relations between the IESE and the CEOSL were conducted almost exclusively by the secretary-general of the CEOSL, Luis Villacrés Arandi, who drew a salary as "adviser" of IESE, rather than with the Executive Committee of the labor confederation as a body. Villacrés had control of the funds coming from the AIFLD. Under Villacrés there were six "activists" who were supposed to be union organizers.

When Torres Lazo arrived as country program director, he came to the conclusion that the six activists were not in fact trying to organize new unions and to service the existing ones, but rather were engaged largely in helping to assure Villacrés his reelection as head of the CEOSL. Torres Lazo dismissed the activists.

Meanwhile, a strong opposition to the leadership of Luis Villacrés had developed in the CEOSL. Villacrés asked for Torres Lazo's help to get reelected in the face of this opposition, but the country program director refused to oblige.

In the face of this opposition, Villacrés twice postponed the scheduled congress of the CEOSL. When it was finally held in the provincial city of Manta in October 1974, there was a split, with two organizations claiming to be the CEOSL, one headed by Villacrés, the other by José Chaves. In the face of this, Torres Lazo offered to split the funds destined for CEOSL, evenly between the two groups, until unity could again be achieved in the organization. José Chaves accepted this idea, but Villacrés rejected it, saying that all of these funds should go to him.

A "unification" congress, on the invitation of the Postal Federation, was finally held in the city of Cuenca in June 1975. According to Torres Lazo, there were representatives of 28 of the 42 regional and industrial federations that had belonged to the CEOSL at this meeting, which the IESE had helped to finance. Most of the delegates came from the Chaves faction, although there were some also that had until then been associated with Villacrés. This congress reelected José Chaves as secretary-general and chose a new Executive Committee.[78]

Meanwhile, Luis Villacrés carried on a violent campaign against not only the Chaves faction of CEOSL, but also against IESE and Agustín Torres Lazo. He sent out a letter to all of the federations of CEOSL denouncing the validity of the unity congress.[79] He also wrote a letter to the minister of labor, protesting the ministry's failure to recognize the Villacrés group as the legal CEOSL and challenging the right of the Postal Employees Federation to issue an invitation to the CEOSL unity congress, or even to belong to the CEOSL, given that government employees' organizations were not legally authorized to belong to central labor organizations.[80] He also circulated a letter to President Rodríguez Lara and the ministers of government and labor, signed by presidents and secretaries-general of the federations affiliated with his CEOS faction, that, among other things, denounced Agustín Torres Lazo as a foreigner who was "corrupting our Trade Union Movement through economic means ... to have a clandestine meeting of the 21st of June in the city of Cuenca," and also raising again the issue of the right of the Postal Employees Federation to belong to the CEOSL.[81]

Torres Lazo responded to these attacks by having Pedro Carlos Ronquilla, "Coordinator" of the IESE, put in the newspapers a paid advertisement announcing that Luis Villacrés was no longer "labor adviser" to the institute; revealing that over time, Villacrés had been paid nearly 500,000 sucres by the institute; and thanking Villacrés for his past services.[82]

The Chaves faction of the CEOSL emerged as the spokesman for that segment of the Ecuadorian labor movement. With the emergence of the new Partido Izquierda Democrática (Democratic Left Party) in the late 1970s as one of the country's principal political parties, the CEOSL tended to be generally aligned with it.

ORGANIZED LABOR DURING THE MILITARY TRIUMVIRATE REGIME

The installation of a new three-man military junta early in 1976 did not bring labor peace. In March, a wave of strikes broke out in Quito, and in a number of cases the strikers occupied their workplaces. Although the minister of labor said that in some instances the union leaders had been responsible for the impasse in negotiations, and in others the fault was with the employers, the government threatened to use force if the workers did not leave the factories. Some of the firms involved threatened to enter into bankruptcy if there was not some quick settlement of their disputes.[83]

Then, as I wrote at the time, "The month of June was marked by strikes and political disturbances. On June 20 a strike of coffee and banana workers began, supported by government employed agronomists and veterinarians," some 600 of whom were dismissed. Then on July 15 there was a one-day strike by policemen in Quito, demanding pay increases, as a result of which 13 senior police officials were arrested.[84]

Finally, on October 15, 1976, the Confederación de Trabajadores del Ecuador declared a general strike in Quito and Guayaquil. However, because the CEDOC and CEOSL did not support this walkout, it failed.[85]

The attitude of the military government toward organized labor hardened in 1977, and as a consequence, "labor unrest ... grew even more pronounced," as reported by John Martz. In January, as the result of a strike by hospital workers in Guayaquil, 45 union leaders were arrested. Then in May, there was a month-long teachers' strike, and the three labor confederations declared a general strike "in support of demands for salary increases, oil nationalization, agrarian reform, and the resolution of existing labor disputes." John Martz reported that this strike call was "relatively ineffective." As a result of these conflicts, Martz explained, "much of the top labor leadership went underground."[86]

However, the most serious labor conflict of 1977 took place in the sugar plantations along the coast. Most of the sugar workers had been organized, with the help of the Instituto de Educación Sindical Ecuatoriana, and all but one of the unions belonged to a Sugar Workers Federation affiliated with the CEOSL. The unions were of varying strength—one was said by federation officials to be largely dominated by the employer, and others were militant. Only one, the union in the Aztra sugar mill, was controlled by left-wing political elements.[87]

It was at the Aztra mill that trouble broke out in October 1977. On October 18, the union there went on strike, demanding compliance with the collective contract, which called for automatic wage increases when the price of sugar rose—two such price increases had occurred without any wage adjustment. On that afternoon, the strikers, together with many of their wives and children, occupied the mill. They were quickly besieged by 200 armed police, the commander of whom demanded the immediate evacuation within two minutes of the building through a very a very narrow door.

It being impossible for all those people to leave the building through the narrow entrance in front, panic-stricken workers and family members fled by a back door, which opened directly onto a deep irrigation ditch. Numerous people perished in the ditch, some of whom suffered from bullet wounds. The union leaders claimed that 120 people had perished; the government recognized the death of 25.

This massacre was followed by massive protest. On October 20, the three labor confederations called for three days of mourning. On October 24 and 25, the workers of the San Carlos and Valdéz sugar plantations—the country's two largest—went on strike in a protest demonstration.[88]

The year 1978 was marked by considerable less labor militancy than the year before. This was probably due to several causes. For one, the attention of the political parties with influence in the labor movement was to a large degree centered during the first half of the year on the presidential election of July 16. For another, as John Martz wrote, "the rivalry of the three national federations, along with internal divisions of both CEDOC and CEOSL, produced greater disunity within the national labor movement. The customary May Day parades in Quito and Guayaquil were less successful than those of the preceding years. From 20,000 to 30,000 workers participated in Quito, while in Guayaquil there were rival marches by the three organizations."

Also, the CTE suffered particularly from internal quarrels. At one point, the Quito affiliate of the CTE, the Federación de Trabajadores de Pichincha (FTP), was seized by elements of the pro-Maoist Partido Comunista Marxista-Leninista. Although the pro-Moscow Communists soon regained control, "the FTP was left in a weakened condition," according to John Martz.[89]

ORGANIZED LABOR IN THE NEW CIVILIAN GOVERNMENT PERIOD

In August 1979, the first elected civilian president in seven and a half years took office. This was Jaime Roldós Aguilera, with Osvaldo Hurtado as his vice president, the candidates of a coalition of the Concentration of

Popular Forces party with its particular strength in the Guayaquil region and the Christian Democratic–oriented Popular Democracy Party.

As John Martz noted a bit later, "There was considerable apprehension over the Roldós government's attitude toward the working class." However, the CEOSL offered "conditional support" to the new regime, and the CTE "announced that the organization would be independent of the government" and judge it upon the basis of its actions. At its inception, the Roldós government appeared to be friendly disposed toward organized labor—among other things, setting up a procedure whereby the general wage level might be raised and immediately paying government employees the four months of back salary that had been left unpaid by the military regime.[90]

However, the elected government was forced to follow to a modified degree the restrictive economic policies of its predecessor. In January and February 1980, this led to a series of demonstrations of protest by the labor movement. Nevertheless, the CEDOC indicated in April 1980 its support for the government, so as to "benefit the popular sectors and consolidate democracy."[91]

In May 1981, President Roldós was killed in an airplane crash and was succeeded by Vice President Osvaldo Hurtado Larrea. Organized labor indicated its support for the constitutional transfer of power. However, two weeks before Roldós' death, the three central labor groups (through the Frente Unido de Trabajadores—FUT) had called a general strike on May 13, demanding a "rollback of consumer prices; higher income deductions; and a 75 percent increase in the minimum wage." The walkout had the most support among the industrial workers, about half of whom struck. Although the government declared the strike illegal, it did not take any further action against it. None of the strike's objectives were achieved.

The central labor groups continued to have internal problems. This was particularly true of the Confederación de Trabajadores del Ecuador, where the Maoists had finally succeeded in getting control of its Quito affiliate. Maoists were also very influential in the teachers' union, the Unión Nacional de Ecuadores, which had emerged as one of the most important and militant union groups.[92]

In 1982 the slump in oil prices hit Ecuador, and by the end of the year, the national income was actually declining. This economic crisis and the government measures to deal with it provoked strong reaction from organized labor, including two general strikes and the threat of a third.

The first general strike was officially called by the Frente Unido de Trabajadores to last two days, September 22 and 23, supposedly to secure wage increases and a freeze on prices. Although it was supported by the CTE and the teachers' union, it was opposed by the CEDOC, which claimed that its purpose was "destabilizing the administration" and not "furthering class interests." As a consequence of this opposition, the strike was only partially successful.[93] During the walkout, the minister of labor announced the government's willingness to continue to negotiate with the labor movement over the issues between it and the administration.[94]

However, labor unrest continued. On September 27, the Chauffeurs' Federation declared a walkout that lasted until October 2. This walkout was said by David Scott Palmer to have been "fairly successful," in the workers' response to it and in what it achieved.[95]

The most serious showdown between the Hurtado government and the labor movement came at the time of the second general strike called by the Frente de Trabajadores on October 20–22, in response to a government decree a week earlier raising gas prices by 120 percent and the price of flour by 100 percent. This walkout had the support of virtually the whole labor movement and was accompanied by widespread riots and demonstrations.

In the face of the situation arising from the strike, President Osvaldo Hurtado declared a national "state of emergency" and established a curfew. In a public statement in defense of these measures, Hurtado said that "the country has lived sine October 18 in a state of internal commotion that affects the citizens' peace, the stability of the constitutional regime and the permanence of the democratic system." He called on the citizenry to abandon violence.

After the strike was over, the FUT decided to call a "national convention" to plan another "day of protest" against the government's economic policies. However, after consultation with the FUT, the government ended the state of emergency and decreed a general 35 percent wage increase. It also provided for a 50 percent increase in bus fares, to help the drivers pay for the increase that had been decreed in the cost of gasoline. The Chauffeurs' Federation, which had gone on strike even before the general walkout called by the FYT, did not end their strike until after the bus-fare concession had been granted. After the government's moves, the FUT canceled its plans for a new strike in November.[96]

The economic crisis deepened in 1983, with a 3.2 percent decline in the GNP, food price increases of 100 percent, and inflation generally rising to over 50 percent. One cause of this situation was serious damage caused to agriculture by severe floods. The intensive economic crisis generated continuing labor militancy. After a 27 percent currency devaluation, as well as serious fuel price rises, the FUT called yet another general strike, on March 23–24. That walkout had the support of virtually the whole labor movement and, according to David Scott Palmer, was "almost 100 percent effective." It did not achieve its immediate objectives, but the president and Congress approved a substantial increase in minimum wages a few weeks later.

In June and July 1983, the teachers' union went on a month-long strike. It succeeded in winning from Congress a salary increase of more than 25 percent.[97]

In 1984 the still-deepening economic crisis was complicated, from organized labor's point of view, by the election of a right-wing leader of the Social Christian Party, León Febres Cordero, as president. The year generally was marked by mounting violence of various kinds.

In February and March 1984, there was a month-long strike of petroleum workers in the eastern part of the country. This walkout was marked by considerable violence, in which eight people were injured and considerable property was destroyed. Later in the year, on November 1, the FUT declared a national general strike, which was supported by the Unión Nacional de Ecuadores. This walkout was not a success, in part because the new Febres Cordero government declared it illegal, but probably more significantly because the Chauffeurs' Federation did not support it.[98]

Two months later, however, a new general strike call by the FUT on January 9–10, 1985, against the government's decreeing of price increases in food, transportation, and gasoline, was more successful. An assembly at which the strike was called denounced "three anti-popular measures which signify a hard blow to the squalid budget of the people." The meeting adopted a six-point series of demands not only dealing with the government's recent measures, but also calling for an increase in appropriations for education, dismissal of the economic and labor ministers, and "irrestrictive application" of the Agrarian Reform Law. David Scott Palmer noted that "Quito was brought to a standstill and casualties were high—seven killed, 50 wounded, and 500 arrested."[99]

Still another general strike was called by the FUT, for 24 hours, on March 27, 1985. This was supported by the People's Front, a group "composed of student, peasant, worker and teacher associations." This time the walkout was against President Febres Cordero's veto of a bill raising the minimum wage. It was marked by extensive attacks on workers' demonstrations not only by the police but, according to the union leaders, also by private paramilitary organizations operating with the government support.[100]

Labor ferment continued in 1986. There were many demonstrations throughout the year under the sponsorship of FUT and the Popular Front to protest, among other things, the Febres Cordero government's move to privatize a number of government-owned firms. Also, the FUT organized in Quito a "national convention" that drew up a number of demands, including calls for a consumer-protection law and an increase in the minimum wage with a provision for automatic adjustments to keep up with price increases. There were also protests at the convention against the government's insistence on continuing to pay the foreign debt and its relaxing of laws governing foreign investment in Ecuador.

Labor unrest in 1986 culminated in a new general strike on September 17, called by FUT. Although the minister of labor claimed that only 20 percent of the workers participated in this walkout, news reports indicated that the industries, schools, and universities in Quito and Guayaquil were closed down by it.[101]

Early in March 1987, a serious earthquake in Napo province intensified the country's economic crisis, as well as fomented increasing opposition to the Febres Cordero economic policies. The labor movement expressed its unhappiness with the regime with a new 24-hour general strike called by the FUT on March 25, which also had the support of the Chauffeurs' Federation. Although the government claimed that only 25 percent of the workers obeyed the strike call, union leaders claimed that 90 percent of the workers participated. The Izquierda Democrática party said that the strike meant that the Febres Cordero government "must make changes in economic policy, show more tolerance, and strive for real democracy in the country."[102]

ORGANIZED LABOR AND THE RODRIGO BORJA REGIME

The year 1988 saw new elections. The successful candidate for president, Rodrigo Borja of Izquierda Democrática, promised during his campaign a more friendly attitude toward organized labor than the attitude of Febres Cordero and agreed to raise the minimum wage faster than the increase in prices. Representatives of Borja conferred at length with union leaders during the campaign "to harmonize government and labor objectives."[103]

Before the new government took office, there was an additional general strike led by the FUT on June 1. This was preceded by a walkout of the 100,000-strong teachers' union, demanding passage of a bill providing for a 50 percent increase in teachers' monthly salaries and also, according to the president of the Unión Nacional de Educadores, Antonio Cañizares, "to nip in the bud the government's intention of harming again the working class."[104]

The union leaders called the June 1, 1988, general strike a "total success," although the government claimed that 98 percent of the country's companies operated "normally." President Febres Cordero declared a state of emergency and put soldiers out to patrol the streets of the principal cities. Demonstrators raised barricades to block traffic in Quito. The press reported that workers in transport, factories, and state-owned enterprises, as well as the street cleaners, generally obeyed the strike call.[105]

Late in June, about 200 striking teachers went on a hunger strike. But the teachers' strike was finally settled on June 27. The school was extended to make up for the days lost because of the walkout.[106]

The advent to power of President Rodrigo Borja and the Izquierda Democrática party in August 1988 somewhat modified both the political and the economic situations in the country. On the political side, Borja enjoyed the backing in parliament not of his own party but of the more-or-less Christian Democratic Party of ex-president Osvaldo Hurtado and of the Broad Left Front (Frente Amplio de la Izquierda—FADI), the left-wing coalition based on the pro-Soviet Communist Party. This change was significant for organized labor, since ID enjoyed some influence in the Confederación Ecuatoriana de Organizaciones Sindicales Libres, and the pro-Moscow Communists were still the major political element in the leadership of the Confederación de Trabajadores del Ecuador.

However, the economic situation was only marginally improved. Within his first year, President Borja was able to resume at least nominal payments on the country's foreign debt, which President Febres Cordero had suspended just before leaving office, and this assured the disbursement of loans from the World Bank and the Japanese Export-Import Bank, which had been held up. However, inflation continued at a very high rate—69.69 percent in the first 10 months of 1989, compared with 85 percent for the full year 1988, and the 1990 budget provided that 34 percent of its funds would go toward debt service.[107]

The economic situation meant that President Borja had to continue on a broad scale the economic policies followed by his predecessors. He did modify them by providing relatively frequently minor currency devaluations and price increases, rather than less frequent very large ones.

After a few months of relative tolerance of the new government, the labor movement finally moved more aggressively against its economic policies. The FUT called a general strike in November 1988, which was accompanied by what were called "violent clashes."[108]

Then, after a few months of relative labor peace, the Chauffeurs' Federation launched a general strike of its members of June 9, 1989, to which President Borja responded by using the national security law to mobilize transport units, while at the same time moving to curb illegal food exports to Colombia and seizing goods being held off the market in the hope of higher prices.

At the same time, the FUT, which at that point was headed by José Chaves of the CEOSL, called a general strike for June 14, but then postponed it until July 12, to permit further negotiations between the union leaders and the government. The unions were demanding a 100 percent increase in the minimum wage, as opposed to the 20 percent rise that had been enacted by the government.

These negotiations were not satisfactorily concluded, insofar as the leaders of the labor movement were concerned. However, when the July 12 strike did take place, there were only "minor incidents," and the walkout was judged to have been a "flop" by the British publication *Latin American Report*.[109]

By mid-July 1990, the struggle of the organized labor movement to change government economic policy led to still another general strike call by the FUT. Among the things being demanded by the FUT, still led by José Chaves, were an increase in the minimum wage, an end to fuel price rise and to the mini-devaluations of the sucre being carried out by the government, and a variety of other things. Before the strike, the FUT leaders had consultations with the chambers of commerce and industry, but refused to talk with any government officials other than President Borja himself. When the walkout finally took place, it was only "partially observed."[110] Certainly, it did not serve to fundamentally change economic policies that governments had been following for more than a decade.

NEOLIBERALISM AND THE ECUADORIAN WORKERS

It is clear that the organized labor movement of Ecuador and the workers who made it up suffered from the triumph of so-called neoliberalism, which became the accepted wisdom in Latin America (and much of the rest of the world) during the 1980s. This triumph was provoked by a period of severe economic crisis that made the 1980s for Ecuador, as for most of Latin America, "the lost decade" and that led to acceptance of the doctrine and practice of neoliberalism, under the prodding of the International Monetary Fund.

These events came immediately after a period of almost frenzied prosperity in the 1970s, resulting from the discovery and exploitation of important new oil resources in the eastern part of the country, which coincided with the worldwide increase in oil prices. That oil boom had brought an annual increase of 8 percent in the Gross Domestic Product of Ecuador between 1972 and 1981. The product per capita had risen from $260 in 1970 to $668 in 1981. This large and rapid increase in income had acted as a major spur to industrialization.

However, the new prosperity had also converted Ecuador into a favorite customer of the international banking community, which was anxious to find customers to borrow the vastly increased deposits that the international oil boom had brought into their coffers. As a result, the country's foreign debt had risen from $241.5 million in 1970 to $11,180 million by 1989.[111] However, when the oil bonanza came to an end with the drastic fall of oil prices in the early 1980s, the government of Ecuador had to turn to the International Monetary Fund (IMF) for help to deal with its gigantic debt, its balance of payments crisis, and its growing inflation.

The managers of the IMF were willing to extend aid only if Ecuador—like the other Latin American countries—would conform to the philosophy and policies of neoliberalism. This meant, in the short run, to deal with the grave inflation problem, placing "restrictions on government credit, raising interest rates to generate savings, seeking to reduce unemployment through foreign investment, reducing public expenditure through reducing subsidies, congealing wages and opening the economy to international competition."[112] It also meant the large-scale privatization of the state-owned sector of the economy.

The governments of the late 1970s and the 1980s all were forced to follow neoliberal policies (or did so willingly). Although, as we have seen, the administrations of Roldós, Hurtado, and Borja at first sought to resist the implementation of neoliberalism, they were in fact unable to do so.

The implementation of neoliberalism was clearly the major cause of the disturbed labor situation of the late 1970s and the 1980s.

The prescriptions of neoliberalism bore particularly heavily on organized labor. As Galo Chiriboga Zambrano wrote,

Insofar as labor was concerned, there was imposed a series of legal reforms tending to *deregulate* labor–management relations, imposing restrictions on the formation of unions, both in the private and public sectors, creating administrative obstacles for the calling of strikes, facilitating the dismissal of workers by the employers, favoring uncertain employment, destroying labor stability, keeping wages down in the face of inflation; in sum, implementing a labor policy against the interests of the Ecuadorian workers.[113]

ORGANIZATIONS OF RURAL WORKERS

By 1990, a segment of the organized working class that theretofore had played at best a very minor role in the Ecuadorian labor movement had begun to gain strength, and in the years that followed (which are beyond the scope of the present work), it was to become increasingly important in the national economy and polity. This group was that of organized rural workers.

By the end of the 1980s, organized labor in Ecuador remained overwhelmingly an urban phenomenon. However, from at least the early 1930s, the labor movement and the parties associated with it had an interest in trying to make contacts with and even organize the rural workers. Thus, in 1932 the first candidate the Communist Party ran for president was Antonio Ruíz Flores, who was president of the Central Council of Agrarian Unions of Milagro. The Communists continued their interest in trying to gain influence among the rural workers, and particularly the Indians. In 1944 they established the Federación Ecuatoriana de Indios (Federation of Ecuadorian Indians), which elected the head of the Communist Party, Ricardo Paredes, as a delegate to the constituent assembly that was then in session.[114]

As late as 1977, the Communists were said to continue to control the Federación Ecuatoriana de Indios. They also were said to control another rural organization, the Federación de Trabajadores Agrícolas del Litoral (Coastal Farm Workers Federation).[115] Both of these organizations belonged to the Confederación de Trabajadores del Ecuador, and the former was headed by Bolivar Boliños, secretary of the organization of the CTE.[116]

Starting in the early 1960s, various governments launched what they called agrarian reforms. The first administration to do this was that of President Carlos Arosemena. He decreed that the *huasipungos*, the small plots of terrain whose use landowners granted to Indians to build their huts and grow food for their own sustenance, should thenceforward be the property of the Indians, not of the landlords. This decree aroused great opposition from the landowners and was never ratified by Congress before the ouster of Arosemena by the army.[117]

The military government of 1936–1966, which followed the overthrow of President Arosemena, decreed its own agrarian reform law and began modestly to put it into effect. However, after the ouster of that regime, the law became virtually inoperative. Then the "reformist" military regime of General Rodríguez Lara decreed its own agrarian reform law, which one leader of the CEDOC described as really dealing more with ways of increasing agricultural output than with land redistribution.[118]

However, these agrarian reform statutes undoubtedly served to encourage the growth of organizations among the agricultural workers both in the highlands and along the coast. So did the growth of modern commercial agriculture, producing export crops, along the littoral. All three central labor groups sought to take advantage of this tendency, as did elements outside of any of them.

The CEOSL established a Federación Nacional de Campesinos (National Federation of Peasants) in 1969. It had its greatest strength in the province of Guayas, where most of its members, however, were wageworkers rather than independent peasants or tenants. The organization also had some unions in the mid-1970s in the provinces of Loja and Bolivar.[119]

However, of the three national labor confederations, the CEDOC was undoubtedly most successful among the peasants and agricultural laborers. As early as the mid-1960s, it had a Peasants Federation, which claimed to have 25,000 members. At that time, it too worked principally among the coastal rural wage earners and had succeeded in negotiating a few collective contracts with employers.[120] In the mid-1970s the president of the CEOSL's Peasants Federation admitted that the CEDOC was the leader in the field.[121]

The CEDOC's rural organizations, which by the mid-1970s were the Federación Nacional de Organizaciones Campesinas and its affiliate along the coast, the Asociación de Campesinos Agrícolas del Litoral, sought to bring about the full application of the agrarian reform laws, as well as to offer legal aid to peasant groups, which were accused of invading and settling on land belonging to large landlords. The organizations helped rural workers present petitions for land distribution under the agrarian reform laws, but one lawyer for CEDOC, who was involved in presenting these petitions, stated in July 1975 that he did not know of a single case in which such a request had been definitively settled to the satisfaction of the petitioners.[122]

The rural workers' organization of CEDOC on the coast expressed the frustration of the agrarian unionists. It complained in June 1975, "In summation, the Agrarian Reform remains paralyzed throughout the country. While many high personages … never cease to make promises and declarations about their decision to apply the Law." The same statement complained extensively against the failure of the government to give any help to peasant group that were trying to establish cooperatives of various kinds and accused the regime (of Rodríguez Lara) of caving in to the landowners' Chambers of Agriculture, which feared the competition from the peasant cooperatives.[123]

One U.S. anthropologist, who had carefully studied the rural situation in the Andean area of Ecuador, concluded as late as 1988 that relatively few peasants had received land under the agrarian reform laws. However, in some instances, economic factors had brought large landowners to sell part or all of their large estates to the peasants. She also noted that there had been large-scale conversion of tenants and sharecroppers into the wageworkers in upland Ecuador in the previous several decades.[124]

By 1990, it was clear that the rural workers of Ecuador—whether wage earners, tenants, or members of the Indian communities—had become organized to a degree that had never existed in the past. This was demonstrated in May of that year, when 1,000 Indians, representing some 70 different organizations, descended on Quito to present petitions to President Rodrigo Borja. Among other things, they were demanding return of community land to the Indians from whom it had been stolen by private landowners, payment of debts owed by the government to Indian organizations, recognition of Quechua as an official language, payment by oil companies for environmental damage they had done to Indian lands, and funds for both education and public works in rural areas.[125]

CONCLUSION

By 1990, organized labor in Ecuador included within its ranks most of the country's factory workers, a considerable proportion of the plantation workers, and employees of the railroads and in motor vehicle transportation. Also organized were the petroleum workers.

The labor movement had gotten its first real start after the Liberal Revolution of the 1890s, but for many decades had consisted more of mutual benefit societies than of trade unions. It was not until after World War II that the trade unions came to be predominant in organized labor.

Since the early 1960s, the negotiation of collective bargaining contracts had become widely accepted. In accordance with the Labor Code, the Ministry of Labor often intervened in this process through conciliation and arbitration procedures. However, unlike the situation in many Latin American countries, the ministry interfered relatively little in the internal affairs of the country's unions—not intervening either in union elections or in administration of union finances.

The labor movement continued to be divided principally among three central labor groups, the Confederación de Trabajadores del Ecuador (CTE), the Confederación Ecuatoriana Organizaciones Clasistas (CEDOC), and the Confederación Ecuatoriana de Organizaciones Sindicales Libres (CEOSL). For purposes of inter-union solidarity and confronting unpopular government economic policies, the three central labor groups from time to time organized joint actions, particularly general strikes and other protests, through the Frente Unido de Trabajadores (FUT). Although from time to time, one or another of the three groups expressed interest in establishment of a single national central labor group, this proved impossible because of ideological differences among the three existing organizations.

Organized labor proved relatively ineffective in getting successive governments to desist from "economic stabilization" and neoliberal programs, which involved, in varying degrees, limitations on wage increases and other labor benefits and altering legislation in ways designed to weaken organized labor and undermine collective bargaining.

By the last decade of the twentieth century, the triumph of the theory and practice of neoliberalism was raising grave doubts about the future of Ecuadorian organized labor.

NOTES

1. Interview with Pablo Duque, secretary of finances, Confederación de Trabajadores del Ecuador, in Quito, July 4, 1966.

2. Ibid., August 21, 1952, September 6, 1956.

3. Interview with Ezequiel Torres, vice president of Confederación de Trabajadores del Ecuador, in Quito, August 21, 1952.

4. *Hispano Americano,* Mexico City, January 19, 1951.

5. Interviews with Nelson Cháves, president of Federación Ferroviaria, in Quito, August 21, 1952; and Guillermo Calvo Gross, secretary of culture and sports, Sindicato Ferrocarril del Sur, in Quito, August 21, 1952.

6. Interview with Pedro Saad, ex-secretary-general of Confederación de Trabajadores del Ecuador, secretary-general of Partido Comunista del Ecuador, in Quito, August 21, 1952.

7. *El Sol,* Quito, August 20, 1952.

8. Interview with Pablo Duque, op. cit., August 21, 1952.

9. Ibid., September 6, 1956; and interview with Marco T. Oramas, secretary of organization of Confederación de Trabajadores del Ecuador, in Quito, September 5, 1956.

10. Interview with Telmo Hidalgo, president of Federación de Trabajadores de Pichincha, in Quito, September 5, 1956.

11. Interview with Hugo Larrea Benalcazar, member of National Executive Committee of Socialist Party, in Quito, September 5, 1956.

12. Interview with Marco T. Oramas, op. cit., September 5, 1956.

13. Interview with J. Osvaldo Espinosa O., secretary of Cámara de Agricultura de la Primera Zona, in Quito, September 7, 1956.

14. Confederación Ecuatoriana de Obreros Católicas: "A Los Trabajadores del Ecuador," n.d. (circa 1952) (throwaway).

15. Interview with Pedro Saad, op. cit., August 21, 1952.

16. Interviews with Jaime Carrión, an editor of Socialist Party newspaper *La Tierra,* in Quito, September 4, 1956; and William Dustman, first-secretary and labor reporting officer, U.S. Embassy, in Quito, September 5, 1956.

17. Interview with Aquiles Gustavo López Castelo, a leader of Sindicato Único de Chóferes de Pichincha, in Rio Piedras, Puerto Rico, July 15, 1958.

18. Interview with Luis Alfonso Zhannafría T., assistant to inspector of labor of Quito, in Quito, September 7, 1956.

19. Interview with Pedro Saad, op. cit., August 21, 1952.

20. Interviews with Noé Villacréses, president of Federación Nacional de Trabajadores Textiles, in Quito, September 5, 1956; Luis Freire, president of Federación de Calzado y Curtiembre del Ecuador, in Quito, September 5, 1956; and Miguel Carillo, president of Sindicato Textil de Ambato, in Quito, September 5, 1956.

21. Interviews with Hugo Larrea Benalcazar, op. cit., July 4, 1966; and Pablo Duque, op. cit., September 6, 1956.

22. Interview with Warren Deane, political officer of U.S. Embassy, in Quito, July 5, 1966.

23. Interview with Pedro Velasco Ibarra, president of CEDOC, in Quito, August 21, 1952.

24. Ibid., September 5, 1956.

25. Interview with Jacinto Figueroa, secretary of conflicts, and subsequently president of Confederación Ecuatoriana de Obreros Católicos, in Quito, July 5, 1966.

26. "Une Belle Manifestation d'une grande organization," in *Labor,* monthly magazine of International Federation of Christian Trade Unions, December 1957.

27. Interview with Hugo Espinoza, member of Executive Committee of Confederación Ecuatoriana de Obreros Católicos, in Quito, July 5, 1966.

28. Interview with Germán Sanabria Benítez, president of Federación Ecuatoriana de Trabajadores Embarques de Fruta, in Quito, July 5, 1966.

29. Interview with Jacinto Figueroa, op. cit., July 5, 1966.

30. Interview with Vicente Barbarán, president of Juventud Trabajadora Ecuatoriana, youth wing of Confederación Ecuatoriana de Obreros Católicos, in Quito, July 5, 1966.

31. Robert J. Alexander, "Impressions of Ecuador, July 5 1966" (typewritten).

32. Interview with Víctor Sánchez, member of Executive Committee of Confederación Obrera de Guayas, in New Brunswick, NJ, May 16, 1954.

33. Interview Antonio Espinoza, member of Executive Committee of Confederación Obrera de Guayas, in New Brunswick, NJ, May 16, 1954.

34. United States Department of Labor, "History and Structure of Ecuadorian Trade Unions," n.d. (circa 1963) (mimeographed), p. 8.

35. "Panorama de la Educación Sindical en el Ecuador," Primera Conferencia Interamericana de Directores de Educación Sindical, Enero 13–17, 1964, Informe de la Confederación Ecuatoriana de Organizaciones Sindicales Libres (CEOSL), Instituto de Capacitación Sindical, p. 1 (mimeographed).

36. United States Department of Labor, "History and Structure," op. cit., p. 2.

37. "Primera Conferencia Interamericana," op. cit., p. 2.

38. United States Department of Labor, "History and Structure," pp. 8–9.

39. "Primera Conferencia Interamericana," pp. 2–9.

40. Interview with Pedro Cantos, member of staff of Instituto de Educación Sindical Ecuatoriana, in Quito, July 11, 1975.

41. Interview with Eduardo Donoso Baquerizo, technical adviser of Cámara de Industria de Guayaquil, July 16, 1975.

42. Richard Lee Milk in Gerald Michael Greenfield and Sheldon L. Maram (editors), *Latin American Labor Organizations,* Greenwood Press, Westport, CT, 1987, p. 294.

43. Interview with Álvaro Aparicio, president of Federación Ferroviaria, in Quito, September 5, 1956.

44. Interview with Luis Alfonso Zhannafría T., op. cit., September 7, 1956.

45. Interview with Fausto Machuca Ibarra, secretario de justicia y reclamos of Sindicato Ferroviario Ecuatoriano-Comité Local Riobamba, in Rio Piedras, Puerto Rico, July 12, 1962.

46. Interview with Roberto A. Nevárez Ponce, a leader of Sindicato Ferroviario Ecuatoriano, in Rio Piedras, Puerto Rico, July 12, 1962.

47. Milk, op. cit., p. 302.

48. Interview with Pacífico Vega, president of Federación de Chóferes del Ecuador, in Quito, September 5, 1956.

49. Muilk, op. cit., p. 302.

50. Robert J. Alexander, "Impressions of Ecuador," Quito, July 5, 1966 (typewritten).

51. Lynn Ratliff in *1971 Yearbook on Latin American Communist Affairs,* Hoover Institution Press, Stanford, CA, 1971, pp. 80–81.

52. *El Universo,* Guayaquil, July 14, 1971.

53. Interview with Carlos Castro, ex-president of Electrical Workers Federation of Guayas, in Quito, July 13, 1975.

54. Interview with Joaquín Arbito Reinoso, secretary-general, Federación Ecuatoriana de Trabajadores Hoteleros y Ramas Afines, in Guayaquil, July 15, 1975.

55. Interview with Sergio Quiñones Fajardo, secretary-general, Comité de Empresa of Cristelalerías del Ecuador, in Guayaquil, July 15, 1975.

56. Interview with Víctor Recalde, secretary-general of Comité de Empresa of Ingenio San Carlos, at the Ingenio, Guayas, July 15, 1975.

57. Interview with Winfried Bach, representative in Ecuador of Konrad Adenauer Foundation, in Quito, July 14, 1975.

58. John Martz in *1977 Yearbook on International Communist Affairs,* Hoover Institution Press, Stanford, CA, 1977, p. 445.

59. Interview with Jacinto Figueroa Vera, secretary of conflicts, and subsequently president of Confederación Ecuatoriana de Obreros Católicos, in Quito, July 12, 1975.

60. Lynn Ratliff in *1973 Yearbook on International Communist Affairs,* Hoover Institution Press, Stanford, CA, 1973, p. 340.

61. Interview with Cesario Valverde, secretary-general of Federación Provincial de Trabajadores de Guayas (CTE), in Guayaquil, July 14, 1975.

62. Interviews with David Passage, political officer, acting labor reporting officer, U.S. Embassy, in Quito, July 14, 1975; and Remo Ray Garufi, deputy director of Agency for International Development/Ecuador, in Quito, July 11, 1975.

63. Interview with Jacinto Figueroa Vera, op. cit., Quito, July 12, 1975.

64. Interview Remo Ray Garufi, op. cit., Quito, July 12, 1975.

65. John Martz in 1977 *Yearbook on International Communist Affairs,* op. cit., p. 446.

66. Robert J. Alexander in *The Americana Annual 1977,* New York, 1977, p. 189.

67. Lynn Ratliff in *1975 Yearbook on International Communist Affairs,* Hoover Institution Press, Stanford, CA, p. 508.

68. Milk, op. cit., p. 294.
69. David Scott Palmer in *1983 Yearbook on International Communist Affairs,* Hoover Institution Press, Stanford, CA, 1981, p. 86.
70. Milk, op. cit., p. 293.
71. Interview with Bolívar Martínez, member of National Directorate of CEDOC, in Guayaquil, July 12, 1975.
72. Interview with Jacinto Figueroa Vera, op. cit., July 12, 1975.
73. Interview with Winfried Bach, op. cit., July 14, 1975.
74. Interview with Angel Padilla Barahona, secretary-general of Federación Sindical de Trabajadores de Guayas (dissident group of CEDOC in Guayas), in Guayaquil, July 16, 1975.
75. "Alai Entrevista al Presidente de la CEDOC," printed bulletin of Agence Latinoamericaine d'Information, co-sponsored by Federación Latino Americana de Periodistas and Federation Professionelle des Journalistes du Quebec, Montreal.
76. Interview with Jorge Zevallos, president of Partido Izquierda Democrática of Ecuador, in Santo Domingo, Dominican Republic, October 29, 1977.
77. Interview with Pedro Cantos, op. cit., July 11, 1975.
78. Interview with Agustín Torres Lazo, country program director for Ecuador of American Institute for Free Labor Development, in Quito, July 11, 1975.
79. Letter of Luis B. Villacrés Arandi to "Todos Los Presidentes y Secretarios Generales de las Federaciones Provinciales, Regionales, Cantonales y por Ramas de Trabajo y Organizaciones de Base Afiliados a 'CEOSL' " Quito, July 4, 1975 (mimeographed).
80. Letter of Luis B. Villacrés Arandi to "Señor doctor Ramiro Larrea Santos, Ministro de Trabajo y Bienestar Social," Quito, July 2, 1975 (mimeographed).
81. Letter of leaders of affiliates of CEOSL to President Guillermo Rodríguez Lara, Minister of Government and Police Guillermo Durán Argentales and Minister of Labor and Social Welfare Ramiro Larrea Santos, Quito, July 21, 1975 (mimeographed).
82. *El Comercio,* Quito, June 28, 1976.
83. *Los Tiempos,* Cochabamba, Bolivia, April 3, 1976.
84. Robert J. Alexander in *The American Annual 1977,* op. cit., p. 189.
85. John Martz in *1977 Yearbook on International Communist Affairs,* op. cit., p. 447.
86. John Martz in *1978 Yearbook on International Communist Affairs,* Hoover Institution Press, Stanford, CA, 1978, p. 374.
87. Interview with Edmundo Mejía, member of Executive of Federación de Trabajadores Azucareros, at Ingenio San Carlos, Guayas Province, July 18, 1975.
88. Fred Murphy, "Police Gun Down Striking Sugar Workers in Ecuador," *Intercontinental Press,* New York, November 7, 1977, p. 1217.
89. John Martz in *1979 Yearbook on International Communist Affairs,* Hoover Institution Press, Stanford, CA, p. 345.
90. John Martz in *1980 Yearbook on International Communist Affairs,* Hoover Institution Press, Stanford, CA, 1980, p. 353.
91. John Martz in *1981 Yearbook on International Communist Affairs,* Hoover Institution Press, Stanford, CA, 1981, p. 70.

92. John Martz in *1982 Yearbook of International Communist Affairs,* Hoover Institution Press, Stanford, CA, 1982, p. 95.

93. David Scott Palmer in *1983 Yearbook on International Communist Affairs,* Hoover Institution Press, Stanford, CA, 1983, p. 86.

94. "Embajada del Ecuador Bulletin #609, October 1982," Washington, DC.

95. David Scott Palmer in *1983 Yearbook on International Communist Affairs,* op. cit., p. 86.

96. Ibid., p. 86; and "Embaja del Ecuador, Bulletin #610, November 1983," Washington, DC.

97. David Scott Palmer in *1984 Yearbook on International Communist Affairs,* Hoover Institution Press, Stanford, CA, 1984, p. 119.

98. David Scott Palmer in *1985 Yearbook on International Communist Affairs,* Hoover Institution, Stanford, CA, 1985, p. 80; and *El Pais,* Madrid, November 3, 1984.

99. David Scott Palmer in *1985 Yearbook on International Communist Affairs,* op. cit., p. 80.

100. Catherine M. Conaghan in *1986 Yearbook on International Communist Affairs,* Hoover Institution Press, Stanford, CA, 1986, p. 85.

101. Catherine M. Conaghan in *1987 Yearbook on International Communist Affairs,* Hoover Institution Press, Stanford, CA, 1987, p. 88.

102. *Latin American Report,* London, January 28, 1989, p. 11.

103. *Latin American Report,* London, May 18, 1988, p. 1.

104. *Latin American Report,* London, June 9, 1988, p. 4.

105. *Latin American Report,* London, June 16, 1988, p. 5.

106. *Latin American* Report, London, June 20, 1988, p. 11 and, July 7, 1988, p. 10.

107. *Latin American Report,* London, January, 5, 1989, p. 77, and November 2, 1989.

108. *Latin American Report,* London, July 19, 1990, p. 9.

109. *Latin American Report,* London, August 3, 1989, p. 12.

110. *Latin American Report,* London, August 2, 1990, p. 3.

111. Galo Chiriboga Zambrano in Holm-Detlev Köhler and Manfred Wannöffel (coordinadores), *Modelo Neoliberal y Sindicatos en América Latina,* Fundación Friedrich Ebert, México, 1993, p. 149.

112. Ibid., p. 156.

113. Ibid., p. 156.

114. Interview with Ricardo Paredes, founder and longtime secretary-general of Partido Comunista de l Ecuador, in Quito, July 5, 1947.

115. John Martz in 1977 Yearbook on International Communist Affairs, op. cit., p. 447.

116. Lynn Ratliff in *1971 Yearbook on Latin American Communist Affairs,* op. cit., p. 86.

117. Interview with Roberto A. Nevárez Ponce, op. cit., July 12, 1962.

118. Interview with Jacinto Figueroa Vera, op. cit., July 12, 1975.

119. Interview with Cristóbal Vera, president of Federación Nacional de Campesinos, agrarian secretary of Confederación Ecuatoriana de Organizaciones Sindicales Libres, in Quito, July 13, 1975.

120. Interview with Jacinto Figueroa Vera, op. cit., July 5, 1966.

121. Interview with Cristóbal Vera, op. cit., July 13, 1975.

122. Interview with José Gaybort, lawyer for Confederación Ecuatoriana de Organizaciones Clasistas, in Guayaquil, July 16, 1975.

123. "ACAL al Pueblo y al Gobierno del Ecuador," in *Nueva*, monthly newsmagazine, Quito, June 1975, pp. 106–107.

124. Interview with Barbara C. Schroeder, member of Rutgers University Anthropology Department, officer of Office of Educational Policy Studies, in Mexico City, June 11, 1988.

125. *Latin American Report*, London, June 28, 1990, p. 1.

Bibliography

BOOKS AND PAMPHLETS

Alexander, Robert J. Aprismo. *The Ideas and Doctrines of Victor Raúl Haya de la Torre*, The Kent State University Press, Kent, OH, 1973.
————. *International Trotskyism 1929–1984: A Documented Analysis of the Movement*, Duke University Press, Durham, NC, 1991.
American Labor Year Book 1923–24. Rand School Press, New York, 1924.
American Labor Year Book 1931. Rand School Press, New York, 1931.
American Labor Year Book 1932, Rand School Press, New York, 1932.
Añi Castillo, Gonzalo. *Historia Secreta de las Guerrillas*, Ediciones "Mas Alla," Lima, 1967.
Asociaciones de Trabajadores del Ecuador, 1942, Quito, 1942.
Balbi, Carmen Rosa. *Las Relaciones Estado-Sindicalismo en el Peru 1985–1987*, Fundación Friedrich Ebert, Lima, 1988.
Bazan, Armando. *Biografía de José Carlos Mariátegui*, Zig-Zag, Santiago, Chile, 1939.
CGTP III Congreso Nacional 6–10 Marzo 1974, Lima, Peru, Lima, 1974.
Comunidad Laboral: de la Ficción a la Realidad, Junaj, Lima, 1975.
Confederación de Trabajadores del Perú. *Memoria 1964–1967: Un esfuerzo permanente por la dignificación del Trabajador*, Lima, 1967.
Confederación General de Trabajadores del Perú. *CONADET 87: Somos Alternative de Gobierno y de Poder*, Lima, 1987.
El Movimiento Revolucionario Latino Americano, Report of the First Conference of Latin American Communist Parties, Buenos Aires, 1929.
Espinoza, Gustavo. *1° de Mayo: Intervención de Gustavo Espinoza, S-G de la C.G.T.P. en el Mitin del 1° de Mayo de 1972*, Lima, 1972.
Greenfield, Gerald Michael and Sheldon L. Maram (editors). *Latin American Labor Organizations*, Greenwood Press, Westport, CT, 1987.

Guy, Inman. *Latin America—Its Place in World Life,* Willst, Clark & Co., New York, 1937.

Haya de la Torre, Víctor Raúl. *La Jornada de las 8 Horas,* Lima, n.d.

Johnson, Nancy R. *The Political, Economic and Labor Climate in Peru,* Industrial Research Unit, The Wharton School, University of Pennsylvania, Philadelphia, 1979.

Kantor, Harry. *Patterns of Politics and Political Systems in Latin America,* Rand McNally, Chicago, 1969.

Köhler, Holm-Detlv and Manfred Wannöffel (coordinadores). *Modelo Neoliberal y Sindicatos en América Latina,* Fundación Fiedrich Ebert, México, D.F., 1993.

Lozovsky, Alexander, *El Movimiento Sindical Latino Americana—Sus Virtudes y Sus Defectos,* Ediciones del Comité Pro Confederación Sindical Latino Americana, Montevideo, n.d.

Martínez de la Torre, Ricardo. *Apuntes para una Interpretación Marxista de la Historia Social del Perú,* Volume 1, Empresa Editora Peruana S.A., Lima, 1947.

———. *El Movimiento Obrero en 1919,* Lima, 1928.

Movimiento Obrero, Sindicatos y Poder en América Latina, Editorial El Coloquio, Buenos Aires, 1975.

1971 Yearbook on Latin American Communist Affairs, Hoover Institution Press, Stanford, CA, 1971.

1973 Yearbook on International Communist Affairs, Hoover Institution Press, Stanford, CA, 1973

1975 Yearbook on International Communist Affairs, Hoover Institution Press, Stanford, CA, 1975.

1977 Yearbook on International Communist Affairs, Hoover Institution Press, Stanford, CA, 1977.

1978 Yearbook on International Communist Affairs, Hoover Institution Press, Stanford, CA; 1978.

1979 Yearbook on International Communist Affairs, Hoover Institution Press, Stanford, CA, 1979.

1980 Yearbook on International Communist Affairs, Hoover Institution Press, Stanford, CA, 1980.

1981 Yearbook on International Communist Affairs, Hoover Institution Press, Stanford, CA, 1980.

1982 Yearbook on International Communist Affairs, Hoover Institution Press, Stanford, CA, 1981.

1983 Yearbook on International Communist Affairs, Hoover Institution Press, Stanford, CA, 1983.

1984 Yearbook on International Communist Affairs, Hoover Institution Press, Stanford, CA, 1984.

1985 Yearbook on International Communist Affairs, Hoover Institution Press, Stanford, CA, 1985.

1986 Yearbook on International Communist Affairs, Hoover Institution Press, Stanford, CA, 1986.

1987 Yearbook on International Communist Affairs, Hoover Institution Press, Stanford, CA, 1987.

1988 Yearbook on International Communist Affairs, Hoover Institution Press, Stanford, CA, 1988.

Palmer, David Scott (editor). *Shining Path of Peru,* St. Martin's Press, New York, 1992.

Pareja Pflucker, Piedad. *Aprismo y Sindicalismo en el Perú 1943–1948,* Ediciones Rikchay Peru, Lima, 1980.
Payne, James L. *Labor and Politics in Peru: The System of Political Bargaining,* Yale University Press, New Haven, 1965.
Poblete Troncoso, Moisés. *El Movimiento Obrero Latinoamericano,* Fondo de Cultura Económica, México, D.F., 1946.
Primero Congreso Católico Nacional, Quito, 1935.
Segundo Congreso Nacional de Obreros Católicos Ecuatorianos, Quito, 30 de Junio de al 2 del Julio de 1944, Quito, 1944.
2do Congreso Nacional de Trabajadores del Perú: Conclusiones y Resoluciones CGTP, 1–5 de Diciembre 1971, Lima.
Sulmont, Denis. *El movimiento obrero peruano (1890–1980), reseña histórica,* Tarea, Lima, 1981.
The Americana Annual 1977, New York, 1977.

NEWSPAPERS AND PERIODICALS

AFL-CIO News, Washington, DC.
Allied Labor News, pro-Communist news service, New York City.
Amauta, periodical edited by José Carlos Mariátegui in Lima in the 1920s.
Análisis Laboral, scholarly monthly dealing with "Social-Economic and Legal Aspects," Lima.
Boletín Diario de Jornada, daily newspaper, Lima.
Boletín Latino Americano del CIO, periodical of Congress of Industrial Organizations, Washington, DC.
The Call, Socialist Party daily, New York City.
Chicago Daily News.
Claridad, Socialist periodical, Buenos Aires.
Combate, daily newspaper, Lima.
Daily Worker, newspaper of Communist Party of U.S., New York City.
Democracia y Trabajo, organ of Communist Party of Peru during first Prado administration, Lima.
El Comercio, daily newspaper, Quito.
El Comercio, daily newspaper, Lima.
El Nacional, daily newspaper, Caracas, Venezuela.
El Obrero Textil, official newspaper of Textile Workers Federation, Lima.
El Popular, official daily of Confederación de Trabajadores de México, México City.
El Siglo, daily newspaper, Quito.
El Trabajador, pro-Communist periodical of early World War II period, Quito.
El Telégrafo, daily newspaper, Quito.
El Universo, daily newspaper, Guayaquil, Ecuador.
Expreso, daily newspaper, Lima.
Foreign Affairs, periodical of Council on Foreign Relation, New York.
Fortune, news and feature magazine, New York.
Hispanic American Historical Review, scholarly journal.
Hispano Americano, newsmagazine, Mexico City.
Hoy, daily newspaper, La Paz.
Inter-American, magazine, New York City.

Inter-American Labor News, New York City.
Intercontinental Press, periodical of Socialist Workers Party, New York City.
International Labor Review, monthly of International Labor Office, Montreal.
International Press Correspondence, periodical of Communist International.
La Antorcha, Quito newspaper.
Labor, monthly magazine of International Federation of Christian Trade Unions.
La Correspondencia Sudamericana, periodical of South American Secretariat of
    Communist International, Buenos Aires.
La Defensa, weekly periodical of Centro Católico de Obreros, Quito.
La Justicia, origin of Unión General de Empleados de Comercio, Quito.
La Nueva Crónica, daily newspaper, Lima.
La Prensa, daily newspaper, Buenos Aires.
La Prensa, daily newspaper, Lima.
Latin America, weekly newsmagazine on Latin America, London.
Latin American Report, weekly periodical on Latin America, London.
La Tierra, newspaper of Partido Socialista del Ecuador, Quito.
La Tribuna, daily newspaper of Partido Aprista Peruano, Lima.
Los Tiempos, daily newspaper, Cochabamba, Bolivia.
Marka, news and features magazine, Lima.
Metal, periodical of International Metalworkers Federation.
Mother Earth, anarchist magazine edited by Emma Goldman, New York.
National Catholic Welfare Conference News Service, Washington, DC.
New York Herald Tribune, daily newspaper, November 23, 1930.
New York Times, daily newspaper.
Noticiario Obrero Norteamericano, publication of American Federation of Labor,
    Washington, DC.
Noticiero de la C.T.A.L., publication of Confederation de Trabajadores de América
    Latina, Mexico City.
Nueva, monthly newsmagazine, Quito.
ORIT Notes, occasional periodical of Organización Regional Interamericana de
    Trabajadores, México, D.F.
Prensa Sindical, labor periodical, Lima.
Presente, newsmagazine, Lima.
RILU Magazine, organ of Red International of Labor Unions, Moscow.
Solidaridad, official organ of Federación Textil and Federación Obrera Local, Lima.
The Times of the Americas, biweekly newspaper, Miami.
Trabajadores, periodical of Federación de Trabajadores de Pichincha, Quito.
Ultima Hora, daily newspaper, Lima.
Unidad, newspaper of pro-Soviet Partido Communist del Perú, Lima.
Vanguardia, magazine of Eudosio Rabines, Lima.
Voz Obrera, pro-Nazi paper, Quito.

INTERVIEWS

Abarca, Alfredo, editor of *Unidad,* weekly newspaper of pro-Soviet Partido
    Comunista del Perú, in Lima, July 17, 1975.
Aguero, Héctor Petrovich, secretary of organization, Lima Light and Power
    Company *sindicato,* in New Brunswick, NJ, February 24, 1954.

Alcazar Sarmiento, Antonio, secretary of defense of Sindicato Ferrocarril Central del Perú, in New Brunswick, NJ, February 24, 1954.

Amott, John C., labor reporting officer, U.S. Embassy, in Lima, August 29, 1956.

Aparicio, Álvaro, president of Federación Ferroviaria, in Quito, September 5, 1956.

Aramburu, Carlos, secretario de hacienda, Confederación de Trabajadores del Perú, in Lima, August 29, 1956.

Arbito Reinoso, Joaquín, secretary-general, Federación Ecuatoriana de Trabajadores Hoteleros y Ramos Afines, in Guayaquil, Ecuador, July 15, 1975.

Arca Parro, Alberto, senator, one of founders of Socialist Party of Peru, in Lima, June 27, 1947.

Arévalo Silva, Armando, northern secretary of Confederación de Trabajadores del Perú, in Rio Piedras, Puerto Rico, July 9, 1962.

Aspillaga, Eduardo, secretary-general of Federación de Obreros Panaderos "Estrella del Perú," in Lima, June 24, 1947.

Avalos, Rafael, president of Federación Nacional de Campesinos del Perú, in Lima, July 13, 1971.

Bach, Winfried, representative in Ecuador of Konrad Adenauer Foundation, in Quito, July 14, 1975.

Barbarán, Vicente, president of Juventud Trabajadora Ecuatoriana, youth wing of Confederación Ecuatoriana de Obreros Católicos, in Quito, July 5, 1966.

Bastidas C., Celestino, member of Executive of Aprista-controlled Federación de Trabajadores de la Construcción Civil del Perú, in Rio Piedras, Puerto Rico, July 29, 1959.

Benitez, José, president of Federación Gráfica del Perú in Lima, August 18, 1952.

Benítez, Marcial, president of Federación Campesina del Norte of FENCAP, and CTP, in Lima, July 13, 1971.

Brauer, Carl, first secretary, U.S. Embassy, in Lima, July 13, 1953.

Brown, David, adviser to the Ministry of Agriculture, economist from Iowa State University, in Lima, July 1, 1966.

Calvo Gross, Guillermo, secretary of culture and sports, Sindicato Ferrocarril del Sur, in Quito, August 21, 1952.

Cano Sánchez, Humberto, secretary of hygiene of Federación de Panadores "Estrella del Perú," in Lima, August 18, 1952.

Cantos, Pedro, member of staff of Instituto de Educación Sindical Ecuatoriana, in Quito, July 11, 1975.

Carillo, Miguel, president of Sindicato Textil de Ambato, in Quito, September 5, 1956.

Carranza, Manuel, secretario de la Selva of Federación Nacional de Campesinos del Perú, in Lima, July 8, 1971.

Carrasco, Raúl, secretary of organization, Federación Campesina del Perú, in Lima, July 10, 1972.

Carrión, Jaime, an editor of Socialist Party newspaper *La Tierra*, in Quito, September 4, 1956.

Castillo, Luciano, founder of Partido Socialista del Perú, in Lima, June 26, 1947, July 13, 1953, August 18, 1952, August 29, 1956.

Castillo, Mary, member of National Executive of Partido Socialista del Perú, wife of Luciano Castillo, in Lima, April 6, 1962, July 18, 1975.

Castro, Carlos, ex-president of Electrical Workers Federation of Guayas, in Quito, July 13, 1975.

Cevallos Hidrobo, Miguel Angel, president of Federación de Trabajadores de Pichincha, in Quito, July 8, 1947.

Chang Crespo, Julio, president of Federación de Trabajadores Libres de Guayas, in Guayaquil, July 15, 1975.

Chau Villanueva, Wilfredo, secretary-general, Federación de Trabajadores de Hospitales, in Lima, July 10, 1972.

Cháves, Nelson, president of Federación Ferroviaria, in Quito, August 21, 1952.

Cotillo, Rogelio, member of Executive of Santa Corporation Workers Union of Peru, in Annapolis, MD, September 28, 1963.

Cox, Carlos Manuel, Aprista member of the Senate, in Lima, June 29, 1966.

Creagan, James, labor reporting officer, U.S. Embassy, in Lima, July 17, 1975.

Cruzado, Julio, secretary-general of Confederación de Trabajadores del Perú, in Lima, July 18, 1975.

Cruzado, Leonidas, president of Federación de Trabajadores Azucareros del Perú, in Lima, July 7, 1971.

D'Angles, Lucio, secretary of organization of Federation of Private Employees in La Libertad, Peru, in Annapolis, MD, September 28, 1963.

Deane, Warren, political officer of U.S. Embassy, in Quito, July 5, 1966.

Delgado, Carlos, subchief of Sistema Nacional de Apoyo de la Mobilización Social (SINAMOS), ex-Aprista, in Lima, July 13, 1971.

del Piélago, Tomás, ex-Aprista, pro-Peronista leader of Graphic Workers Federation, in Lima, August 18, 1952.

de Santillana, Geraldo, political officer of U.S. Embassy, in Lima, June 30, 1966.

Donos Baquerizo, Eduardo, technical adviser of Cámara de Industria de Guayaquil, in Guayaquil, July 16, 1975.

Dulanto, Octavio R., founder and ex-president of Sindicato de Trabajadores del Ferrocarril Central del Perú, in Lima, August 29, 1956.

Duque, Pablo, secretary of finances, Confederación de Trabajadores del Ecuador, in Quito, August 21, 1952, September 6, 1956, July 4, 1966.

Dustman, William, first secretary and labor reporting officer, U.S. Embassy, in Quito, September 5, 1956.

Echegaray, Mariano M., national secretary of Indian Affairs, and Cleofe Túpac Yupanque de Saenz, head of Women's Section of same secretariat of Aprista Party, in Lima, June 21, 1947.

Espinosa O., J. Osvaldo, secretary of Cámara de Agricultura de la Primera Zona, in Quito, July 4, 1947, September 7, 1956.

Espinoza, Antonio, member of Executive Committee of Confederación Obrera de Guayas, in New Brunswick, NJ, May 16, 1954.

Espinoza, Gustavo, secretary-general, Confederación General de Trabajadores del Perú, in Lima, July 12, 1972.

Espinoza, Hugo, member of Executive Committee of Confederación Ecuatoriana de Obreros Católicos, in Quito, July 5, 1966.

Espinoza Segovia, Hernán, secretary of culture of Confederación General de Trabajadores del Perú, in Lima, October 6, 1987.

Fernández Stoll, Jorge, director general of labor under presidents Benavides and Prado, in Lima, June 20, 1947.

Figueroa, Jaime, editor of *Unidad*, weekly newspaper of pro-Soviet Partido Comunista del Perú, in Lima, July 12, 1971.

Figueroa Vera, Jacinto, secretary of conflicts, and subsequently president of Confederación Ecuatoriana de Obreros Católicos, in Quito, July 5, 1966, July 12, 1975.

Freire, Luis, president of Federación de Calzado y Curtiembre del Ecuador, in Quito, September 5, 1956.

Frías, Ismael, former Trotskyist leader, supporter of Velasco regime, journalist of *La Crónica* of Lima, in Lima, July 13, 1971.

Gamarra Ramírez, Isidoro, president of Confederación General de Trabajadores del Perú, in Lima, July 17, 1975.

García, Elias, trade union secretary of Communist Party of Peru, in Lima, June 20, 1947.

García Calderón, Major General, former subsecretary of labor in government of President Juan Velasco Alvarado, in Washington, DC, January 18, 1977.

Garufi, Remo Ray, deputy director of Agency for International Development/ Ecuador, in Quito, July 11, 1975.

Gaybort, José, lawyer for Confederación Ecuatoriana de Organizaciones Clasistas, in Guayaquil, July 1, 1975.

Gaybort Rada, Humberto, member of Executive Committee of Federación Provincial de Trabajadores del Guayas, secretary-general of Partido Socialista of Guayaquil, in Guayaquil, July 1, 1947.

Gilmore, Eugene, economic counselor of U.S. Embassy, in Lima, August 2, 1954.

Gomero Gomero, Medardo, member of Executive of Sindicato de Chóferes de Servicio Público de Lima, in Rio Piedras, Puerto Rico, July 29, 1959.

Green, James, official of United States Agency for International Development in Peru, in Lima, June 30, 1966.

Greene, David, economist of United States Agency for International Development in Peru, in Lima, July 24, 1968.

Guimare, Mario, secretary of discipline, Confederación de Trabajadores del Perú, in Lima, July 10, 1972.

Guzmán, Migual Angel, vice president of Confederación de Trabajadores del Ecuador, Socialist, in Quito, July 4, 1947.

Haya de la Torre, Víctor Raúl, founder and "Jefe" of Partido Aprista Peruano, in Lima, June 18, 1947.

Hernández, A., president of Asociación de Empleados del Perú, in Lima, June 22, 1947.

Hidalgo, Telmo, president of Federación de Trabajadores de Pichincha, in Quito, September 5, 1956.

Jara, Fortunato, head of Buro Nacional de Sindicatos of Aprista Party, member of Executive Committee of Confederación de Trabajadores del Perú, in Lima, June 19, 1947, September 3, 1956.

Jáuregui, Arturo, exiled Peruvian labor leader, in Montevideo, Uruguay, July 29, 1952, in México, D.F., August 16, 1963.

Larrea Benalcazar, Hugo, member of National Executive of Socialist Party, in Quito, September 5, 1956, July 6, 1966.

Latorre, Juan, onetime secretary-general of Sindicato de Chóferes de Lima, in Lima, June 18, 1947.

Lizarzaburu, Alberto, a leader of Textile Workers Federation, in New Brunswick, NJ, March 2, 1954, in Lima, July 31, 1954, September 3, 1956.

López, Augusto, secretary of economy of Federación de Chóferes del Perú, in Lima, September 1, 1956.

López Castelo, Aquiles Gustavo, a leader of Sindicato Único de Chóferes de Pichincha, in Rio Piedras, Puerto Rico, July 15, 1958.

Luna, Juan P., former secretary-general of the Confederación de Trabajadores del Perú, member of Chamber of Deputies under first Prado regime, in Lima, June 28, 1947, August 19, 1952, July 25, 1968.

Machuca Ibarra, Fausto, secretary of justicia y reclamos of Sindicato Ferroviario Ecuatoriano—Comité Local Riobamba, in Rio Piedras, Puerto Rico, July 12, 1962.

Maldonado Tamayo, Luis, secretary-general of Partido Socialista, Ecuatoriano, in Quito, July 6, 1947.

Martínez, Bolívar, member of National Directorate of CEODC, in Guayaquil, July 12, 1975.

Martínez de la Torre, Ricardo, a founder of Communist Party of Peru, leading historian of early Peruvian labor movement, in Lima, June 27, 1947, July 13, 1953.

Mejía, Edmundo, member of Executive of Federación de Trabajadores Azucareros, at Ingenio San Carlos, Guayas Province, July 18, 1975.

Méndez Williams, Máximo, secretary of press and propaganda, Federación Nacional de Trabajadores Ferroviarios, in Lima, June 23, 1947.

Mendoza, Julio Miguel, press secretary; Julio César Abarca, secretary-general, and Alfonso Luna, member of Cuzco Local of Aprista Party, in Cuzco, June 9, 1947.

Mendoza Benavides, Pompeyo, delegate of Unión Sindical de Pasco to Confederación de Trabajadores del Perú, in Lima, July 24, 1968.

Miranda Donayre, Juan, secretary-general of Sindicato Mixto Central de Generación y Similares de Electrolina, in New York City, February 24, 1979.

Mujica, Nicanor, Aprista leader, leader, minister of the presidency of Peru, in New York City, June 10, 1986.

Navarro, José, secretary-general, and Juan P. Pérez, press secretary of Federación Campesinos y Yanacones, in Lima, June 23, 1947.

Negreiros, Luis, secretary-general, Unión Departamental de Empleados Particulares de Lima, former secretary-general of Federación Tranviaria, in Lima, June 22, 1947.

Nevárez Ponce, Roberto A., a leader of Sindicato Ferroviario Ecuatoriano, in Rio Piedras, July 12, 1962.

Oramas, Marco T., secretary of organization of Confederación de Trabajadores del Ecuador, in Quito, September, 5, 1956.

Padilla Barahona, Angel, secretary-general of Federación Sindical de Trabajadores de Guayas (dissident group of CEDOC in Guayas), in Guayaquil, July 16, 1975.

Palacios Sáenz, Carlos, leader of Socialist Party of Guayaquil, in Guayaquil, July 2, 1947.

Paredes, Ricardo, founder and secretary-general of Partido Comunista del Ecuador, in Quito, July 5, 1947.

Parra, Pedro, leader of Frente de Unidad y Independencia Sindical, ex-anarchist, ex-Communist, member of Partido Socialists Auténtico, in Lima, June 25, 1947; secretary-general, Federación de Chóferes del Perú, in Lima, September 3, 1956.

Passage, David, political officer, acting labor reporting officer, U.S. Embassy, in Quito, July 14, 1975.

Payne, James L., scholar of Peruvian labor movement, in New Brunswick, NJ, January 20, 1962.

Pérez, Alberto, secretary of Grievance Committee, Sindicato Municipal de Transportes of Lima, in New Brunswick, NJ, September 13, 1963.

Pita, Leopoldo, former (and future) head of Sugar Workers Federation of Peru, in San José, Costa Rica, August 29, 1952, in Lima, July 6, 1957.

Pringle, Sandy, second secretary and labor reporting officer, U.S. Embassy, in Lima, August 18, 1952.

Purcell, Arthur, labor attaché of U.S. Embassy, in Lima, July 9, 1971, July 10, 1972.

Quiñones Fajardo, Sergio, secretary-general, Comité de Empresa of Cristalerías del Ecuador, in Guayaquil, July 15, 1975.

Rabines, Eudosio, founder of Peruvian Communist Party, in Lima, June 23, 1947.

Ramírez, Salas, Manuel, secretary-general, Federación de Chóferes y Anexos del Perú, in Lima, July 10, 1972.

Recalde, Víctor, secretary-general of Comité de Empresa of Ingenio San Carlos, at Ingenio San Carlos, Guayas, July 15, 1975.

Roa, Raúl, secretary-general of Glass Workers Federation, in Lima, June 23, 1947.

Romualdi, Serafino, assistant secretary of ORIT, in Santiago, Chile, July 30, 1956.

Rosales, Julio, Peruvian representative of the International Federation of Free Teachers Union, in Lima, July 18, 1975.

Saad, Pedro, first secretary-general of Confederación de Trabajadores del Ecuador, a major Communist leader, in Guayaquil, July 8, 1947; in Quito, August 21, 1952.

Sabroso, Arturo, secretary-general of Confederación de Trabajadores del Perú, in Lima, June 17, 1947, August 18, 1952, July 12, 1953, August 30, 1956.

Salazar, Abelardo, a leader of Communist Party in Cuzco, in Cuzco, June 12, 1947.

Sanabria Benítez, Germán, president of Federación Ecuatoriana de Trabajadores Embarques de Fruto, in Quito, July 5, 1966.

Sánchez, Luis Alberto, one of principal leaders of Partido Aprista Peruano, in Salvador, Brazil, August 9, 1962; in Lima, July 9, 1971.

Sánchez, Víctor, member of Executive Committee of Confederación Obrera de Guayas, in New Brunswick, NJ, May 16, 1954.

Sandoval Morales, José, adviser to Confederación de Trabajadores del Perú, former head of Textile Workers Federation, in Lima, June 29, 1966.

Sarmiento, Augusto, Eduardo García, José Lira Rojas, René Somocurso, Ladisláo Valdivieso, secretary-general, delegate to Federación de Trabajadores de Cuzco, member of defense organization, president of the cooperative and secretary of culture, respectively, of Sindicato de Chóferes de Cuzco, in Cuzco, June 8, 1947.

Schroeder, Barbara C., member of Rutgers University Anthropology Department, officer of Office of Educational Policy Studies, in Mexico City, June 11, 1988.

Sime Rivadeneira, Juan Ancres, director of Maritime Workers Hour, head of Dock
    Watchmen's Union of Callao, in New Brunswick, NJ, March 12, 1954.
Tabada, Juan, secretary-general of Sindicato Petrolero de Talara #1, in Washington,
    DC, November 26, 1967.
Temoche, Ricardo, international secretary of Partido Aprista Peruano, former
    of Executive of Confederación de Trabajadores del Perú, in Lima, July 7,
    1971.
Torres, Ezequiel, vice president of Confederación de Trabajadores del Ecuador, in
    Quito, August 21, 1952.
Torres, Víctor, secretary-general, Federación de Azucareros del Perú, in Lima, July
    8, 1971.
Torres Lazo, Agustín, country program director for Ecuador of American Institute
    for Free Labor Development, in Quito, July 11, 1975.
Townsend Ezcurra, Andrés, a major leader of Partido Aprista Peruano, in New
    York City, November 15, 1975.
Uria, Guillermo, chief of Estrella Section of Fabrica Huascar-Estrella, in Cuzco,
    June 11, 1947.
Valdivia Fulchi, Eugenio, leader of Aprista students in University of San Marcos,
    in Lima, October 6, 1987.
Valverde, Cesario, secretary-general of Federación Provincial de Trabajadores de
    Guayas (of the CTE), July 14, 1975.
Vargas, Emilio, Enrique de la Fuente, Julio Oliveiro, secretary-general, treasurer,
    and subsecretary, respectively, of Federación Gráfica del Perú, in Lima, June
    24, 1947.
Vega, Pacífico, president of Federación de Chóferes del Ecuador, in Quito,
    September 5, 1956.
Vela, Mike, former representative in Peru of Clerical and Office Workers Trade
    Secretariat, in New York City, January 25, 1965.
Velasco Ibarra, Pedro, president of Confederación Ecuatoriana de Obreros
    Católicos, in Quito, July 7, 1947, August 21, 1952, September 5, 1956.
Vera, Cristóbal, president of Federación Nacional de Campesinos, agrarian
    secretary of Confederación Ecuatoriana de Organizaciones Sindicales
    Libres, in Quito, July 13, 1975.
Viale, Francisco, a leader of Socialist-controlled Petroleum Workers Federation,
    Socialist member of Chamber of Deputies, in Lima, August 18, 1952.
Villacorta, David, secretary of coordination of Federación de Construcción Civil,
    in Lima, June 23, 1947.
Villacréses, Noé, president of Federación Nacional de Trabajadores Textiles, in
    Quito, September 5, 1956.
Vizcarra Rosas, Abraham, president of Sociedad Mutua de Empleados, organizer
    of Federación de Empleados y Obreros de Cuzco, in Cuzco, June 11, 1947.
Wheeler, Charles, AIFLD country program director of Peru and Bolivia, in Lima,
    July 17, 1975.
Yzaguirre, Virginia, member of National Executive of Partido Aprista Peruano, in
    New York City, May 11, 1964.
Zavala Núñez, Leobardo, official of Sindicato Unido de Obreros y Empleados de
    la International Petroleum Company of Callao, in Rio Piedras, Puerto Rico,
    June 5, 1958.
Zavala V., Víctor, a leader of Socialist-controlled Petroleum Workers Federation,
    Socialist member of Chamber of Deputies, in Lima, August 19, 1952.

Zevallos, Jorge, president of Partido Izquierda Democrático of Ecuador, in Santo
    Domingo, Dominican Republic, October 29, 1977.
Zhannafría T., Luis Alfonso, assistant to labor inspector of Quito, in Quito,
    September 7, 1956.

MISCELLANEOUS

"Alai Entrevista al President de la CEDOC," printed bulletin of Agence Latino-
    Américaine d'Information, co-sponsored by Federación Latino Americana
    de Periodistas and Federation Profesionelle des Journalistes de Quebec,
    Montreal.
Alexander, Robert J. "Impressions of Ecuador, July 5, 1966" (typewritten).
Associated Press.
Confederación de Trabajadores del Perú, "Manifesto a Todos Los Trabajadores de
    la República y Opinión General del País," Lima, n.d. (but circa May 1956).
Confederación Ecuatoriana de Obreros Católicos: "A Los Trabajadores del
    Ecuador," n.d. (circa 1952) (throwaway).
Confederación Latinoamericana de Sindicalistas Cristianos: "Manifiesto de la
    CLASC en Torno al Problema Laboral del Perú," Santiago, Chile, December
    22, 1962.
"Consejo Directivo Nacional de la CTP (Periodo de 1973–1976)" (typewritten).
Costilla Larrea, Emilio. "Apuntes para la Historia de la Lucha Social en el Perú"
    (manuscript).
"Embajada del Ecuador, Bulletin #609, October 1982," Washington, DC.
"Embajada del Ecuador, Bulletin #610, November 1982," Washington, DC.
Federación Azcareros of CTP "Modificación del Decreto-Ley No. 17,716
    (mimeographed).
Foreign Broadcast Information Service, Washington, DC.
"Informe Sobre el Balance del Paro Nacional Unitario y Popular del 19 de Mayo de
    1987, Aprobado por el Consejo Nacional de la CGTP" (mimeographed).
"The Interamerican Confederation of Labor Refutes the Junta Militar de Gobierno
    of Peru," Santiago, Chile, December 28, 1948, signed by Arturo Jáuregui
    and Isidoro Godoy.
Letter of leaders of affiliates of CEOSL to President Guillermo Rodríguez Lara,
    Minister of Government and Police Guillermo Durán Argentales and Min-
    ister of Labor and Social Welfare Ramiro Larrea Santos, Quito, July 21, 1975
    (mimeographed).
Letter of Luis B. Villacrés Arandi to "Señor doctor Ramiro Larrea Santos, Ministro
    de Trabajo y Bienestar Social," Quito, July 2, 1975 (mimeographed).
Letter of Luis B. Villacrés Arandi to "Todos Los Presidentes y Secretarios Generales
    de las Federaciones Provinciales, Regionales, Cantonales y por Ramas de
    Trabajo y Organizaciones de Base Afiliados a 'CEOSL,' " Quito, July 4, 1975
    (mimeographed).
Letter of Víctor Carrión and Manuel España of Workers' Departamental Trade
    Union Federation of Junín to George Meany, January 20, 1949.
Letter to the author from Luis Maldonado Tamayo, secretary-general of Partido
    Socialista Ecuatoriano, December 5, 1947.
"Ley de Seguridad Interior de la República," Lima, July 1, 1949.
"Manifesto de la Confederación de Trabajadores del Perú," Lima, July 15, 1945
    (mimeographed).

"Manifesto de la Confederación de Trabajadores del Perú," Lima, November 20,
      1948 (mimeographed).
Naft, Stephen. "Labor Organizations in Latin America," unpublished manuscript.
"Nuevo Crimen Aprista Contra la Clase Obrera," n.d. (probably May 1947)
      (throwaway).
"Panorama de la Educación Sindical en el Ecuador," Primera Conferencia Intera-
      mericana de Directores de Educación Sindical, Enero 13–17, 1964. Informe
      de la Confederación Ecuatoriana de Organizaciones Sindicales Libres
      (CEOSL), Instituto de Capacitación Sindical (mimeographed).
Unión Departamental de Empleados Particulares de Lima, n.d. (throwaway).
United States Department of Labor. "History and Structure of Ecuadorian Trade
      Unions," n.d. (circa 1963) (mimeographed).
United States Department of Labor, "Peru: Guide to Program Officers, Team
      Managers and Lecturers," n.d. (circa 1963) (mimeographed).

Index

ABOUT THE AUTHOR

ROBERT J. ALEXANDER is Professor Emeritus of Economics and Political Science, Rutgers University, where he taught for fifty-five years. He is a distinguished scholar with forty-six earlier books to his credit, including *The Bolivarian Presidents: Conversations and Correspondence with Presidents of Bolivia, Peru, Colombia, and Venezuela* (Praeger, 1994).